# SOCIALIST
# DILEMMAS

# SOCIALIST DILEMMAS
## East and West

Edited by
**HENRYK FLAKIERSKI**
**and THOMAS T. SEKINE**

**M. E. SHARPE, INC.**
Armonk, New York · London, England

Available in the United Kingdom and Europe from
M. E. Sharpe, Publishers, 3 Henrietta Street, London WC2E 8LU.

**Library of Congress Cataloging-in-Publication Data**

Socialist dilemmas : East and West
Henryk Flakierski and Thomas T. Sekine, editors.
p.    cm.
ISBN 0-87332-687-3
1. Communism—1945–
2. Communist countries——Politics and government.
3. Communist countries—Economic conditions.
I. Flakierski, Henryk.
II. Sekine, Thomas T. (Thomas Tomohiko), 1933–
HX44.S5858    1990    90-8616
335.43′09′045—dc20    CIP

Printed in the United States of America

MV    10    9    8    7    6    5    4    3    2    1

# Contents

# Introduction

During the decade of the 1970s the political economy of the world underwent dramatic changes. The previously uncontested supremacy of the United States suddenly receded in the aftermath of the Vietnam fiasco; and in the West a more pluralistic, and hence less stable and predictable, international relations emerged in its place. The optimistic notes of affluence and economic growth could no longer be sustained as, on the morrow of the demise of Bretton Woods, world trade wavered under the influence of exchange volatility, erratic capital flows, and constant threats of protectionism. Twice hit by oil crises, moreover, the industrialized nations of the West floundered helplessly in the grip of severe stagflation. This time Keynesian fiscal remedies did not work wonders. The way out was a costly and frustrating zero-sum process, bound to intensify social conflicts. Thus ended the happy marriage of the welfare state and free enterprise; the half-socialist and half-capitalist "mixed economy" no longer held together. In the 1980s neoconservatism arrived to signal the end of the grand Keynesian dream.

No less problematic was the political and economic climate in the East. Even with the Sino-Soviet rift, the communist nations of the Eastern Bloc had high hopes, during the 1960s, of eventually winning the economic race with the "capitalist" West. But this illusion was shattered in the 1970s. Frequent crop failures hampered planned advances in industrial production. Productivity remained low and mechanization lagged. The Brezhnev-era effort to introduce Western capital and technology in order to strengthen the industrial base had only limited success, as the combined balance of payments deficit of the CMEA countries vis-à-vis the West steadily worsened, despite Soviet exports of natural gas and gold. By the end of the decade the Soviet Union found its energy production inadequate to meet the increasing need of its CMEA neighbors. The burden of foreign debt and energy shortage led many of them, especially Poland, to the brink of economic collapse. The malfunctioning and stagnation of the command economy, long held captive to bureaucratic control and political patronage, could no longer be easily dismissed as temporary aberrations. As the

1980s dawned it became clear that mere decentralization, marketization, and greater discretion on the part of socialist enterprises would not solve the problem. A much more radical, if proportionately more perilous, change, involving nothing less than alternative forms of ownership of the means of production, had to be faced. The dream of the "victory of socialism" also faded away, leaving a sense of despondency and frustration.

Thus in the second half of the 1980s neither the West nor the East was as sanguine or monolithic as both had been two decades before. With both in the grip of political and economic uncertainties, the ideological confrontation seemed to lose its sharp edge. Furthermore, the urgency of concern over the quickly deteriorating living environment began to be felt just as acutely in the East as in the West. When American and Soviet scientists found themselves in substantial agreement over the dreaded scenario of nuclear winter, only the most fanatical continued to be moved by the false doctrine of nuclear deterrence. The crippling cost of military preparedness could no longer be imposed on either populace. Not confrontation, but cooperation between the two superpowers claimed priority on the global agenda.

Thus the political economy of the world has changed. No longer are the accepted dogmas and political ideologies of the past valid or convincing. The presuppositions of the debate on comparative economic systems are now in need of fundamental revision.

It was in this perspective that the Political Economy Workshop at York University featured a series of lectures on socialism in its 1988 session. About a dozen presentations were made by York University scholars and invited guest speakers covering a wide range of issues related to both the idea and the reality of socialism. The organizers were pleasantly surprised to find that there was a fair degree of unanimity and consensus, rather than a sharp contrast of opinions, over the past record and present status of socialism. Everyone agreed that the East European experiments were disappointing and that a radical new departure was required if they hope to be plausible alternatives to the Western-type economies. It was also generally agreed that the social democracies of the West had made too many politically expedient concessions to big business. They abandoned much of their original socialism and reconciled themselves with the private sector, their former enemy, to the extent of embracing the market ideology which their forebears had strictly enjoined them to oppose. In other words, socialism, whether in its "actually existing" version in the East, or as a "viable alternative" in the West, never really amounted to what had originally been claimed for it. This much was agreed without question. Differences arose only over what to make of this sobering fact, and what one might now expect the future of socialism to be.

All of the articles assembled in this volume are based on presentations in the workshop. The first four, which reflect mainly the East European experiences of "actually existing" (or "real") socialism, are ordered from the relatively more philosophical and theoretical to the relatively more empirical and factual.

The Pokorný paper begins with reflections on the fundamental distinction between "political community" and "civil society." After critically examining Marxism's lopsided emphasis on the latter to the exclusion of the former, the author comes to the important conclusion that "socialism can regain a meaning only if it rejects the positivism hidden in the 'administration of things.'" By the "administration of things" the author means the planning of economic life governed by "the technocratic rule, rational only to itself." The paper intends to demonstrate that the neglect of "the realm of ethics as to content and of politics as to process" was responsible for the failed socialist experiments of the East.

The Brus paper reexamines the Marxist and Schumpeterian presupposition of an inevitable "march into socialism" in light of empirical evidence after World War II, and repudiates it. This thesis that capitalism inevitably develops out of itself into socialism was, in fact, rejected by James Burnham as long ago as 1941, but economists have generally chosen to ignore the question. This paper may constitute the first open admission of this conclusion by an Eastern economist with impeccable credentials, in light of what transpired both in the West and in the East in the post–World War II decades.

The Kowalik paper examines the neoliberal call in Poland for the privatization of the state sector, which he judges as having "little chance of succeeding for the time being." Instead the author suggests a transformation of most of the state sector into a socialized sector based on a variety of forms of intermediate group ownership of the means of production (self-managed, cooperative, municipally owned, etc.), warning against "dualistic" thinking in terms of either state or individual-private ownership.

The Flakierski paper then focuses on the "relationship between pay differentials and the socioeconomic characteristics of the self-management system in Yugoslavia." It offers a detailed empirical study of the Yugoslav distributional pattern, which is "characterized by low levels of skill differentials and high levels of interbranch and interfirm differentials," concluding that the latter go against "the sacred socialist principle of distribution according to work."

The paper by Laski makes, at the most empirical level, a comparison of economic performance in Poland and Spain, deliberately choosing two average developed countries, each belonging to a different bloc, instead of the two superpowers which represent them or the two blocs as wholes. The paper breaks new ground in studies in comparative economic systems. The conclusion that Poland does not compare favorably even with Spain seems to clinch the argument that the "march into socialism" was an illusion.

The next three articles are based on Western experiences and conceptions of socialism. This time they are arranged from the relatively more empirical and realistic to the relatively more theoretical and speculative.

Thus the Panitch paper addresses the present state of social democracy in the West, focusing especially on recent developments in the British Labour Party. It is not so much the absence of "economics of feasible socialism," the author argues, but rather the lack of "politics of feasible socialism" that explains the crisis of the Left in the West. Conventional social democratic policies are not enough to overcome the crisis of the welfare state supported by Keynesian economics. After examining various attempts at transcending such policies, the author concludes that the inability of the party and the state to democratize their own structures lay at the root of past failures.

The Lefeber paper asks the following fundamental questions: Is it at all possible to transform a semi-developed country such as Greece, tightly locked into the international capitalist system, into a socialist society? Can such a transformation be accomplished by democratic means? The Greek experience does not seem to have provided an answer. Although PASOK, the Greek Socialist Party, can claim to have been successful in some areas, it has distinctly failed to render the economy dynamic. While sacrifices were needed in the short run, the government did not provide an adequate social-support system to mitigate their impact. It did not create the necessary decentralized institutions and did not eliminate corruption. The political costs were high.

The Sekine paper is in two parts. In the first half it criticizes the conventional notion of socialism with the claim that it has inherited from capitalism the abstract-universal way of thinking as reflected in modernism, scientism, industrialism, and economism, while neglecting the aspect of humans as concrete species-beings. In the second half it outlines an economic organization upon which a proper socialist society might be built. Although this part is frankly exploratory and somewhat utopian, its argument is supported by a *tableau économique* in three sectors which explains the circular flows of two types of goods and two types of services. The author writes in the Japanese (rather than Western) tradition of Marxism, strongly influenced by Kozo Uno and Yoshiro Tamanoi, whose works are not well known in the West. Of the two critiques of capitalism by Marx—one that it is unjust and the other that it is inverted and inhuman—Uno emphasizes the latter, and thus readily connects with Tamanoi's radical call for a new economic paradigm which integrally allows for the thermodynamic implication of economic life. Sekine also absorbs much, through Tamanoi, from the seminal works of Karl Polanyi.

The editors regret that some important contributions to the workshop (in particular, papers dealing with Third World development strategies and with women's perspectives) could not be made ready for inclusion in this volume. These are conspicuous gaps. But the comprehensiveness of coverage is not necessarily the virtue that the editors sought as the first priority. They are satisfied with the fact that many, if not all, of the new dimensions of socialism are touched on by one or more authors in this volume, and that all available contributions are of a quality and originality to make the publication of this collection worthwhile.

Finally, it devolves on the editors to thank certain individuals whose selfless cooperation made their task far easier than it would otherwise have been. They especially thank Dr. Colin Duncan of Queens University, Mr. Brian MacLean of Dalhousie University, and Mr. Kenneth Stokes of the International University of Japan for kindly editing many of the articles collected here. This was an enormous task given that most of the eight contributors are non-native English speakers. The editors also wish to thank Ms. Pat Cates and her team in the Secretarial Services of the Faculty of Arts, York University, for their patience in preparing many versions of the typescript of this book.

HENRYK FLAKIERSKI
THOMAS T. SEKINE

# SOCIALIST
# DILEMMAS

# Socialism

## Reflections on an Idea

### DUŠAN POKORNÝ

If one were to write a history of socialism in a hundred words or less, it might well read like this: "Socialism" first appeared as a demand of justice on men's free will—and nothing came of it. Then the idea became a claim of history on history: a claim of historical laws, acting through the political movement of an oppressed social class, on history as a flow of events. This time, there were results; but they did not inaugurate justice or freedom. "Socialism" became a huge machine efficient in producing, apart from weapons, mainly more unrepentant oppression.

Now, the voices demanding reform are stronger than ever before. Yet both the content and the fate of the endeavor remain uncertain. Much will no doubt depend upon how the malady will be diagnosed and what framework will underlie the attempted remedy.

The discussion to follow is intended to contribute to the testing of this vast ground.

### I

To begin at the beginning, we have to go back to the distinction between political community and civil society—or rather to the prehistory of that distinction. That is, we have to return to the interpretations and reinterpretations of Aristotle's statement that man is a *political* animal.

In the philosopher's own mind, the *polis* seems to have been for men what nature was for other beings: it was presented as the language-based, culture-dominated *locus* of their existence.[1] It was the distinguishing feature of human

---

The author is at the Departments of Political Science and Economics, University of Toronto.

language to "declare what [was] just and what [was] unjust,"[2] while culture demanded that man's life be guided by customs and laws as expressions of dispassionate reason.[3] Of course, this reason was not accessible to men directly or immediately. But the mediator between "reason always out there" and "reason here and now" was not a philosopher-king, or Plato's coming together of knowledge and power.[4] For absolute knowledge must necessarily be situated outside of the actual community of men; and the power that makes this knowledge socially effective is then also an outside power, not the power of the *polis*, or political power properly speaking. For Aristotle, the *polis* as a *type* of the human group's organization is before the individual,[5] and true laws exist even before they are promulgated.[6] However, the identity of an *actual* community is formed conjointly with that of its members,[7] and the elimination of "passion" from laws has to be the work of men, even the best of whom are not totally free of passions.[8] Thus the mediator between "reason out there" and "reason here" is the *polis* itself—or rather the historical, albeit *telos*-oriented, process of the true community's formation. This, then, is how politics became an extension of ethics; and the *polis*, or the state, was where the ideal of good life was to be attained.

But history was not kind to the theory, and by the time Aurelius Augustinus, or Saint Augustine, sat down to write his *City of God*, it appeared necessary to take another look at Aristotle's conception of man. Man is by nature a *social* animal, said Augustinus, and even the life of the blessed in heaven is a social life. But man is not a political animal, at least not by nature. The state as a machine of authority, subjugation, and coercion is the consequence of the Fall of man and should not be seen as a vehicle of God's grace.[9] Since those were the dying days of the Roman empire, the immediate message was that *this* state was no longer to be considered as having a privileged, God-ordained place in the history of mankind. The conclusion of the argument was, however, phrased in terms of *any* state. Man's road to salvation (or its opposite) was that of an individual situated among (some) other (nameable) individuals. His ultimate fate depended neither on his attitude to the social whole, nor on the political structures characteristic of it. Indeed, the doctrine has been seen as pointing to a kind of "withering away of the state."[10] In any case, the first *Utopia* was based on the separation of the social nature of man from the political "superstructures," understood as originating in the historically revealed limits to his ability to socialize. And when, a thousand years later, the *City of God* was secularized, Thomas More placed the Best Order into the realm of the "social man." He proposed that "all men . . . haue and enioye equall portions of welthes and commodities,"[11] rather than relying on moral goodness, or historically developed custom, or the political community to see to it that private property be (as Aristotle had it) put to common use.[12]

But the debate did not end there. Some three hundred years later—after a modern civil society emerged from the disordered political states of the Middle

Ages—Hegel entered the list to propose a new version of Aristotle's position, and Marx to reject it on grounds that were, after all, not that different from those of More and Augustinus (not to speak of Plato himself).

Hegel introduced private property at the most fundamental, but also the most abstract, level of right, where right is a "possibility," a "warrant"[13] as yet unutilized, in short a blank waiting to be filled in. In order to become contentful, private property had not only to be (re)connected with particular interests at the level of the individual's welfare but also with his part in the "war of all against all" characteristic of the civil society. Moreover, private property had to submit to the state as "the actuality of the ethical Idea," that is, to politics as the sphere of action where universal interest attains its ultimate concreteness. Only in this way, Hegel thought, could freedom be both subjectively present and objectively possible.[14]

Marx, by contrast, treated politics as a matter of particular interests—among which predominates the interest of the economically most powerful class—and made the social ownership of the means of production the socioeconomic base of the socialistic society. In this way, the new, "human" society was to be erected squarely on the grounds previously occupied by the old, civil society.[15] Politics was assigned the merely transitory role of bringing about the momentous change. Its role was that of a midwife out on a suicidal mission: she will bring the child into the world—and then bow out of it. In its ultimate form, freedom excluded politics.

Today, with history older and sadder, we have especially pressing reasons to look into the justification of these two perceptions of politics.

## II

We have already seen how, in Hegel, "private property" is to start with a kind of place-holder. It is central to the very concept of bourgeois society (for it was in this constitutive role absent in the feudal one), though still empty, and powerless to fill up the void except by transgressing itself. It is only as it comes to be confronted with the multiplicity of social contexts in which it is to be used—a multiplicity inherently belying the initial stolid identity of a right which is, after all, the same for all—that "private property" gradually attains content. Indeed, the process is not finished until the state[16] is placed atop all the levels of mediation to give the ultimate, fully structured, and hence in a variety of ways limiting, meaning to "right," and to its first, originally unbounded expression, "private property." For here, as everywhere else, it is only through the particular that the abstract universal can become a concrete one.

Marx, too, starts the conceptual construction of the new society with the bare bones of its institutions, with the social ownership of the means of production and *ex ante* planning of economic activities. He is also keenly aware of the necessity to concretize these abstract universals with a view to this or that historical situation. The discussion of "permanent revolution" is indeed in a number of ways an outstanding example of the particular mediating the transformation of the abstract into the concrete: ultimate goals must not be confounded with intermediary goals.[17] One is tempted to say, however, that what Marx giveth with one hand he taketh away with the other. Criticizing Hegel, he writes that the abolition of bureaucracy as a merely imaginary, unreal universal class is possible only when the universal interest—that is, the interest of the society as a whole, or rather that of history as a process of man's emancipation—becomes the particular interest of a real class, the class of the workers.[18] In this case, clearly, "particularity" is a class distinction. It refers to the general features distinguishing the proletariat partly from the ruling classes of "these" times, partly from the subjugated classes of previous historical periods. "Particularity" refers to what all the workers share, not to what may be the role, in the identity formation of each, of this or that family background, of the profession or trade one is engaged in, or of the traditions of the nation to which the individual belongs.

This is not the only meaning of "particularity" to be found in Marx's philosophy of history, but it is the one that dominates both his and Lenin's concept of the postrevolutionary state.[19] In fact, the assumed identity of the working class's particular interest and the universal interest—the interest of all, including those of the generations to come—dominated this crucial part of their argument to a point where it became virtually impossible to ask (at the level of the philosophy of history, not merely at that of the tactics of the revolutionary struggle) a question that in the twilight hours between night and day must surely have haunted even the intrepid: What if the particular revolts against the universal? Or rather: What if the *actual* particular fails to measure up to the *presumed* universal? In the extreme case, what if the working class, seen now as a multitude of varied interests, attitudes, values, decides to discontinue the experiment with the postrevolutionary society and return to (a modified version of) the old one?

As it turned out, the question was not an idle one. In Russia, an imperialist war lost and a civil war won left the working class exhausted and spread too thinly over a huge ground; while their potential allies among the peasantry remained confused and inarticulate.[20] By 1921 it became clear that "if the working classes were allowed to speak and vote freely, they would destroy the dictatorship."[21] And this became, in fact, the rallying call of the Kronstadt revolt: the soviets ought to be in reality what they were in name, that is, councils of freely chosen delegates of workers and peasants, elected bodies expressing the will and the interests of the people, rather than serving as mere agents of the Bolshevik party which had seized power and excluded anybody else from sharing in that power.[22] The sailors of the Red Navy were not seeking the restoration of the old regime, but they did demand the abolition of the dictatorship that had been, since Marx's time, considered a *sine qua non* of the revolution's success.

Clearly, it would have required a great deal of patient political work—political in the sense of mediation of interests, not in that of the crushing force with which the Kronstadt uprising was suppressed—to help the working people to create a society which would be *both* as radically new as history was deemed to require *and* in the image of them as they actually *were*. Still, some Marxists, among them Rosa Luxemburg,[23] thought that this was the road to take. However, the party leadership, including Lenin and Trotsky, decided it did not have the time for that political work; and the party took it upon itself to govern on the basis of what the workers and poor peasants *ought* to be. Not surprisingly, the "ought" of the historical role quickly became the "ought" of personal power. Concomitantly, universality was installed in its pure, abstract, vacuous form: the true revolutionary must owe nothing to family or nation, to professional integrity or moral conviction. By the same token, particularity lost the mediating role assigned to it in the true dialectic of individuals and societies. From a necessary link between universal interest as a bare abstraction and universal interest as concrete and living, particularity was relegated to a source of error and trespass.

Marx's identification, in the present context, of the universal and the particular—that is, his treatment of the latter as an absence of differentiation, rather than an expression of it—was certainly not a sufficient condition for that gigantic turn of the screw; but it was a necessary condition. Moreover, it had, in its turn, prerequisites rooted in even deeper layers of Marx's thought.

## III

Marx praised Hegel for having realized that man made himself by labor.[24] In fact, Hegel himself spoke of two kinds of labor: labor in the usual (and also in Marx's) sense of the word was termed "sensory seizure," and labor in the sense of "giving names" to what is "out there" was called "unsensory occupation."[25] In fairness, we have to note that these formulations are taken from Hegel's manuscripts that remained unpublished throughout Marx's life. But the distinction is present also in works that Marx knew and commented upon. The first kind of labor is man's *act on* nature, a project of the human mind being imposed on a thing offering resistance,[26] while the second is a precondition of *inter*actions *between* people. For it is through language that one self-consciousness exists for another. One *is* in being *recognized* by the other,[27] and language is the ground—the "first actual community"[28]—where these recognitions take place. Keeping all this in mind, it ought to be said that Hegel's men "make themselves" by labor *and* language as *the* means of mutual recognitions.

"Recognition" figures prominently also in Hegel's discussion of property. Within the framework of abstract right, there are three aspects to it. Property exists, first, as an external thing and, second, as an "embodiment of [my] will," meaning that "I hold property by means of . . . my subjective will." Finally, however, I must be able to hold property "by means of another person's will as well." That is, I hold it by virtue of his accepting my title as valid and respecting it. Moreover, this will be true also of his property. In this respect, he will hold it by virtue of my accepting his title and respecting it. It is in this way that I am (he is) said to hold property in virtue of my (his) participation in a "common will"; and the mediations establishing it occur in what Hegel calls "the sphere of contract." But the first precondition of contract is that "the parties to it recognize each other as persons," that is, as "capacities for rights."[29] In other words, it is the presence of "person" as a *universal* actor-role that distinguishes the bourgeois society from the feudal one, and the recognition of all by all as "persons" becomes thus the foundation of the new social order.

Marx agrees that "language is practical consciousness that exists also for other men."[30] He is also prepared to say that (a) "the *material* of my activity [is] given to me as a *social* product"; and he immediately adds that (b) "the language in which the thinker is active" is also a social product.[31] Since he speaks of the activity of a scientist, the "material" is either society or nature. If it is the latter, the first statement (a) may be interpreted as follows. Man is never just a passive observer of what is "out there." He is always an actor, taking a position vis-à-vis what he encounters, a position that affects the very perception of the "what." It relegates the nature-given thing to the status of an "object," in the sense of that which is to be acted upon, and simultaneously constitutes that man as the "subject," as the entity that forms mental projects negating the *status quo* and imposes them on the outside world. But this subject itself is a social creation—the attitude that characterizes it is historically generated—and so the object, too, is a social product. What is, then, the meaning of statement (b)? If language is, as everybody agrees, a social product, has it been historically created as a purely *neutral* vehicle just *reporting* what *is* "out there," or is it an *active,* "biased" tool always already giving *meaning* (human meaning, for there is no other) to the "out there"? Does the thought really owe nothing to the word—or do we have to admit that the "what" is inseparable from the "how"? Marx opts for the first alternative: he would not agree that "*les choses . . . dépendent des mots.*"[32] His main reason is no doubt a social one. The revolutionary cannot depend just on the *meaning* of things and situations; for the meaning can never be established by him alone. He must know what things and situations *are.* It is the privileged access to objective truth that is presumed to give him the warrant for acting on his own, independently of consensus.

As for "recognition," it is not a standard part of Marx's vocabulary, but there is a passage where he returns to it. And, what is more, he uses the term in an argument about property.

> This *material*, immediately *perceptible* private property is the material perceptible expression of *estranged human* life. Its movement—production and consumption—is the *perceptible* revelation of the movement of all production until now, i.e., the realisation or the reality of man. Religion, family, state, law, morality, science, art, etc., are only *particular* modes of production, and fall under its general *law.* The positive transcendence of *private property,* as the

appropriation of *human* life, is therefore the positive transcendence of all estrangement—that is to say, the return of man from religion, family, state, etc. to his *human*, i.e., *social*, existence. Religious estrangement as such occurs only in the realm of *consciousness*, of man's inner life, but economic estrangement is that of *real life*; its transcendence therefore embraces both aspects. It is evident that the *initial stage* of the movement amongst the various peoples depends on whether the true *recognised* life of the people manifests itself more in consciousness or in the external world—is more ideal or real. Communism begins from the outset (*Owen*) with atheism; but atheism is at first far from being *communism*; indeed, that atheism is still mostly an abstraction. The philanthropy of atheism is therefore at first only *philosophical*, abstract philanthropy, and that of communism is at once *real* and directly bent on *action*. We have seen how on the assumption of positively annulled private property man produces man—himself and the other man: how the object, being the direct manifestation of his individuality, is simultaneously his own existence for the other man, the existence of the other man, and that existence for him.[33]

In the present context, the following three propositions are crucial: (a) human existence is social existence; (b) recognized life need not be the true life; (c) collective property is to serve as a means of one man's "producing" another man.

(a) To be man is to be a social being, and "society" is where we all ought to be at home with one another. Yet the institutions of private property and the state exile man into a world consisting on one hand of things and violence, and on the other hand of myths and other forms of false consciousness. In the market, relations between men assume "the fantastic form of relations between things."[34] (Individual labor becomes social labor—or my labor in relation to yours—only as "abstract" labor, that is, as the determinant of the ratio at which the things produced are exchanged. Turning to plainer language, we often say that a thing "changes hands," as if the "hands" were just so many accessories to the thing and men merely the means of *its* movement.) As for the state, "the political constitution has [become] the religion of national life, the heaven of generality over against the earthly existence of its actuality,"[35] which is the suppression of one class by another. In all these ways, the *life* of men becomes a denial of the life of *men*.

(b) The "recognized life of the people," or the "world" in which they picture themselves as living, may be false or true. But the transition from the former to the latter is not a matter of knowledge alone. To the extent that the market, the state, the religion *make* the actual world non-transparent and hence unrecognizable, "cognition" must take the form of "*action*." Having (to start with, unwittingly) created these obstacles to transparency, men can, and must, remove them. If human relations are to be "understood" (in the sense of *known*), they must represent "understandings" between the people concerned (i.e., binding mutual promises *constituting* social reality). In this sense, the "true recognized life of the people" presupposes mutual identity-forming recognitions between the individuals themselves.

(c) If the phrase "man produces man" meant simply that A satisfies by his labor the needs of B and vice versa, the reference could be to any society based on the social division of labor. But that is clearly not what was intended: the validity of the statements is made dependent on the presence of the social owner-ship of the means of production. It is in this light that we have to see also the remainder of the quotation. Initially, the object (the product) is a manifestation of, say, A's individuality in the sense that it embodies a project that originated in his mind; but that is true of any act of labor, whatever the social (institutional) conditions under which it is performed. If the social ownership of the means of production is to make a difference, the projects of A and B must be coordinated beforehand with a view to the genuine needs of both. Thus the formation of the individuality of A becomes expressly interwoven with the formation of the indi-viduality of B, that of both with that of C, etc. If we think of all of them taken together, the interweaving is the function of economic planning made possible by the social ownership of the means of production. This is, then, how Hegel's abstract universal of "contract" operating at the level of "persons" and made concrete in a series of mediating steps culminating in the category of the "state" is replaced by a universal called "economic plan" that "works" at the level of the new, human civil society and the corresponding role of producer-citizen. This is a universal that is concrete in the sense of operating as an all-inclusive, omnipresent vehicle of mutual recognition of all by all.

But this is not the end of the story, yet. Rather, we have to take another look at the proposition we have ended up with.

## IV

To begin with, let us return to the concept of labor. If we isolate an act of labor from all the social conditions under which it is performed, then, in both Hegel and Marx, labor will be exhaustively described in terms of the subject (the producer and his "purpose" in the sense of the "image" of the product), the object (the nature-given, or already pre-formed, thing to be changed in accor-dance with the present project, and ultimately so changed) and the means of the subject's object-transforming action (the tools, machines, etc.).[36] Having deliberately abstracted from the social context of the act, we are entitled to take the "purpose" as given. The presupposition precludes an inquiry into the project's justification (or the lack of it). We cannot ask whether the "purpose" (the image of the product in the producer's mind) is good or bad. Nor is there any need to exclude cunning or artifice,[37] for they are directed against the object, not against another subject. In brief, the concern is only with the relation between the end (taken as a datum) and the means (whose range is also taken as given). This "labor process"[38] is then the sphere of the legitimate application of instrumental rationality ($R_1$), demanding the most efficient choice, and the most economic use, of the means to achieve the end sought. This rule (i) is technical in the sense of aiming at a change in the physical world,[39] and (ii) while allowing the end to be determined outside any criterion of rationality, it does so by presupposition (the social situation is for the moment abstracted from), not by an assertion about states of affairs or by a prescriptive judgment.

Both Hegel and Marx treat the "labor process" as an analytical construct: in actuality the act of labor is always "embedded" in a set of social institutions and cannot be separated from them. Put another way, behind the immediate "purpose" (the image of the product) is an idea of what the product will be good for, and what is good for me may be bad for somebody else. More generally, the "purpose" may become the "picture" of a whole new *state of affairs* (rather than just the "image" of a new form of a *thing*) and the change in the situation (whether personal or national) is justified by "intention," that is, by my individual welfare or happiness.[40] If we then interpret the "end" in $R_1$ as the "intention" (rather than the "purpose"), we enter the arena of strategic reason ($R_1^s$), whether it takes the form of the neoclassical economist's algorithm of maximizing utility (profit) or that of Kant's categorical imperative.[41] The rule is (i') formal in prescribing only a procedure, but this time the decision is about what I will do to the *people*, rather than to an object; and (ii') the exclusion of ends from the jurisdiction of reason is justified, not by a temporary presupposition, but descriptively (this *is* what people do) or normatively (this is what people *ought* to do).[42]

Hegel argued that Kant's inward-directed morality, one that is "the active self's very own,"[43] can provide only a conditional justification of the ensuing action. Ultimately, to act rationally is to act "not as a particular individual, but in accord with the concepts of ethics in general,"[44] that is, in accord with norms that are shared as a part of a historically developed "form of consciousness," or a scheme of how to give (human) meaning to what merely is, or occurs, "out there." This notion of practical reason ($R_2$) is grounded in norms that are (unlike the rules of $R_1$ and $R_1^s$) "substantive." They may be said to "regulate legitimate chances of the satisfaction of needs" and in this way to define "intersubjectively binding expectations of behavior."[45] In their turn, these norms become the basis of *inter*action *between* man *and* man, as distinct from man's *action on* (passive) nature: the unilaterality of the latter is sharply distinguished from the bilaterality, or multilaterality, of the former.

Marx's position may be characterized as one which cuts across the dividing lines between $R_1$, $R_1^s$, and $R_2$.

(a) On the formal side, he propounds the rule of minimizing labor time. The normative principle is introduced in the context of minimization of production costs (recalling $R_1$), but it is also meant to provide "time for the full development of the individual."[46] In this respect, the rule was no doubt intended to go beyond strategic reason ($R_1^s$). On the whole, however, the principle leaves an impression of vacuity. "Economy of time" does not appear as a matter of deliberate choice of techniques of production: rather, it seems grounded in the very "logic" of the production process itself.[47] And maximization of free time says in itself nothing about how the "saved" time will be divided between idle time and time for "higher activity."[48]

(b) On the substantive side, Marx rejects Hegel's historically given *Sittlichkeit*[49] as class-biased and puts forward the notion of human emancipation through praxis. While "emancipation" is certainly a prescriptive term—something which *ought* to be attained[50]—it follows directly from what is presented as a description, namely, from the essence of man as a demiurge of (social) reality.[51] On second thought, of course, one is tempted to add that this is precisely the point where the boundary dividing description and prescription must be transcended; for emancipation is fundamental human interest, a *practical* interest of *pure* reason.[52] But this is not, and cannot be, Marx's argument. In its turn, "praxis" or "revolutionary," "practical-critical" activity[53] is closely associated with the assertion that "what individuals *are*, coincides with their *production*," even if this production "presupposes the intercourse between individuals with one another,"[54] or what we have called interaction between men themselves. In a secular perspective, of course, the dependence is that of production relations on the forces of production, even though "feed-backs" are allowed for.[55]

From what has been said it is clear that, in order to understand the meaning of "praxis," we have to start with labor. In Marx's eyes, the *trans*formation of nature—the shaping of the nature-given thing in accordance with man's image of the product—is already a revolutionary act. And so it is. But it is a revolutionary act *within* the framework of man-to-nature relations where that "other" may be legitimately used as a means because the other is a thing. Yet this fundamental distinction tended to be forgotten, both by Marx and by many of his followers. One of them was Georg Lukács whose *History and Class Consciousness* had "praxis" as its "central concept." In 1967, looking back at the text he had written in 1922, he said that his treatment of "praxis" had not been correct. "Praxis," he now argues, has its "original model and form" in labor, and not to understand that it is so, is to "relapse into idealistic contemplation."[56] So "praxis" must be modeled after labor—that is, after physical activities legitimately guided by instrumental rationality ($R_1$). And at the other end of the line is just "contemplation." No mention here of the boundless field in between, namely, of interactions between men themselves, of the "understandings" constituting social reality proper in accordance with practical reason ($R_2$).

All in all, we can hardly escape the conclusion that, in Marx, "the production activity which regulates the material interchange of the human species with its natural environment, becomes the paradigm for the generation of all categories; everything is resolved into the self-movement of production." In this way, "communicative action" (or the language-mediated interactions between people, interactions governed by substantive norms) is reduced to "instrumental action,"[57] guided by the principle of the most economic use of the means available for attaining given ends.

As a consequence, the emancipatory role of "praxis" is fatally compromised:

Efficiency in the employment of means may parade as justice in the choice of ends—and liberation from hunger as liberation from servitude.

There is no dividing line between "forcing things" and forcing people: requirements of production may legitimately include the deformation of men.

The subjectivity of *labor* (guided by $R_1$) is separated from, and superimposed upon, the subjectivity of the *people* performing that labor (the subjectivity to be expressed within the framework of $R_2$).

## V

Marx demanded that labor (man's act on nature) be recognized as appropriation (within the sphere of man-to-man relations). This required that the material means of production become the producers' property—more especially, their collective property—by the right of revolution (occurring, of course, in the domain of relations among men themselves). The title thus acquired would guarantee the producers' access to land, buildings, machines, etc., that is, their possession of the material means of production (a matter of man's acts on nature). And all this was to occur within the boundaries of the "human" society as an heir in good standing of the old civil society.

Turning first to *possession*, we shall note that nothing is said about the possession of the product. To say that once the product leaves the last producer's hands it is already the property of all is also to say that possession as a distinct relation between the producer and the product disappears. This did not mean much to the factory worker who had been in this position ever since wage labor started to emerge from simple commodity production. But it did matter a lot to the peasant who was thus deprived of the implicit, traditionally respected "right" to subsistence production. Moreover, the possession of the means of production themselves was grounded exclusively in the collective ownership of it. Without the latter as an ever-present "living" relation of all to all, "possession" in this field could be expressed only negatively: by destruction or sabotage, by a sit-in without production, by a strike, etc. And once the latter two were outlawed and "social ownership of the means of production" was rendered vacuous (which was in both cases a matter of the political state, not that of the civil society), there existed no legal form of possession of the means of production. To put the same thing in different words, there was full employment—in some sectors over-employment relative to the actual needs of the production process—but the basis of it was not the *right* to work. Rather, it was the *permission* to work. This is obvious in the case of higher bureaucrats, managers, and professionals whose access to "this" job has always been treated as a privilege that could be withdrawn at the pleasure, or rather displeasure, of the powers that be. However, as the "dissidents" of various persuasions were to learn, *any* person could be refused permission to work and then be prosecuted for living off illegitimate earnings, or simply for "anti-social behavior" defined as not participating in the society's production endeavor.

As for *property*, the fundamental difference between the old and the new civil society was that the bourgeois, even when deprived of his participation in the political process, could go back to his property,[58] while the socialist producer, when he suffered the same fate, had nowhere else to go, had no independent basis to retreat to. In this respect, his position was similar to that of a tribesman whose clan was divested of the birthright of access to land by the chief of the tribe, using first the power of symbols (say, the seizure of a sacred drum) and later the manipulation of consensus in the interpretation of the clan's *own* customary law:[59] the loser had *no* economic basis *from* which to defend his right *to* an economic basis. The collective ownership right of the soviet producer was exhausted by his right of participation in the decisions regarding what social goals the means of production will serve and in what manner. He *had* only his political right to *protect* his political right—and that left him too vulnerable to political abuse and naked violence. In Hegel's terms, the right of joint ownership was absolute at the level of law,[60] but without a particularized existence at the level of the civil society. Consequently, the realization of the right became the province of the political state. Therefore, when Stalin *disfranchised* the producers in the sphere of politics, they were also left *expropriated* and *dispossessed* in what was to be the realm of the human society.[61]

All this brings us back to economic *planning* and the "withering away" of the state.[62] On the technical side, the plan is intended to ensure that the sectors producing material means of production are able to satisfy (in terms of values in use and concrete labor) the demands of the sectors producing the articles of consumption, and to do so (at least in principle) under conditions of expanding reproduction. In this context, the organization of production equals the "administration of things,"[63] and labor itself is seen only from the *outside* as a duty to be accomplished and a deed duly entered into the public "account of labor."[64] In its pure form, this is the sphere of jurisdiction of instrumental rationality ($R_1$).

But labor has also its *inside:* the "how" of the activity and the "what" it is aimed at. It is in this general context that Marx speaks of expanded reproduction whose pace is "dictated by social needs." Their content is indicated merely by citing "the full development of the individuality," subject to "the existing productivity of society."[65] Beyond that we learn nothing about how "social needs" are determined.[66] Yet the reference to them is sufficient for concluding that economic plan in the sense of technical control over production as a relation between men and nature is to be understood as a response to an underlying social compact about which individual wants will be (given the productivity constraint) sanctioned as social needs, which is of course a matter of relations between men themselves. "Economic plan" in the sense of administration of things gives expression to a social concord on "who is who" in the sense of which of "your" wants, and which of "mine," will become the needs of all. It is only in this manner that the social ownership of the means of production can function as a universal means of mutual recognition. By rights, this is the domain of practical reason ($R_2$).

If one were to try to translate this argument into the more tangible language of economics, one could begin with this question: Given the state of the productive basis of the economy at some starting point and a set of assumptions about the efficiency of future investments, is there a unique, scientific way of determining which allocation of investment funds between the two departments—the sectors manufacturing the means of production and the sectors producing articles of consumption—will maximize consumption? The temptation might be to reply that the best thing is to give all the available investment funds to the consumer goods department. But Soviet theorists of planning discovered already in the 1920s that the longer the time horizon of the maximization problem, the higher share of the funds—but not all of them—must go to the first department, manufacturing the means of production.[67]

In other words, it all depends on the time horizon: will it be ten years or a hundred years? Will we maximize the consumption of the present generation of the producers—or will we maximize the stock of the means of production to be handed over to the next generations? This is not a technical question, nor can it be answered in technical terms. In this respect, no one is allowed to hide behind science, pure and simple. As Sartre was wont to say, albeit in a different context, we cannot escape our freedom. The decision is about norms as the basis of interpersonal relations, norms which will determine whose needs are intended to be satisfied and whose will have to remain unheeded, norms which will, in that sense, determine *who* will have the chance to become *whom*.[68] The realm is that of ethics as to content and of politics as to process.

At this point, however, we have to remind ourselves of the way Marx perceives the first phase of the postrevolutionary situation. For when he speaks of "all," he really means "some." Or rather, he means "all who count" and that immediately poses the question of who will count for the purpose of determining who will count, and so on, and so on. This looks like false infinity—but it duly finds its end in Stalin. Politics in the sense of unbridled use of power in pursuit of a spurious universal interest eliminates politics as the workers' and peasants' participation in the decisions making the universal interest concrete and thus true. The resulting expropriation and dispossession of the presumed collective owners amounts to an abrogation of all mutual recognitions and to an arbitrary determination of whose individual wants will become the society's alleged needs. Hence the sense of profound injustice that has now pervaded the Soviet society for more than seven decades.

On this score, then, the short message of the story is that "socialism" can regain a meaning only if it rejects the positivism hidden in the pure administration of things; readopts social justice as its ethos; and, in order to give it concreteness, restores politics to its proper function of the medium through which any initial notion of universal interest (a notion to start with always necessarily abstract) is confronted with a wide range of varied particular interests, so that "society" does not become an enclosed void.

## VI

This argument has been conducted in terms of Marx's own perception of the society of free producers and hence in terms of directive economic planning. But the conclusion stands even if allowance is made for a movement toward market relations in several of the Soviet-type societies. For the strengthening of the "civil society" requires more, rather than less, "politics," albeit in the above sense of mediation, not suppression. One need not take Hegel's (or Keynes's) word for it. Western societies offer plenty of empirical evidence to support the claim.

It would be wrong, of course, to think of the reforms, actual or planned, as introducing market relations into a virgin land where they had never existed. In fact, "socialist" societies have always been producing commodities (in Marx's sense of the unity of value in use and value in exchange) by default. Whenever the socialization of individual labor through the plan failed—that is, whenever the alleged production of values in use did not correspond to the actual structure of "social needs" (in principle satisfiable within the "existing productivity of society")[69]—it was likely that market relations would "step into the breach" to deal with the discrepancy.[70] That they often did is amply documented by the presence of the "black market," by bribes being demanded and paid for a number of services (sometimes including health care), and ultimately by the emergence of a whole "secondary" economy.

An intentional introduction of market relations into the "primary" economy is, of course, a quite different matter. To say that all consumer goods production will be oriented toward actual rather than presumed final demand, that most capital goods (as a Western economist would call them) will be traded between enterprises (rather than allotted to them by the central authority), that an enterprise that does not stand the test of economic efficiency will be allowed to go bankrupt (rather than being eternally bailed out by the state)—to say all that is to express a commitment to a change that goes right to the essence of the traditional understanding of "socialism." Alas, the magnitude of the intended change is proportionate to the problem on hand. It has turned out that no industrially developed economy[71] of any size can operate in a rational manner on the basis of centralized directive planning, whether "rational" is understood in the context of $R_1$, $R_1^s$, or $R_2$. To be sure, the method of "material balances" may be used with various degrees of competency, but the core of the difficulty is in the method itself. It goes back to Marx's idea of an *ex ante* integration of all economic activities in terms of values in use (the physical qualities and quantities of the various material means of production) and concrete labor (the quality and quantity of the labor employed to produce this or that product).[72]

Since one would not want to overstate a good case, it ought to be granted that planning in terms of material balances may be understood as an iterative technique that, in principle, does lead in a finite set of steps to the "right" input-output table.[73] Even that, however, does not get us very far. Apart from considerations of a more detailed or technical character—such as the effects of limited plant capacities and of inflexible supply of labor of various kinds[74]— there is, in the first place, the matter of size and complexity. Once it is realized that the Soviet Union produces now more than a million different products, it becomes evident that duly interlocking material balances will, even at the level of the so-called "basic proportions," amount to a jigsaw puzzle so gigantic that it defies solution on informational grounds alone.[75]

In addition, there is the matter of costs. Again the argument ought not to be couched in terms of absolutes. It is true that a suitably adjusted input-output matrix does imply a unique set of "accounting prices" expressed in units of homogeneous labor; in effect, these are Marx's values seen as underlying the actual prices.[76] But all this merely shows that prices in a Soviet-type economy *need not* be so many aberrations divorced from actual data, that is, from the cost basis—*given* a final demand structure that may have been self-servingly presumed and a "grid" of intersectoral relations that in part "solidifies" previous arbitrary production and investment decisions. Even if for a moment we abstract from the size factor, which is formidable even in countries that have less than a million production processes distinct at least in their final stages, it is obvious that the possibility of an *ex post* calculation of "reasonable" prices by no means excludes the actuality of an irrational structure of costs in an *ex ante* sense of the word, costs as they enter the decision-making processes.

In this crucial respect, then, the reforms call for a rational calculus based on an internally consistent price system, meaning one that conveys correct information on the "terms on which alternatives are offered."[77] In its substance, the call is not new. As early as in 1918, Lenin wrote that, while "confiscation" requires merely determination, "socialisation cannot be brought about without the ability to calculate." To bring the point home, he added: "*economically*, state capitalism is immeasurably superior to our present system," suffering, as it was, partly from the notion that it was unbecoming to a revolutionary to count and reckon, partly from the uncultured calculativeness of the petty bourgeoisie.[78] The seventy years that elapsed between then and now have, of course, changed the country in very many ways. What comes first to mind is that, then, it was abysmally poor, but "on the go," even if the direction of the movement was a matter of much legitimate dissent. Today, the society is richer but, despite some recent jolts, still frightfully stale. On inspection, however, we will note another difference. Reading Lenin, one has the impression that the "capitalist" calculation can be grafted on the socialist system without a major conflict; the former tends to be seen as just a tool of the latter. These days, there is a degree of awareness that, at least in the transitional period, a lot of tension will exist between the two. It may be worthwhile, therefore, to take a closer look at the market as a domain of counting and reckoning and its relation to the social environment.

## VII

For the sake of brevity, let us consider just two "divisions" of this vast terrain: prices (with a postscript on foreign trade) and investments.

Traditionally, the case for economic reforms has been made in terms of enterprises maximizing profit subject to parametrical prices. As a rule, such prices would be determined by competition; as an exception, limited initially to cases of basic social interests, the price would be fixed by the state. This latter approach might have to be used also in the case of monopolistic markets,[79] unless a sufficient degree of competition could be engendered by imported goods. Whether such import-based interventions are economically feasible is not of our concern. For the present purpose it will suffice to note that in all the instances cited the enterprise is seen as a price-*taker*. However, one may also want to take into account that quite a few capitalist firms operating in oligopolistic markets, mainly the corporations employing very modern technology, are now often seen as the *makers* of prices that are based on the cost of production and a "normal" profit markup. The freedom of the price-setter is then constrained partly by oligopolistic competition, partly by trade unions attempting to prevent a redistribution of net income in favor of the owners of capital and, more generally, aiming at wages (meaning also wage differentials) that are "fair."[80] The point to hold on to is that this behavior is *not* a part of the supply-demand mechanism ensuring that the labor market is cleared. Rather, it is an exogenous factor reflecting *social* concerns and the role of institutions designed to articulate them, if need be even at the cost of a measure of unemployment.[81]

It is widely assumed, and feared, that oligopolistic enterprises in reformed Soviet-type economies would also act as price-makers; and, if so, the question arises: what income-distribution constraints could be placed on *their* freedom in price-setting? The obvious answer is that the state will step in to determine the principles of income distribution.[82] That, however, need not be sufficient. For at issue are not the broad outlines of an income policy; rather, of concern is the structure of the wages and salaries in this or that enterprise or a group of enterprises, and that requires a much more direct participation of the workers and their organizations. But there is more to the story than just this. The distinction between the supply-demand mechanism of the market and the social environment within which it operates brings to mind the three concepts of rational behavior discussed earlier. The market is, of course, the province of instrumental and strategic reason ($R_1$, $R_1^s$). Social attitudes and concerns open room for norm-based interaction ($R_2$), although there is no a priori way of knowing how much of that room will actually be occupied by it. It is clear that striving for rational calculus ($R_1$, $R_1^s$) ought not to be understood as denying the legitimacy of the social concerns best articulated (or at least expressible) within the framework of practical reason ($R_2$).

At this point it will be useful to bring in foreign trade. While nearly all countries are engaged in it, that does not necessarily make them open economies. In principle, a closed economy is merely an open economy without currency reserves (and with no possibility of obtaining credit). In real life, of course, a lot depends on the conditions under which an open economy becomes, in this sense of the word, a closed one, and on the consequences of that fall from grace. A particularly interesting, and frightening, case has been described as follows:

> There have been sufficient reserves to support an expansion in its early stages; but without the point being reached at which expansion becomes "self-sustaining," the reserves are exhausted (and cannot be supplemented by foreign borrowing). The country is then in the dire position that its current level of employment, *and* its current level of real wages, are levels that it cannot sustain, cannot possibly sustain. . . . It may be possible, by desperate efforts, to avoid exchange depreciation; but that cannot be done, unless the expansion is cut back severely; the whole of the shock must then be taken by employment. Exchange depreciation diminishes that shock, but at the cost of aggravating inflation. . . . But since inflation is an ineffective way of cutting real wages, some part of the shock will still have to be borne by employment. Thus, as a result of the crisis, there is exchange depreciation, increased inflation, and rising unemployment, all (more or less) at the same time.[83]

This case is, of course, of special importance for countries that are poor in natural resources and at the same time regard full employment as their adopted, or "natural," goal. But the lesson to be drawn from this special case is completely general. The point is that the allocative function of prices is not the same thing as their social function, and that one may get into conflict with the other (for reasons which are by no means limited to the lack of currency reserves). Needless to say, this is not to suggest that the allocative function be neglected; as already noted, the history of Soviet-type economies is replete with proofs that this kind of error is exceedingly costly. But the social function of prices (including wages and interest rates) must not be neglected either, whether it concerns unemployment or, say, regional disparities. Moreover, one of the reasons for keeping in mind this latter function of prices is precisely the difficulties we often face in the context of the former: "a world in which optimum efficiency is attainable through free use of a price-mechanism is very far off."[84]

An internally consistent price structure has been insisted upon not only as the basis of production decisions (and consumer choices), but also as the point of departure for investment decisions (and, in due course, savings decisions, too).

This is, no doubt, a valid and important consideration. Yet it may help to add that even in Western countries investment and saving decisions are not necessarily seen as located in the market place, or at least not unconditionally so. In the Keynesian framework, the reservation is expressed as follows. The decision to invest depends on the interest rate which is "a highly psychological," or "highly conventional," phenomenon. Furthermore, if technological change has to be taken into account, the dependence is also on the marginal efficiency of capital, which is seen as an "expected yield," conditioned by "the state of confidence," and so an "outcome of mass psychology." In their turn, savings decisions are governed by the propensity to save, the obverse of the propensity to consume, associated with a "fundamental psychological law."[85] In this last case, the savings behavior is regulated by a social convention according to which an increase in income is responded to by a *less-than-proportionate* increase in consumption. In the preceding two instances, the departure from pure market conduct is even more pronounced. The present is made to depend on a picture of the future, so that facts, *including* those "produced" by the market, are of importance to the degree to which they change socially generated expectations.

Somewhat surprisingly, the argument starting from the neoclassical premises is even more radical. The conclusion deserves to be quoted in almost "so many words." Let us assume

> conditions completely favorable to the satisfactory working of the price system. The amount of saving any one household undertakes (out of a given income and at a given rate of interest) will depend upon the goods and services it expects those savings to be able to purchase in future years—upon the expected level of prices. . . . But the prices which will actually prevail in the future depend upon the savings decisions of other households, now and in the future. This is so not only on the demand side, but also because the savings of all households together determine the rate of capital formation—and thus the future supply of goods and services. No one household has any way of knowing what other households intend to do. The market does not provide it with the information it requires to make a rational decision. This is perhaps one of the more important senses in which the rate of saving (and investment) is unavoidably 'political'. The ordinary mechanism of the market cannot handle it. The ballot box, or something else, must be substituted for the price system.[86]

Before going any further, let me say that, to my knowledge, no reform proposals have aimed at a complete marketization of investment decisions. Yet the reasons for "holding back"—at least the rate of accumulation is to be decided by the state—have been usually associated with the characteristic features of the "socialist" economies themselves.[87] Now it turns out that the grounds are inherent in the nature of investment (and savings) decisions, no matter under what institutional conditions they are made and whether or not the price system functions in a satisfactory manner. Once socially generated expectations are excluded by assumption, or proved insufficient for dealing with the problem of uncertainty in respect to the future, explicit political compacts become necessary. And if they are to be truly *political*, they cannot be guided by instrumental or strategic rationality ($R_1$ or $R_1^s$): this is the rightful province of practical reason ($R_2$).

## VIII

It is no doubt possible that a society would freely opt for a lesser degree of efficiency in exchange for more social justice. In the present case, however, the loss of efficiency has been too blatant and crippling. Moreover, the custom has been to "resolve" the consequences by adding to inequities in the sphere of distribution and to injuries in the social and political life as a whole. The market is, of course, known to have limitations of its own. The individual actor's influence on its performance is proportionate to his or her income, wealth, or economic position; moreover, there is a "leverage coefficient" to be considered, positive in the case of the well-to-do or well-placed, negative for those who are poor or disadvantaged. Besides, the dynamism of the market has to be "bought" at the price of increased uncertainty in many walks of life. This will remind us of the sad fact that even an alienated way of life may become a refuge when threatened—perhaps only by the unknown—and that security is sometimes defended, even if it is only the security of oppression. For these reasons and others, already discussed, the change must be visible not only in what is done with regard to the present, but also in what is done about the past. For the identity of a people, being the product of their having accepted history and transcended it, cannot be restored as a collective head with a hole the size of the Kremlin. To gain legitimacy, the reform cannot cite just efficiency. It must be shown that the rational calculus ($R_1$, $R_1^s$) is a tool, not a master: that there is a genuine move toward practical reason ($R_2$) that tests the validity of ends, not merely the efficacy of means. For, otherwise, the change would be only from an irrational bureaucratic rule to a technocratic one, a rule rational only to itself.

## Notes

1. Martin Heidegger writes—albeit within a context different from ours—that the "*polis* is the historical place, the there *in* which, *out of* which, and *for* which history happens." *An Introduction to Metaphysics*, translated by R. Manheim (New York, 1961), p. 128.

2. *Politics*, 1253a, quoted according to E. Barker's translation (New York, 1962).

3. Ibid., 1287a.

4. *Republic*, 473d.

5. *Politics*, 1253a.

6. Law is not a mere covenant (*Politics*, 1280a). But it has an element of convention, which is the necessity to have the law declared (not enacted) by legislators. *The Politics of Aristotle*, edited and translated by E. Barker, p. 367 (editor's commentary on the treatment of justice, law, and equity in Aristotle's *Ethics*).

7. Replying to Socrates's claim that the greater the unity of the state the better (*Republic*, 463b), Aristotle says, in effect, that unity should not be mistaken for sameness. Indeed, there is a point at which a polis, seeking unity, will cease to be a polis (*Politics*, 1261a, 1263b).

8. Ibid., 1286a, 1287a.

9. *City of God*, edited by V.J. Bourke (New York, 1958), mainly Book XIX, chs. 5 (the life of saints is social) and 15 (God meant no man to have domination over man; servitude is the result of sin). At the same time, Augustinus appears to approve of individual property (e.g., XV, 16 and XIX, 21) and even of slavery, at least to the extent that it is penal (XIX, 15).

10. P. Laslett, "History of Political Philosophy," in P. Edwards, ed., *The Encyclopedia of Philosophy* (New York and London, 1967), vol. 6, p. 374.

11. *Sir Thomas More's Utopia*, edited by J.C. Collins (Oxford, 1964), p. 44.

12. *Politics*, 1263a.

13. G.W.F. Hegel, *Philosophy of Right*, translated by T.M. Knox (London, 1967), § 38.

14. Ibid., § § 257, 258, 261.

15. "Theses on Feuerbach," no. X, K. Marx and F. Engels, *Selected Works*, vol. 1 (Moscow, 1973), p. 15.

16. Ultimately, the state itself is a level of mediation: as the mind of a nation, a mind "restricted" by having "a history of its own," it "passes into the universal world history, the events of which exhibit the dialectic of the several national minds—the judgment of the world." *Hegel's Philosophy of Mind, Part Three of the Encyclopedia of Philosophical Sciences* (1830), translated by W. Wallace (Oxford, 1985), paras. 341, 352, 548. See also the *Philosophy of Right*, §§ 341, 352.

17. "Permanent revolution" appears for the first time in Marx's article "On the Jewish Question," written in 1843. See K. Marx and F. Engels, *Collected Works*, vol. 3 (New York, 1975), p. 156.

18. "Contribution to the Critique of Hegel's Philosophy of Law," ibid., p. 48.

19. See mainly Marx's address "The Civil War in France," part III, *Selected Works*, vol. 2 (Moscow, 1977), pp. 217–30; and Lenin's "The State and Revolution," chs. III and V, *Selected Works* (Moscow, 1977), pp. 286–300, 320–34.

20. Isaac Deutscher, *The Prophet Unarmed: Trotsky 1921–1929* (London, 1959), pp. 9–16.

21. I. Deutscher, *The Prophet Armed: Trotsky 1879–1921* (London, 1954), p. 506.

22. Ibid., pp. 510–14.

23. Rosa Luxemburg, *The Russian Revolution*, translated by B.D. Wolfe (New York, 1940), mainly chs. V, VI, VIII.

24. "Economic and Philosophic Manuscripts of 1844," *Collected Works*, vol. 3, pp. 332–33.

25. *Hegel and the Human Spirit, A Translation of the Jena Lectures on the Philosophy of Spirit (1805–6)*, translated with commentary by Leo Rauch (Detroit, 1983), pp. 93, 112.

26. *Philosophy of Right*, § 52. The resistance resides in the sheer positivity of the object's being—not in a counter-project, which would imply negativity and which is the prerogative of the subject.

27. G.W.F. Hegel, *Phenomenology of Spirit*, translated by A.V. Miller (Oxford, 1977), paras. 178, 191, 508, 652.

28. Herbert Marcuse, *Reason and Revolution: Hegel and the Rise of Social Theory* (Boston, 1960), p. 75. In speech, writes Hegel himself, "self-consciousness, *qua independent separate individuality*, comes as such into existence, so that it exists for others" *Phenomenology of Spirit*, para. 508.

29. *Philosophy of Right*, §§ 71, 36.

30. "German Ideology," ch. I; *Selected Works*, vol. 1, p. 32.

31. "Economic and Philosophic Manuscripts of 1844," p. 298. Emphasis mine.

32. Henri Lefebvre, *Le langage et la société* (Paris, 1966), p. 38. See also pp. 19–20 where Lefebvre contrasts the Hegel-based position of Merleau-Ponty and of modern linguistics with the Marx-based position of Sartre.

33. K. Marx and F. Engels, "Economic and Philosophic Manuscripts of 1844," *Collected Works*, vol. 3, pp. 297–98.

34. K. Marx, *Capital*, vol. 1 (Moscow, 1971), p. 71.

35. K. Marx, "Contribution to the Critique of Hegel's Philosophy of Law," *Collected Works*, vol. 3, p. 31.

36. G.W.F. Hegel, *Phenomenology of Spirit*, para. 400. K. Marx, *Capital*, vol. 1, p. 174, "The Labour Process. . . ."

37. *Philosophy of Right*, § 52R.

38. This is Marx's term; see again *Capital*, vol. 1, ch. VII.

39. Jürgen Habermas, *Toward a Rational Society: Student Protest, Science and Politics*, translated by J.J. Shapiro (Boston, 1971), pp. 91–93.

40. G.W.F. Hegel, *Philosophy of Right*, §§ 119–23.

41. " 'Rationality' is to be understood as the consistent choice of action calculated to achieve what is desired, given the possibilities. . . . The question of rationality or irrationality is therefore a question of the appropriateness of means, given the ends, and neither requires or implies any judgment about the ends." G.C. Archibald and R.G. Lipsey, *An Introduction to a Mathematical Treatment of Economics* (London, 1973), p. 157. As for Kant, see Jürgen Habermas, *Theory and Practice*, translated by J. Viertel (Boston, 1974), p. 151.

42. Roughly speaking, classical utility theory (starting with Bentham) was normative, while the neoclassical economic theory sees itself as descriptive: "the consumer's market behavior is explained in terms of preferences, which are in turn defined only by *behavior*." The "individual confronted with given prices and confined to a given total expenditure *selects* that combination of goods which is highest on his preference scale." Paul A. Samuelson, *Foundations of Economic Analysis* (New York, 1971), pp. 91, 97–98. Emphasis mine. There are, of course, various intermediary positions. For instance, R.D. Luce and H. Raiffa write that "game theory is not descriptive, but rather (conditionally) normative. It states neither how people behave nor how they should behave in an absolute sense, but how they should behave if they wish to achieve certain ends." *Games and Decisions* (New York, 1967), p. 63.

43. *Phenomenology of Spirit*, para. 603.

44. *Philosophy of Right*, § 15A.

45. Thomas MacCarthy, *The Critical Theory of Jürgen Habermas* (Cambridge, Mass., 1982), p. 313. The first quotation is from Habermas's "Wahrheitstheorien," in H. Fahrenbach, ed., *Wirklichkeit und Reflexion* (Pfüllingen, 1973), p. 251. Habermas agrees with Hegel that the norms that guide our behavior toward others ought to be substantive, that is, contentful (see $R_2$). However, he is also aware that Hegel does not provide a framework for the change of norms. Therefore, Habermas introduces procedural rules to govern the practical discourse within which it is to be established which hypothetical, or actually proposed, norms are *valid*. This is, of course, not the same thing as the procedures by means of which norms (including the valid ones) are actually "*produced*"; the latter is a matter of the constitutional provisions governing political processes. It ought to be noted, however, that—to the extent that he opts for *procedural meta-rules* for the validity tests—Habermas is returning to the Kantian tradition of cognitivistic ethics. See, e.g., *Moralbewusstsein und komunikatives Handeln* (Frankfurt, 1983), pp. 53, 113–14.

46. K. Marx, *Grundrisse, Foundations of the Critique of Political Economy (Rough*

*Draft)*, translated by M. Nicolaus (Harmondsworth, 1973), p. 712.

47. Saving of labor is said to be "identical with development of the productive force." This statement denies that "abstinence from consumption" is involved. Yet to the extent to which new technologies are "embodied," they require material investments that in any economic system compete with immediate consumption demands. (See also section 5 below.) From the point of view of the "direct production process," saving of labor time can be "regarded as the production of fixed capital, this fixed capital being man himself." The creativity with which this kind of capital is endowed will then "react back upon the productive power of labor as itself the greatest productive power." Ibid., pp. 711–12. The description concentrates on the labor process legitimately guided by instrumental rationality ($R_1$), rather than pointing to man stepping out of this process to make socially responsible decisions about new technologies which will affect not only things, but also the people themselves (so that the choices properly belong to the sphere of $R_2$).

48. Ibid., p. 713.

49. The German word *Sittlichkeit* is derived from *Sitten*, meaning "customs." In its turn, the last term is understood as "ethical life" (*das Sittliche*) in the sense of the "general mode of behavior" characteristic of individuals who "are simply identified with the actual order." This is also why Hegel writes that the "state exists immediately in custom," that is, in man's initial immersion in the norms he was born into. *Philosophy of Right*, §§ 151, 257. It is not difficult to see that this framework was seen by Marx as static, fixed, and inimical to the interests of the working class that needed a fundamental change in the society's norms and its perception of needs. One of the best known expressions of this attitude is his and Engels's statement that, to the proletarian, "morality" is just one of the "bourgeois prejudices, behind which lurk in ambush . . . bourgeois interests." "Manifesto of the Communist Party," *Selected Works*, vol. 1 (Moscow, 1973), p. 118. The word "morality" covers here both the morality of Kant and the "ethical life" of Hegel.

50. This is the basis of Steven Lukes's analysis of "morality" in Marx; see his *Marxism and Morality* (Oxford, 1985), mainly chapter 3.

51. See, e.g., the quotation cited in note 33, above.

52. Jürgen Habermas, *Knowledge and Human Interests*, translated by J.J. Shapiro (Boston, 1971), pp. 197–200.

53. "Theses on Feuerbach," I, p. 13.

54. "German Ideology," p. 20.

55. See, for instance, "German Ideology," chapter I, section 4, "The Essence of the Materialistic Conception of History"; and "Theses on Feuerbach," no. III, "the educator himself needs educating." *Selected Works*, vol. 1, pp. 13, 24–26.

56. *History and Class Consciousness*, translated by R. Livingston (Cambridge, Mass., 1986), p. xviii. It remains, of course, a question to what degree was Lukács's self-criticism a voluntary act. In addition, Lukács ought to be given credit for having initiated the discussion of some of the concerns expressed in this paper's view of Marx.

57. J. Habermas, *Theory and Practice*, pp. 168–69.

58. Except, of course, for the unlikely case of a wholesale expropriation of the owners.

59. Such expropriations did in fact take place. See, for instance, D. Pokorný, "The Haya and Their Land Tenure; Property Rights and the Surplus Problem," *Rural Africana*, The African Studies Center, Michigan State University, no. 22 (Fall 1973), pp. 93–124.

60. In the *Encyclopedia*, Hegel treats property and contract under the heading of Law, or Right as Right (both being synonyms for formal, abstract right). *Hegel's Philosophy of Mind*, § 487.

61. While in exile, Leon Trotsky acknowledged that Soviet bureaucracy attained a higher degree of independence from the "dominating" class than had bureaucracy in any

other state, past or present, with the exception of Hitler's Germany and fascist Italy. However, he still argued that the Soviet "apparatus" of the party, the state, and the armed forces failed to attain the position of a ruling class; the reason being that its "independence" was not based on the property relations characteristic of the society. In other words, even under Stalin, social ownership of the means of production prevailed and the workers formed the "dominant" class. The main proof of this contention was that bureaucracy "has not yet created social supports in the form of special types of property," such as stocks, bonds, or inheritance laws allowing for the transfer of bureaucratic positions from father to son. See *The Revolution Betrayed*, translated by M. Eastman (Garden City, N.Y., 1937), pp. 248–49. See also I. Deutscher, *The Prophet Outcast: Trotsky 1929–1940* (London, 1963), pp. 202–8, 302–11. Unfortunately, Trotsky failed to see that the bureaucratic rule *itself* amounted to a transfer of property to the wielders of power. If a peasant is tied to his village for life; if he cannot leave his domicile without permission from the authorities even for a short span of time; if his son cannot attend a university or go to work in the town without such a permit: then it is a misuse of language to say that he is a co-owner of the kolkhoz in question. On the contrary, it is the bureaucracy that "owns" him through the perverted institution of "kolkhoz." However, this critique is not meant to detract from the importance of the stress—in Trotsky's later works—on politics and democratic processes in a reformed Soviet system.

62. See, for instance, K. Marx, "Economic and Philosophic Manuscripts of 1844," *Collected Works*, vol. 3, p. 296; F. Engels, "On Authority," *Selected Works*, vol. 2, p. 378; and V.I. Lenin, *The State and Revolution*, ch. I, section 4.

63. F. Engels, " 'Socialism' Utopian and Scientific," *Selected Works*, vol. 3, pp. 121, 147.

64. V.I. Lenin, "The State and Revolution," *Selected Works* (Moscow, 1977), p. 333.

65. K. Marx, *Capital*, vol. 3 (Moscow, 1971), p. 876.

66. This is, unfortunately, true also of Hegel's "system of needs."

67. E. Domar, "A Soviet Model of Expansion and Growth," in A. Nove, D.M. Nuti, eds., *Socialist Economics* (Harmondsworth, 1976), pp. 149–72; the reference is mainly to pp. 164–68. The article—reprinted from E. Domar's *Essays in the Theory of Economic Growth* (London, 1957), pp. 223–61—is devoted to the exposition and analysis of the work of G.A. Feldman. The main source is two of his articles, both entitled "K teorii tempov narodnogo dokhoda" and published in *Planovoe khoziaistvo*, November 1928, pp. 146–70, and December 1928, pp. 151–78.

68. See section III, paras. (b) and (c).

69. See section V above.

70. See, for instance, Charles Bettelheim, *Economic Calculation and Forms of Property* (New York, 1975), pp. 51–53, 78–87. Similar is the view of Ota Šik, *Plan and Market under Socialism* (Prague, 1967), pp. 168–70. See also J. Kosta, J. Meyer, S. Weber, *Warenproduction in Sozialismus* (Frankfurt, 1973), pp. 119–22.

71. Gunnar Myrdal was not alone in believing that "comprehensive and complete planning" is likely to be beneficial in the "initial stages of underdevelopment." *Beyond the Welfare State* (New York, 1967), p. 103.

72. See, for instance, K. Marx, "Critique of the Gotha Programme," *Selected Works*, vol. 3, p. 17.

73. One of the less technical discussions of such iteration is to be found in J.M. Montias's article "Planning with Material Balances in Soviet-type Economies," *American Economic Review*, December 1959, pp. 963–85. The article is reprinted in A. Nove and D.M. Nuti, eds., *Socialist Economics* (Harmondsworth, 1976), pp. 223–51.

74. In principle, these limitations could be overcome by the application of the techniques of mathematical programming. In practice, however, these techniques have been

used not as a basis of planning, but only as a kind of check on the procedures adopted by the actual planners. One of the first attempts of this kind is discussed in J. Kornai's paper "Mathematical Programming as a Tool of Socialist Economic Planning," reprinted in *Socialist Economics*, pp. 475–88.

75. The meaning of "basic proportions" is usually decided *ad hoc*, depending on the purpose of the analysis. Invariably, products have to be replaced by product aggregates, at least for a substantial part of the calculations. It can be easily seen that in the long and tortuous vertical data flows—from the enterprises to the planning centre and back—a lot of the information is lost, partly literally, partly due to incompleteness, error, clogging (too many data to process efficiently) and misinterpretation.

76. M. Morishima and F. Seton, "Aggregation to Leontief Matrices and the Labour Theory of Value," *Econometrica*, 1961, no. 2. Their procedure was to derive values from technical data and prices. V. Nemchinov is one of those who proceeded, as Marx had, from values to prices. "Basic Elements of a Model of Planning Price Formation," *Voprosy ekonomiki*, 1963, no. 12, pp. 105–21. Excerpts from the article are reprinted in *Socialist Economics*, pp. 406–34.

77. The term—borrowed by Oskar Lange from P.H. Wicksteed—is by no means limited to cost-based prices: it goes even beyond price in the usual sense of the word, that is, the exchange ratio of two commodities in the market. O. Lange, "On the Economic Theory of Socialism," in B.E. Lippincott, ed., *On the Economic Theory of Socialism* (New York, 1964), pp. 59–60. The reference is to Wicksteed's *The Common Sense of Political Economy* (London, 1933), p. 28.

78. " 'Left-wing' Childishness and Petty-Bourgeois Mentality," *Selected Works*, pp. 436, 440. Lenin's emphasis.

79. See, for instance, Włodzimierz Brus, *The Market in a Socialist Economy* (London, 1972), p. 146. Also, Šik, pp. 272–75; Kosta, Meyer, and Weber, pp. 199–201. The institutional basis of the present (late 1980s) "wave" of economic reforms in the USSR is still in the process of formation. It seems, however, that, even if the range of centrally determined prices were reduced substantially (from the pre-reform number of 500,000), they would still prevail in all "essential" ("staple") products (such as "fuel, electricity, the most important raw materials, rolled steel machinery, and some consumer goods"). As for monopolies, the intention is to "end" them, partly by administrative measures, partly by the creation of "parallel enterprises or economic organization." Abel Aganbegyan, *The Economic Challenge of Perestroika*, translated by P.M. Tiffen (Bloomington, Ind., 1988), pp. 119, 128, 131, 134–35.

80. John Hicks, *The Crisis in Keynesian Economics* (Oxford, 1975), pp. 23–24, 62–66. Also Nicolas Kaldor, "Inflation and Recession in World Economy," *Economic Journal* (86), December 1976, pp. 703–14. The distinction between fixprice markets and flexprice markets goes back partly to J.M. Keynes (as noted in Hicks's work), partly to Michal Kalecki. See for instance J.B. Burbidge, "The International Dimension," in A.S. Eichner, ed., *A Guide to Post-Keynesian Economics* (White Plains, N.Y., 1978), p. 144.

81. In the fixprice regime, the loss of output (employment) is larger than in the flexprice world because the adjustment to a fall in demand affects only quantity, not also the price (the wage rate).

82. Brus, pp. 130–40; Šik, pp. 188–89; Radoslav Selucký, *Economic Reforms in Eastern Europe: Political Background and Economic Significance* (New York, 1972), p. 141. (The reference is not to a general statement, but to the description of the late 1960s Hungarian reforms. These reforms were, however, of special importance because—after the discontinuation of Czechoslovak reforms in 1969—they became the sole representatives of more incisive changes, as compared with the narrowly circumscribed reform attempts in the GDR and USSR.) As for the present Soviet economic reforms, it appears

that the state will continue to implement "an overall wages policy, mainly through a centrally established system of pay scales for workers." Also the "incremental norms" (roughly, the coefficients of wage growth per one percent of output growth, linked also to productivity growth) would be determined centrally. See Aganbegyan, pp. 165–67. F.I. Kushnirsky, "Soviet Economic Reform: An Analysis and a Model," in S.J. Linz and W. Moskoff, eds., *Reorganization and Reform in the Soviet Economy* (Armonk, N.Y., 1988), p. 46. In this way, the linkage between wages and the enterprises' economic performance would still be mediated by a rather unwieldy system of overall, exogenously determined indicators.

83. Hicks, p. 83.

84. Ibid., p. 85.

85. J.M. Keynes, *The General Theory of Employment, Interest and Money* (London, 1954), pp. 96, 136, 149, 154, 170, 202–203.

86. J. de V. Graaff, *Theoretical Welfare Economics* (Cambridge, 1967), p. 103. The argument presupposes an absence of perfect forward markets for all commodities, markets extending indefinitely into the future—but that is one of the most realistic assumptions to be introduced into economic reasoning.

87. E.g., Brus, p. 140; Šik, p. 231; Selucky, p. 141 (as in note 82, the reference is to Hungary). See also Kosta, Meyer, and Weber, pp. 183–84.

# The "March into Socialism"

## Expectations and Reality

A general reflection on socialism need not be just another end-of-the-century pastime, in which one confronts past hopes about reality on the occasion of a conventional calendar divide. It may help to bring out the cumulative effects of the continuous flow of change, and provide vital clues to understanding present-day problems.

With this thought in mind, I am moved to consider the validity of the traditional Marxist notion that the very development of capitalism leads inexorably to its replacement by socialism. That traditional notion is closely linked with the claim of socialism's economic rationality, its superiority over capitalism. "No social order," says Marx, "perishes before all the productive forces for which there is room in it have developed; and new higher relations of production never appear before the material conditions of their existence have matured in the womb of the old society itself." [1] The link between the maturity of capitalism and the rationale for socialism was also accepted by Schumpeter, from whom I have borrowed the first part of the title of this paper. For Schumpeter, however, the "march into socialism" was not to be welcomed but to be taken as an "observable tendency," the most important component of which was allegedly the waning of the entrepreneurial function—the cornerstone of Schumpeter's own theory of economic development. [2]

The simple and probably not surprising proposition put forward in this paper is that the unfolding of history has failed to confirm the belief that socialists have history on their side, a proposition that applies to both the traditional Marxist and the Schumpeterian notion of the "march into socialism."

---

The author is at Wolfson College, Oxford.

I

The 1917 October Revolution became the first challenge to the alleged historical regularity of the transition to socialism from mature capitalism. Faithful to their doctrine, most non-Bolshevik Marxists, including such luminaries as Karl Kautsky, denied the socialist character of a revolution in a predominantly peasant country with mere islands of industrial development and scant cultural and organizational conditions for planned management of the economy. Since then quite a number of Marxists have consistently refused to accept the socialist credentials of the Sòviet Union and the countries that followed in her footsteps; they also deny validity to socialism's claim of economic rationality and human emancipation, in the light of the Communist experience. In their view, both Marxism and socialism remain unscathed by this bastard product of rape on history.

On the other hand, there have been numerous attempts to reconcile the main body of the theory with this deflection from the predicted line of the dialectical interaction between the development of the productive forces and of production relations. In the aftermath of World War I, and perhaps during the interwar period as a whole, the arguments of this strand could not be entirely ignored. Those less committed argued simply that the incongruity of the victory of the revolution in Russia coupled with the defeat in Germany and lack of revolutionary situations in other major industrialized countries ought to be regarded as a historical accident, a temporary and freak accident unfit for generalizations. The dominant line, adopted by the communist wing of Marxism and made part and parcel of the official ideology in all countries of real socialism, was by far more assertive, trying to justify the actual developments in a positive way. Based on Lenin's (and to some extent also Trotsky's) formula of the "uneven development" of capitalism in its imperialist stage, the postulate of maturity was reinterpreted as applying to the capitalist system as a whole on the world scale. With world capitalism being economically sufficiently advanced for socialist transformation, the revolutionary break of the chain in the politically weakest link becomes legitimate. The Great Depression of the 1930s—by throwing the capitalist economy into an unprecedented downswing, bringing disastrous misery to many millions around the world, and causing acute instability in political relations— seemed to add weight to the argumentation: capitalism survived owing to the political skills and brutal physical force mobilized by the bourgeoisie against the laws of socioeconomic development; this made its survival costly, and ultimately only temporary. There can be little doubt that it was the turbulence in the capitalist economy at the time and the growing perception of the need to resort to interventionist and redistributive state economic policies to combat the crisis that also made many non-Marxists more receptive to the idea of the "march into socialism"; one can easily detect such a connection in the case of Schumpeter.[3] A related factor was the apparent contrast between the capitalist world and the picture of rapid growth and elimination of the plague of unemployment presented by the Soviet economy—with the dark side of the socialist moon well hidden behind the curtain of secrecy and gullibility.

It is not my intention to probe now into the validity of these arguments, and particularly into the question of the true Soviet performance of the time. The only point I want to make here is that despite the setbacks to the socialist revolution in industrialized countries, the realities of the interwar period still left enough room for interpretations compatible with the Marxist concept of historical regularity of the movement toward socialism.

In the very aftermath of World War II, this type of interpretation could still be argued for, though with its plausibility diminishing over time. On the credit side were placed first of all the Soviet war success presented as an unequivocal test of the socialist system's viability and strength, then the very fact of further expansion of socialism to new countries and continents, and finally the widespread view that problems of postwar reconstruction and restructuring in the industrialized part of the world required socialist methods of economic management in order to prevent repetition of the interwar debacle. On the other hand, however, the Marxist version of the "laws of motion" toward socialism suffered severe blows. The expansion into Eastern Europe was evidently imposed by force. In cases where a claim to the endogeneity of the transition to socialism could be made with any justification, it was in one instance (Yugoslavia) a country at a level of development comparable to that of prerevolutionary Russia, and in others (such as China, later Cuba and Vietnam) countries in which communist parties came to power under conditions of decidedly deeper economic retardation. Combined with the survival of the capitalist order in the leading industrial countries, this could not be so easily explained again either as a freak accident or as a manifestation of the "uneven development of capitalism in its imperialist stage." The suspicion of something like reverse regularity—the lower the level of economic and social development, the better the chances for a socialist revolution—was inevitably looming larger. Not the classical Marxian conflicts between the proletariat and bourgeoisie were the driving forces of such a revolution, but the struggle against colonial exploitation and national subjugation; and not the fuller utilization of the economic potential created by capitalism, but the promise of deliverance from underdevelopment, destitution, and ignorance made socialism attractive. This was acknowledged by Joan Robinson, who—sympathetic to socialism, but free from Marxist insistence on the laws of history—tried to generalize the empirical evidence in a new formula of socialism not "as a stage beyond capitalism but a substitute for it—a means by which the nations which did not share in the Industrial Revolution can imitate its technical elements, a means of achieving rapid accumulation under a different set of rules of the game." [4]

The notion of socialism as not a successor to, but a substitute for, capitalism in less developed countries was obviously unacceptable to Marxists, and numerous attempts were made to refute it. Among others, I myself argued that although it was true that imitation of the capitalist road of development—apart from very exceptional circumstances—would be impossible for the less developed countries in the second half of the twentieth century, the rationale of the socialist way was asserting itself not because of their immaturity but in spite of it.[5] It was hardly a convincing argument, not only in view of the mixed evidence of the comparative success of the capitalist and socialist strategies of fighting backwardness, but mainly because it missed the point about the historical regularities that—regardless of the results achieved under a socialist system in the less developed parts of the world—must be tested in the leading countries. And it was precisely in this testing ground that the second half of the twentieth century began to undermine forcefully the concept of the "march into socialism," in both its Marxist and Schumpeterian versions.

Unlike in the interwar period, the surviving capitalism has this time avoided plunging into depression. On the contrary, fluctuations—relatively mild by the standard of the 1930s—notwithstanding, the Western industrial economies displayed for at least a quarter of a century since the end of the postwar recovery a truly remarkable dynamic capacity: high rates of growth of output and of popular consumption, low (in many cases practically nil) unemployment, strong propensity to innovate both in methods of production and in final products, and substantial widening of social provision ("welfare state"). Even discounting cases of exceptional dynamism (for instance, Japan), the capitalist West looked in this period like anything but a system of production relations putting fetters on productive forces. There were obviously differences in performance among individual countries, but not of the kind that would allow easy categorization in systemic terms or in terms of relative levels of development (Italy, Greece, and Spain surged ahead along with France, Germany, and Scandinavia); several Asian market economies—South Korea, Taiwan, Hong Kong, Singapore—managed a dramatic leap from underdevelopment to the hastily established category of NICs ("newly industrialized countries"). Moreover, the process of rapid technological change, emergence of new centers of modern industry, greater interdependence of individual economies owing to powerful expansion in the international movement of goods, capital, and labor—all this caused a wideranging transformation of the population structure in the developed capitalist West, weakening the familiar social factors relied upon by the Marxist expectations of the "march into socialism." The relative, as well as the later sharp absolute fall in the number of manual workers generally, and of those employed in the traditional proletarian strongholds of the "smokestack" industries particularly, coupled with a marked increase in prosperity and ownership of consumer wealth (houses, durables) not only reduced the scale of support for socialist political militancy but also provided an unmistakable push to the advance of what may be described as "middle class attitudes"—a tendency to seek improvement within and not outside the existing socioeconomic system.

For a time capitalism's new dynamism was ignored by Marxist literature, especially in communist countries, but elsewhere as well. When the problem could no longer be ignored and was faced, mainly by the protagonists of "open Marxism," the attempted defense of the historical trend toward socialist transformation went in the direction of explaining the reasons for success by the socialist nature of the policies applied: the rise of state interventionism bordering in some cases on macroeconomic planning, substantial growth of the public sector in production, and even greater increase in the share of public spending in total expenditures, and a host of other forms of regulatory and redistributive measures undertaken by the "visible hand." In other words, capitalism was being saved by letting socialism gradually in, which was to be read as a sign of the historical tendency reasserting itself. Moreover, it was alleged that the resolution of the conflict that continued to be generated by the still dominant private capital would require further extension of the socialist components in the economic system. In this way the validity of the "march into socialism" was kept alive.

It is outside the scope of this paper to examine the factors determining or influencing the postwar Western economic performance. What is beyond doubt is the correlation in time between the major period of economic progress and the increase in the role of the state. However, such a correlation must not necessarily be interpreted as evidence in favor of the "march into socialism." Even at the peak of state interventionism, Western economies remained basically regulated by the market. The state interfered with the operation of the market, but at no stage was there the prospect of replacing the market by direct allocation of resources of the kind envisaged in the original Marxist blueprint. In particular, the room for entrepreneurship was preserved and, contrary to Schumpeter's expectations, the entrepreneurial function flourished, resulting in the explosive spread of new technologies and new products in commercial use throughout the world.

Around the mid-1970s the long Western boom came to an end; the familiar problems of excess capacity and unemployment returned to the economic agenda. However, the response to these problems was by no means auspicious for the traditional socialist direction—neither politically, nor in the actual evolution of the economic system, nor even intellectually. Politically—what could be taken as at least a partial reflection of the social changes mentioned before—nonsocialist parties were on the whole gaining at the expense of the left. In the economy the trend shifted to deregulation and privatization, while the attempts to widen the public sector and to strengthen the planning component (France, Greece) were rather quickly put into reverse. Intellectually, not only the rise of a laissez-faire ideology among those leaning politically to the right or to the center became manifest, but even on the left the radical socialist solutions were losing support relative to the modern stand; characteristic from this point of view was the strong revival of the idea of "market socialism" in the British Labour Party, not just as a temporary pragmatic compromise but as a fundamental systemic feature.[6]

## II

Needless to say, a mighty factor prompting these trends in the West, and particularly the spread of intellectual disillusionment with the socialist idea, was the experience of real socialism. On the political and human rights side—which I can only mention in passing here—the iron fist of totalitarianism reached its peak in postwar Stalinism, despite the fact that the Soviet Union ceased to be a single socialist country suffering capitalist encirclement; the disclosures at the twentieth party congress in 1956 and elsewhere confirmed the assertions, branded earlier as anticommunist, of unprecedented terror and deprivation suffered under the name of socialism. Later developments, although in many respects improving the state of affairs, have not changed the substance of the monopolistic rule of the single hierarchically organized party ("mono-archy" in my terminology), and were punctuated by the brutal suppression of popular revolts, including movements that had "socialist renewal" as their objective.

On the economic side, the Soviet system of command (centralistic) planning was soon after the war extended to Eastern Europe and to China, a clear sign that it was regarded not as a product of special circumstances in Russia (*inter alia* her vast untapped resources) but as a general model for the functioning of a socialist economy. By and large, a number of differences notwithstanding, it was used for policies similar to those in the USSR in the 1930s: a rapid industrialization drive through massive investment in new industrial capacity, particularly in extractive industries, metallurgy, and heavy engineering. The command system was geared to maximal physical utilization of capital and labor in defiance of conventional cost calculations, which contributed to the elimination of unemployment in Eastern Europe. The immediate results resembled the prewar Soviet ones as well: reportedly high rates of growth with low real wages, the latter to some extent offset by the effects of structural transformations (increased employment opportunities, urbanization, upward social mobility), more egalitarian income distribution, and broader access to education and health care. Soon, however, not the analogies but the differences began to matter most:

First, the performance of socialist economies had to be set against the background of a more successful capitalism: even the crude official rates of growth of national income (the credibility of which have been put in grave doubt in the Soviet Union itself)[7] ceased to look strikingly superior, and the comparisons of change in living standards were strongly unfavorable for the socialist side.

Second, the perception of the command system as a general model meant that basically the same economic mechanism was applied to countries on various levels of development, with various economic structures and cultures, and various degrees of interdependence with the world economy. It soon became evident that the gains were smaller and the losses higher the more modernized the particular national economy was. On the whole Eastern Europe fared, in comparative terms, worse than the Soviet Union, and among the East European countries Czechoslovakia did worst in those terms (East Germany must be treated as a special case).

Third, the time dimension changed: in the prewar USSR the command system operated barely ten years, and any scrutiny of its true merits and demerits was overshadowed by the victory in the war. After the war the command system continued well beyond the period of responding to the Soviet First or Second Five-year Plan—in most cases it has been still around in the 1980s—which made a long-term evaluation possible; and it is from this point of view that the failures become singularly manifest.

It would be, in my opinion, an exaggeration to judge the economies of real socialism as being threatened with collapse in the long run (although individual cases of collapse cannot be ruled out), but they clearly present a picture of relentlessly fading dynamism, or—as in China before the change of course at the end of the 1970s—diminishing capacity to overcome backwardness. The falling rates of growth are only the tip of the iceberg: low propensity to innovate outside the few top-priority sectors such as armaments and space exploration, scant ability to absorb even innovations embodied in imported technology (as amply demonstrated by the periods of East European borrowing or of Soviet windfall profits from oil and gas exports), inferior quality and maladjustment to demand, excessive input intensity (labor-, energy-, material-, capital-intensity) of production, obsolete sectoral structure of industry, composition of foreign trade with the West resembling that of underdeveloped countries—these are the faults widely acknowledged nowadays by most communist leaders themselves. The result is what I like to call "conservative modernization"[8]: the economies of the "real socialist" countries have been modernized—in the sense of changed proportions between industry and agriculture, urban and rural population, skilled and unskilled employment, etc.—but they display peculiar imperviousness to endogenous change, as if producing antibodies preventing the generation of a momentum of their own.

Since Stalin's death there have been numerous attempts to improve the working of the economy. The predominant line was to use economic policy measures, as distinct from systemic changes: reduction of the degree of tautness of the plans, reallocation of resources between sectors (particularly in favor of hitherto neglected agriculture), etc. It would be wrong to deny some positive effects of these measures in alleviating certain of the most glaring imbalances and allowing to improve somewhat living standards, especially in the 1960–75 period. Organizational devices were tried, too: the Khrushchevian shift from sectoral to territorial lines of command, advancement of intra-CMEA cooperation, more advanced techniques in central planning with the help of computers—at best, however, without conclusively favorable results. In China the policy swings were much more violent and ideologically loaded, with correspondingly worse consequences.

Over almost the entire post-Stalin period, an alternative approach to fight the economic malaise was advocated as well: the replacement of the command system by, according to this author's terminology, a system of "central planning with a regulated market mechanism." In other words—systemic changes, known nowadays ubiquitously as economic reforms. It is more than thirty years since the first attempt at such a reform was undertaken (Poland 1956–57), followed by a considerable number of subsequent ones in all countries of "real socialism," including the USSR in 1965. Despite this, the command system survived with minor modifications in all countries except Hungary within the CMEA and Yugoslavia outside it, obviously a separate case since 1948. There is no possibility to discuss here the complex reasons for the failure of reforms so far. Let us note, however, that from time to time, especially in the Soviet Union and in Maoist China, full-fledged ideological crusades against the "revisionist protagonists of market socialism" accompanied the resistance to change.

Against this background, the turnabout that occurred in respect to market orientated reforms since the end of the 1970s is truly remarkable. Reform became the party line not just in one or a few of the smaller countries but in the two citadels of world communism—the USSR and China. In the course of the better part of the past quarter of a century Moscow and Beijing were locked in a fierce ideological battle over primacy in communist orthodoxy, only to find themselves converging on this previously unlikely ground. Moreover, the concept of the reform has become much more radical than in the earlier abortive attempts: not merely the product market but also the capital market is either on the agenda or even in the process of trial implementation; the sacrosanct ownership structure with the state ownership of means of production absolutely dominant as "the highest form of socialist ownership" is under scrutiny, while a variety of other— private and mixed—forms have emerged or are being considered, in some countries with a pledge to grant them equality of opportunity in competing with the state sector; entrepreneurship is the most sought after attribute of economic behavior, with remuneration linked to profitability and hence much more strongly differentiated than under the old rules; joint ventures with foreign capital, not axiomatically on the basis of state majority equity holding, are increasingly favored, as is the postulated openness to the world market through the relaxation and perhaps even disbanding of the traditional monopoly of foreign trade; and the market clearing principle is the aim of the comprehensive reform of the system of price formation. A most important element of this new reform thinking is the acknowledgment in official quarters of the link between economic and political change.

Of course, one ought to beware of overestimating this new tendency. Even discounting the instances of lack of reform zeal (GDR, Cuba, North Korea, to name but a few from three continents), as well as the inclination to avoid certain notions as too embarrassing (e.g., "market socialism"), the gap between verbal declarations and reality remains enormous, leaving the possibility of reversal still wide open; not only potent group interests, but especially the paramount question of the compatibility of reform with the existing sociopolitical order may stand in the way of meaningful change.

Nonetheless, the intentions of the "revolutionaries from above" look genuine, and reflect the frustration with the failure of all the reform-circumventing measures tried in the past. The assertion of certain Western scholars that not only Marx but also Hayek was wrong because "planned economies could survive and they have survived"[9] provides evidently too small a consolation for the leaders of most communist countries who want their system not simply to survive but to be successful. That is why they press for reform, sometimes with astonishing urgency. Symptomatic of this attitude is the rather willing acceptance of the proposition that the far from brilliant, and sometimes outright negative, results of the already implemented reforms (Yugoslavia, Hungary, and to a degree also China within the state sector) are caused not by the general direction of marketization as such, but by insufficient degree of depth and consistency. Hence the raised level of radicalism of the reform concepts.

In the context of the proper subject of this paper, both the earlier and the latter experience of "real socialism" are relevant. They show that the resort to institutions and methods of economic management regarded as befitting the traditional notions of socialism is in the long run fallacious, and that a return to institutions and methods previously deemed capitalist becomes necessary, at least to a substantial degree. And it is not the fledgling socialism emerging in conditions of immaturity, as in Lenin's NEP, which had to tolerate the market temporarily, but to the contrary—the more complex the economy the more apparently it needs the market mechanism. Taken together with the absence of a socialist trend in the countries of mature capitalism, as well as with the marked inverse correlation between the level of development and the likelihood of a socialist revolution, this seems to point sufficiently strongly to the fallacy of insisting on the objective historical tendency of a "march into socialism." Apart from other implications, this conclusion—if correct—undermines the Communist parties' claim to their so-called leading role, meaning monopoly rule, which they try to legitimate by presenting themselves as the conscious proletarian vanguards endowed by Marxist-Leninist theory with the unique capability of reading the course of history.

## III

I would like to conclude with a few words about possible wider implications of this discussion for understanding the very concept of socialism and its relevance in the contemporary world. In my view, the renunciation of socialism as an inevitable outcome of the historical "laws of motion" should not be taken as tantamount to renunciation of the socialist idea as such. There is a lot to be said in favor of policies inspired by the socialist idea, and not only in ethical terms of fairness or of conditions for genuine popular participation in the political process, but in economic terms as well. What can hardly be upheld, however, is the concept of socialism as a grand design transcending in each and every element the institutions developed in the past, and hence by definition postulating their replacement, if not immediately at least in the long run. To the contrary, any new institution—public enterprise, macroplanning, redistributive mechanisms, etc.— ought to undergo pragmatic scrutiny and be put in place only if and insofar as the old institutions have proven inadequate to reach the objectives democratically chosen by the community. Needless to say, such scrutiny cannot be purely technical—it has to be put always in the context of the interplay of social forces. But within this context socialism should be regarded, in my opinion, not as a bounded system but rather as an approach to socioeconomic problems and conflicts of interests, which have to be confronted without the millennial prospect of their vanishing. I see in this a strong case for gradualism, even for the reversibility of certain institutional changes habitually regarded as socialist (nationalization or collectivization of means of production may serve as a prime example). On the other hand, discontinuities at some turning points cannot be precluded either.

As far as gradualism is concerned, it may rightly be said that this is an old idea, especially since Eduard Bernstein's writings almost 100 years ago,[10] and it should not necessarily be linked with the challenge to the "march into socialism." After all, Bernstein himself (in the work referred to above) acknowledged that "the theory which *The Communist Manifesto* sets forth of the evolution of modern society was correct as far as it characterized the general tendencies of that evolution, and that it was mistaken only with regard to timing and forms." This is certainly true. It seems to me, however, that in the light of the evidence accumulated over the twentieth century against the "general tendencies" themselves, the case for gradualism has acquired new relevance. My own views on this problem have undergone a significant transformation under the impact of this evidence, in particular under the impact of the negative experience of "real socialism" that has surged ahead in defiance of the gradualist approach only to find itself now in urgent need to backtrack. Whether a shift into reverse gear can prove to be at all possible under the circumstances, however, is another matter altogether.

## Notes

1. Karl Marx, Preface to *A Contribution to the Critique of Political Economy*, in vol. 1 of Marx, Engels, *Selected Works in Two Volumes* (London: Lawrence & Wishart, 1950), p. 329.

2. Joseph A. Schumpeter, *Capitalism, Socialism and Democracy*, 5th ed. (London: Allen & Unwin, 1976).

3. Ibid.

4. Joan Robinson, "Marx, Marshall, and Keynes," in *Collected Economic Papers* (Oxford: Basil Blackwell, 1980), vol. 2, p. 15.

5. Włodzimierz Brus, *Socialist Ownership and Political Systems* (London: Routledge & Kegan Paul, 1975), p. 13.

6. *Market Socialism. Whose Choice? A Debate.* Fabian Society Pamphlet, no. 516 (London: 1986).

7. G. Khanin and V. Seliunin, "Lukavaia tsifra" [The Cunning Figure], *Novyi mir*, 1987, no. 2 (in Russian).

8. Włodzimierz Brus and Tadeusz Kowalik, "Socialism and Development," *Cambridge Journal of Economics* 7 (1983), pp. 243–55.

9. Clark Kerr, *The Future of Industrial Societies. Convergence or Continuity/Diversity?* (Cambridge, MA: Harvard University Press, 1983), p. 26.

10. Eduard Bernstein, *Evolutionary Socialism*, English translation (New York: Schocken Books, 1961).

# Toward a Mixed Socialist Economy

TADEUSZ KOWALIK

In attempting to assess the possibility of a monocentric communist system evolving toward a "mixed socialist economy," one can ill afford to ignore the system's suppression of the non-communist left, a suppression that may have a major impact on current and future political decisions determining the system's evolution.[1] In Poland, radical social movements, especially the agrarian and workers' movements, were suppressed, and organizations, journals, and publishing companies were liquidated. (The journal *Robotnik* [The Worker], which now appears in limited circulation as an underground publication, stands out as a symbol of the destruction of the Polish Socialist Party.) Behind such suppression and liquidations was an incredible degree of hypocrisy that nearly doomed non-communist socialist thinking to oblivion.

The younger generations are almost totally unaware that the overwhelming majority of the socialist party leaders of the Second International, together with the intellectual heavyweights of that organization, and even some of those of the socialist left who resolved to join the communists (a resolution that often led to a tragic end), all agreed about one thing when looking at the Bolshevik program and tactics. Karl Kautsky, Otto Bauer, Rudolf Hilferding, George Plekhanov, L. Martow, and, in Poland, Ludwik Krzywicki, Mieczysław Niedzialkowski, Kazimierz Pużak, Zygmunt Zaremba, and many others knew perfectly well from the very beginning that the Bolsheviks were not building a socialist system. Even the "orthodox" at the time, such as Rosa Luxemburg (whose *The Russian Revolution* has not yet been published legally in her country), foresaw the consequences of a one-party dictatorship by a minority. In fact, even Edward Abramowski, a Polish socialist thinker, psychologist, and philosopher, could

---

The author is at the Polish Academy of Sciences, Warsaw.

deduce as early as in 1902 the main features of the Stalinist and post-Stalinist systems from the very simple assumption that a group of revolutionaries monopolize power in enforcing a communist system. Oskar Lange, too, though inclined to cloak himself in official terminology, would state in private conversations the following: "I am an old Menshevik and I have never believed that the Bolsheviks were building socialism."

But he and some other democratic socialists were in favor of cooperation with the communists, because in their eyes the communists were "modernizers." The political realism of such a "desperate follower" of the united front with the communists as Julian Hochfeld, and even of such a thinker of "socialist humanism" as Jan Strzelecki, stemmed from similar considerations. Some of them erred disastrously, and the author of this paper must include himself among them. Let me therefore say immediately what that error was.

## A substitute for capitalism

In the 1960s Joan Robinson won a wide acceptance of her theory that central planning *cum* public property had come to play the role of a substitute for capitalism, i.e., for capitalist modernization.[2] But did not the Austrian Otto Bauer argue much along the same lines, way back in the mid-1930s, and support his argument with even more convincing evidence?[3] Put very briefly, Bauer's idea was that the Stalinist five-year plans were creating modern industry with a modern working class, and that that working class would inevitably become the gravedigger of the Stalinist dictatorship. Lange (and with him a host of revisionists) also based his (and their) argument for "socialist democratization" on Bauer's old theory.

The past quarter-century has shown how very one-sided that idea was. The deep-cutting and enduring depression of the 1930s gave many observers the impression that capitalism had exhausted its capability for development, that it no longer could expand, and in particular that capitalism was incapable of industrializing the "backward" countries. The spectacular successes of the first five-year plans (the true costs of which were either kept secret or were not obvious at the time), on the other hand, seemed to indicate that all-embracing central planning had such capabilities. Indeed, the all-out mobilization of resources and manpower concentrating on a few selected goals (as a rule mainly on heavy industry and defense) produced many successes that seemed to bear out that faith. The revolution in education unfolding alongside with the early reforms seemed to be laying a solid foundation beneath a future "welfare state." Strumilin, a converted Menshevik who was regarded highly as the Nestor of the Soviet economists, came forward with the convincing-sounding quip that Stalin dragged Russia out of its barbarity using barbaric methods. The new superpower's nuclear success, especially after the shock caused by Sputnik, made the West take Khrushchev's challenge of catching up with and overtaking the United States very seriously.[4] One of the most prestigious Sovietologists today reacted to the events at that time by coming forward with two scenarios for the USSR: an optimistic one that showed the Soviet Union catching up with the United States within fourteen years, and a pessimistic one according to which that was going to take thirty years—until today.

That was the most reasonable justification for "real socialism" in Eastern and Central Europe, as well as the foundation of what Władysław Bienkowski (a former communist and the author of *Theory and Reality* [London, 1981]) called the "orientalization" of socialism and Marxism. Of course, many observers were aware of the excessive waste of resources involved in central planning, of the huge disproportions between particular sectors, and of the ill-fitting adjustment of production to demand. But the very high rate of growth of industry was clinching the evidence for them. Again, let me mention a good case in point, which, though it looks exotic today, was really typical of the predominant way of thinking at the time. Peter Wiles wrote in the very prestigious *Economic Journal* that if Soviet consumers could not find toothbrushes while there were too many shoebrushes around, that was only a temporary development, since the Soviet economy was growing so fast that it was sure to turn out a surfeit of all kinds of goods.[5]

Now, a quarter-century later, we are in a very different situation indeed. The West is in the longest-ever boom in the history of capitalism. The slower rate of growth after 1973 did not stop the revolution in technology and information. Japan became the second industrial power, and most recently the newly industrialized countries of the Far East have produced impressive records of expansion, thus at least partly denying the view (partly because Latin America has not managed to scramble from its backwardness) that capitalism is no longer capable of modernizing underdeveloped economies.

The communist countries, for their part, have not only failed to carry out their promise to catch up with and overtake, but are also falling more and more behind capitalist economies. They have been seized in an enduring stagnation that has many features like those observed during the Great Depression. It has become obvious in all those countries (that there is no exception is itself a very telling fact) that "socialist industrialization" stops when the extensive economy runs out of steam, and that it is a "conservative modernization"[6] at heart. If this type of modernization goes beyond the point of extensive mobilization of idle resources, its cost becomes prohibitive and overwhelmingly deleterious for the population's standard of living.

This brings us to the error of Bauer and Lange. The case of Poland seems to indicate that the large industrial working class, the product of that conservative modernization, is indeed digging the grave of the system. This is not because, living in the "socialist welfare state," the workers will no longer stand for a lack of democracy, but because a communist system is incapable of creating such a welfare state. The communist economies are unable to cope with their most fundamental requirements. Briefly, even in its role as a substitute for capitalism, which the system has not yet proven itself to be, it cannot succeed without a thorough reform or reconstruction. Yet there is so far no evidence that a recon-struction will work and not lead to a simple repudiation of the system.

I personally hope that there is a "third road" between the monocentric com-munism and the all-out development of a private market economy (even a nine-teenth century version if need be, according to some). And this third road is, I am deeply convinced, not only a value choice but also the least costly of all roads out of the present crisis. This option might be lost, however, because, at least in Poland, there is such a sweeping drift to the right that it puts not only the Communists but also all the left on the defensive.

### Ownership: A turnabout in the reform

Previous reform bids concentrated on decentralization and marketization. Ownership was never really among the main issues of reform programs. That is true of the reform programs the Polish government came forward with in 1981–82, and Solidarity's own programs did not differ much from the government's. When private farmers had their future guaranteed by an amendment to the Constitution in 1983, and when more freedom was given to private small businesses (the private sector outside of agricul-ture doubled its employment in the 1980s), these two developments could be understood as pointing to the stabilization of the present system.

In the mid-1980s, the crisis reached a new stage. The abandonment of central commands as the main tools of planning (but with central allocations of material and financial resources preserved) failed to strengthen the independence of state enterprises. A system of indirect centralism with millions of bureaucratic inter-ventions into the operation of enterprises was created. Moreover, the party *nomenklatura* embracing practically all managerial positions remained intact.

The political crisis over the faltering reform, as I see it, was partly caused by a growing sense of helplessness in the state and party leadership vis-à-vis the huge bureaucracy left virtually intact. For this latter was able to paralyze quietly all modernization bids the central authorities might want to put through. That partic-ular situation bred what came to be called the second stage of the reform and a desire to speed it up. Particularly from the fall of 1988, the reform has entered a new stage (with the term "reconstruction" becoming increasingly popular in that connection), which largely amounts to a "reconstruction" of ownership relations. What follows is a brief presentation of its most important features.

The principle of equal status for all forms of property got its legal safeguard in the law on economic activity of December 1988, which enacted simplified procedures for starting enterprise activity (would-be enterprise holders need not get permission; they must only notify the relevant office). The law was supple-mented both by a government promise to treat all ownership sectors equally regarding the purchase of raw materials and tools, and by certain steps to reduce rationing. Another important (but alas much less consistent) supplement of the same vintage is the law on business operations with foreign capital, and accom-panying government declarations designed to attract foreign investment to Poland. In an amendment to the civil code and particularly the law of enterprise finances, the public property of means of production was divided into two parts: one owned by the treasury (for which the enterprise must pay "dividends") and the other belonging to the enterprise (created by the enterprise's own investment).

These liberalization measures have already resulted in the expansion of the private sector in recent months. In January 1989 alone, several tens of thousands of new private businesses (mostly in the service sector) were registered. Also, it has become very "fashionable" in Poland to create companies. While joint-stock companies are not numerous as yet, limited liability companies have been mushrooming. Some are created by private individuals, others by state enterprises, and some are joint ventures.

It is becoming increasingly common to offer state enterprises for lease to private individuals. The authorities have also aired their intention to "de-statize" cooperatives, as well as to turn over part of state property to local authorities, creating a new form of municipal property. The same process has been unfolding in Hungary and China, as well as in the USSR (but on a smaller scale, usually as lease contracts). Nothing suggests that this is merely a short-lived process, and there is much to show that similar tendencies are beginning to sweep most of the communist countries.

These processes are being accompanied by deep changes in official propaganda. The Polish ruling party organ *Trybuna Ludu* has proudly declared that "a lot of people of power . . . have recently gone into private business." One of the Prime Minister's deputies publicly stated that "the only true self-management is management of your own individual business." Another deputy coined a slogan of "Liberty, Equality, and Competition" as the essence of the recent law on economic activity, a slogan that greatly resembles a well-known ironic slogan of Marx in *Das Kapital*: Liberty, Equality, Property and Bentham (with Property and Bentham standing here for Competition).

These new events have touched off a flurry of emotional reactions, ranging from enthusiasm to fears about a "sell-out of socialism," from accusations of escaping under the wings of capitalism to suspicions of "enfranchising the *nomenklatura*."

### Triumphant comeback of liberals

The most important new phenomenon of the 1980s in Poland and other socialist countries is the emergence and fast development of liberalism, of which the most dynamic is a conservative liberalism or neoliberalism. Extremist neoliberals from the West linked to political conservatism, in particular American ones, are being eulogized as the latest idols of economists. The new movement's gospels are F. Hayek's *Road to Serfdom*, Milton and Rose Friedman's *Free to Choose*, George Gilder's *Wealth and Poverty*, Michael Novak's *The Spirit of Democratic Capitalism*, and a number of articles by these authors or about them. All of these works have been published illegally, but recently this new current has spread to official publications, to the leading Catholic journals, and also to non-Catholic and left-wing journals.[7]

The official press for its part has begun to flaunt the new model formulated by Bronisław Łagowski, a party member from Kraków, the strongest center of the neoliberals. He is publicly trying to persuade the party leadership that to move the nation toward capitalism is the surest way to economic revival. In an unusual move for a communist country, the Polish authorities have entrusted the industry portfolio to one of Poland's richest private businessmen, a man who makes no bones about his hostility toward workers' councils (even though they have not ceased to be one of the pillars of the official program of reform) and his enthusiasm for a daring privatization program. In one of his widely known speeches, he said he would be happy if half of Polish industry could be made private. Thus there can be no doubt that the neoliberal current is making headway even inside the ruling Communist party.

The Polish neoliberals articulated their credo in the Charter of Private Enterprise approved at a conference held at the Catholic University of Lublin in April 1987.[8] In clear opposition to Pope John Paul II's encyclicals *Laborem Exercens* and *Solicitudo Rei Socialis*, the charter eulogizes the virtues of private entrepreneurship, acknowledging its faults only in connection with the lack or limitation of a free market.[9] In the same year the Kraków Industrial Society emerged, the unquestionable bastion of neoliberals. It is interesting to note that the society was registered with a modest program of equal rights for private enterprise in a multisectoral economy. But only a couple of months later it published a declaration demanding an all-out privatization of state industry, seeing in that move the only way of getting out of the crisis and putting an end to bureaucratization. The ideas of private enterprise and free competition are also being embraced uncritically by many clubs, associations, and political parties now being founded in Poland.

This explosion of the neoliberal sentiment (which has been described skillfully by Andrzej Walicki, a Polish historian now teaching in the United States)[10] leaves other ideological currents barely visible. Solidarity is reentering the public scene obviously split. Most of its economic advisers have moved far away from its 1981 program "For a Self-governed Republic" of which self-management was an integral part. A Polish Socialist Party founded late in 1987, a weak organization torn by internal strife, has managed to define its own position vis-à-vis the communist system several times. But it has said little about its economic program and does not react to the excesses of the triumphant liberals.

The bureaucratic structure of cooperatives is also under fire from the general public. This institution has never been able to recover from the "statization" of cooperatives and of the cooperative movement, even though recently some changes in legislation have been adopted to increase the autonomy of cooperatives. Cooperatives are all but nonexistent among the present flood of newly founded business undertakings. Not a peep has come from the Cooperative Research Institute linked with the "statized" cooperatives. The much vaunted idea of municipal ownership of property, the first foundations of which are being laid now, may also come to naught because there are no cadres linked with that tradition, although before the war municipal property played an important part.

In these conditions, workers' self-management bodies are the most promising social movement for reform, for they are institutions that fight both statism and laissez-faire concepts. It was workers' councils that stood up effectively against attempts to reassert a centralistic regime in the Polish economy (known as Lex-Kubiczek, after a former vice-chairman of the powerful Planning Commission, who was the main author of recentralization in 1986), and they managed to do so even at a time when they were not yet allowed—as a movement—to hold public meetings. But since then they have been allowed to organize meetings bringing together delegates from all over Poland. After painstaking efforts an Association of Workers' Self-Management Activists, which wants to help workers' councils in their work, got itself registered officially. Now this association is in the process of setting up its own research institute.

Yet neoliberalism has wrought havoc even in the self-management movement. While they boldly fight all restrictions imposed upon them by state administration bodies at all levels, workers' councils have been notoriously unable to transform themselves from being merely a participating body with limited power into full-fledged organs of self-management. The tendency to transform state enterprises into companies, which is openly backed by the central authorities, has sent shivers down the spines of many representatives of workers' councils who feel uncertain about the movement's future. Recently public officials as well as Lech Wałesa have come forward with vows of support for self-management. But even that did not dispel this uncertainty: "It seems that neither of them [the Communist Party and Solidarity] love us," said one of the founders of the above-mentioned association.[11]

### Privatization

If this is the political and economic geography of present-day Poland and if it is changing in this manner, does it still make sense to think of a Third Road between the abortive communist monocentrism and a private enterprise market economy? Is there any sense in looking for common points between the dynamic liberal circles in Poland and followers of some version of a mixed socialist economy with a large proportion of intermediate ownership between state and private ownership? Does a dialogue between liberals and socialists make any sense? I am confident that, despite what I have described up to now, which has mostly referred to relatively small circles of the intelligentsia, the reality justifies a kind of guarded optimism.

What do the liberals want? And, more important, what are their chances at present?

They want a private-market economy with the state's role in the economy reduced as radically as possible. They want Western technology (and thus also capital) to come in, for they believe that this can help modernize the Polish economy, if not as brilliantly as in the case of South Korea, then at least as brilliantly as in Spain. The social cost of such an operation, including the massive liquidation of inefficient enterprises (and thus unemployment), is inescapable in their eyes. They claim that the bill will not be prohibitive because "Private enterprise spurs people to action, mobilizing entrepreneurial energies, fresh ideas, initiative, perseverance, a readiness to accept sacrifice, owing to which hidden economic reserves can be put to work, and so even at a small expense of resources a nation can embark on a path of autonomous development." Private enterprise, accordingly, "may be the principal economic driving force that can . . . lift our nation from its plight and reverse its fortunes, that is, that can help the nation overcome the crisis and make the Polish economy viable again." [12]

I do not want to deny the virtues and benefits that private enterprise can bring. In fact many socialists used to preach such views. Oskar Lange, for example, in his well-known article on "Economic Foundations of Democracy in Poland" (1943), demanded that both small and medium industries should be left in private hands, because "they will impart a flexibility and pliability as well as adaptive capability that private enterprise *alone* can provide" [emphasis added]. [13] Still, I think it does make sense to consider critically both the chances of private enterprise in the present conditions, and possible roads to and boundaries for privatization in the Polish economy.

One undeniable merit of the liberals is that they are rebuilding the ethos of private enterprise, relieving it of the odium linked to the contemptuous word *prywaciarz* (this word, by the way, has disappeared from the official press), trying to guarantee equal legal and economic status, and spreading the indispensable knowledge of the commercial code. All those are indispensable conditions for the private sector to grow, and indeed the recent flourishing of the private sector is no doubt largely due to the efforts of the liberals.

Until recently, however, the private sector grew in a no-man's land. As long as such a situation continued, the liberals' natural maximalism, which is the most extreme version of liberalism, was of secondary significance. It could be dismissed as merely a question of short-term tactics. In the initial period, of course, it was less important to flaunt any complete program of action than to give an attractive "ideological shine" to private enterprise, to use the term of Ludwik Krzywicki, a Polish sociologist and economist of socialist creed. The more maximalist their propaganda becomes, the greater their chances of dispelling the "shine" of statist institutions. In private conversations, the liberals often concede they are more anxious to produce a fresh ideological approach to private enterprise and the market economy than to introduce commodity production. But this cannot go on much longer, for they soon face the fundamental question of what should be done with the all-embracing state sector, and with state enterprises?

Various neoliberals have had some rather startling things to say in reply to this question. Here are some samples of their opinion.

Janusz Beksiak, one of the advisers to Solidarity, has for several years been calling on the state to pull out from the economy on the argument that people themselves know best what should be done. He is radically opposed to anything resembling a policy design, which is fundamentally at odds with his staunch liberalism.[14] Again, as long as such opposition amounted to jibes at the state's omnipresence, it even carried with it a certain charm. But I am not sure Beksiak would be willing to take responsibility for such a radical step, if it were to be recommended as a practical policy.

Rafal Krawczyk, a Polish economist, has repeatedly called for an act of endowing all of society with property, issuing shares and changing state enterprises into joint-stock companies. A similar idea is being pushed by two economists from Gdansk, Janusz Lewandowski and Jan Shomburg.[15] But a true liberal, who regards private ownership of wealth as the foundation of all public life, is bound to regard this kind of a "present" as "stolen property." One of the liberals called giving people property for nothing a "peculiar kind of Bolshevism."[16]

Stefan Kisielewski, a Catholic essayist and the longest-standing herald of capitalism in Poland, began to become skeptical about it all just as his dream seemed to be coming true. He worries about whether "Mr. Mieczysław [both the prime minister and the minister of industry have this first name] will have the guts to sell the steelworks in Warsaw's Bielany district. But who would consider buying it? Even the Germans, Mr. Brandt's people, are not going to buy it."[17]

Aleksander Paszyński, the president of the newly established Warsaw Economic Association and a specialist in the housing economy, on the other hand, is more confident. He comes close to Beksiak's position when he charges that the reform is headed nowhere, and he accuses the official reformists of "still trying to design a new system." The most important of all processes under way now is, in his view, a creeping erosion of the system, namely the founding of companies under the protective umbrella of the *nomenklatura* and with its participation. For that is taking the system on the path to self-destruction (on which I will have more to say later).[18]

A short time ago, Stefan Kawalec, an economist of the Central School of Planning and Statistics, published an outline of a privatization program that is perhaps the most realistic idea of its kind.[19] I wish to point out two aspects of his argument. First, he seems to argue that privatization will (and must) be a long process. It should proceed at a pace that will "put at least two-thirds of state property in industry into private hands within the next 15 to 25 years." Secondly, Kawalec makes a plea for a privatization process from "the top down," i.e., a process the state should control all along. These two ideas are designed to avoid social unrest and to make sure that the privatization process amounting to the issuing of stocks should embrace the largest possible number of citizens.

## Group ownership

As an alternative to the above projects of privatization, there are certain proposals of social (non-state) group ownership. They are put forward by staunch liberals, who regard private ownership (in the form of stock) as the most efficient type of ownership, but who for practical reasons advocate "lower" forms of group ownership, and are also supported by moderate followers of group ownership who show little enthusiasm for pure liberal concepts. The former are represented by the aforementioned Tomasz Gruszecki, and the latter by Marek Dabrowski. Both have discussed a gamut of non-private and non-state forms of property, as well as mixed private, group, and state forms.

Dabrowski has distinguished the following forms:

> (a) enterprises owned by the workforce as a group yet without employees' individual property shares (much in the style of Israeli kibbutzim); (b) cooperatives in which membership automatically entails employment; (c) employees' joint-stock companies with stocks held exclusively by employees; (d) employees' joint-stock companies with some stocks being offered to non-employees; (e) enterprises being the property of municipalities; (f) enterprises owned by public organizations, parties, trade unions, and foundations; (g) cooperatives taking on hired labor; (h) enterprises owned by different public institutions, e.g., insurance organizations; (i) derivative enterprises, i.e., those owned by other non-private enterprises.[20]

Pawel Roman's idea for an "Employees' enterprise" fits well into one of these categories, too. He advocates an act for endowing the workforce with property at the request of 75 percent of the workforce. As soon as such a vote has been carried out, Roman suggests, the enterprise concerned should be automatically regarded as no longer subordinated to its state hierarchy (founding authorities). Roman's idea basically is that each employee obtains a share free of charge, and that their shares can be turned over to successors as bequests, but cannot be sold. But the holder (or his inheritor) is entitled to a share in profits only for a period twice as long as the length of employment in each case.[21]

Almost all these versions of what is termed social group ownership (and there is practically no end to all kinds of mixtures in this respect) have their roots in practice. In one or another form, they have existed in Poland or elsewhere. Some of them have been described at length in the literature. The problem, however, is that the general public as a rule knows only the two poles of ownership—state and private. That, too, is true as far as the imagination of reformists goes. I will return to this later on. At this point let me only point out that if Kawalec's program of the gradual transformation of some state enterprises (especially very large ones) into ordinary joint-stock companies could be combined with the program of transforming a large category of enterprises into group-owned organizations (such as cooperatives, state but fully self-managed enterprises, etc.), then the process of changing the entire system could perhaps take much less time than Kawalec presupposes. The whole reconstruction could probably also be done at a smaller social cost and against less dogged resistance from the members of the general public who are against the idea of privatization.

I am not saying anything definite on the relative effectiveness of all the above forms of ownership. To the best of my knowledge the literature is pretty inconclusive on this subject. But even if private enterprises are indeed the most efficient ones in the narrow sense of the word, it should be realized that all those other ownership versions promise to be more efficient than the ordinary state enterprises in their monocentric context.

Yugoslavia is the favorite case mentioned by those who want to dissuade others from the idea of worker self-management. Let me therefore quote Harold Lydall, one of the staunchest critics of the Yugoslav system both as a theory and for the way it works in practice:

> For those who start from a Soviet-type command economy . . . the introduction of self-management, even without any fundamental reduction in the monopoly power of the Party, offers a great step forward in economic efficiency, the encouragement of initiative and enterprise, the liberalization of some aspects of political life and the increasing application of the rule of law. . . .
> In any case, self-management is the only hope for the people now governed by the Russian system. It is not surprising, therefore, that all movements for liberalization in the Soviet empire have tried to move in this direction. Although it is easy to find weaknesses and unsolved problems in a self-management system, especially in the complex political and national environment of Yugoslavia these arguments should not be used to discourage workers in these countries from making self-management one of their principal demands.[22]

This conclusion of an Oxford don known for his first-rate neoclassical education should be remembered above all by the neoliberals of the latest vintage, who seem to have made an about-face without any qualms. But is there any reason to believe that the particular version of self-management we know from theory books (for even the most successful self-management bodies have as yet reached at most the stage of participation, and most of them are on the level of the more modest version of workers' control) is the only possible one? That version, and similar ones, must be improved in a process of learning by doing.

### An aside: Panamization as the fourth road

Let me briefly return to Paszyński's ideas about the "creeping" erosion of the system as a way of taking it toward self-destruction. Here is what he is telling those who fear that the state authorities may soon give the now fashionable tendency to found companies short shrift:

> For the time being the economic administration, and even the state and party apparat, are interested in founding as many companies as possible. They see chances for themselves to sit on various company councils and even to hold company stocks. That by itself presents no threat to companies as profit-making organizations; the apparat is only whetting its appetite for profits that companies can provide them with, and so not only is it not trying to hamper

the growth of companies but it is even making life easier for companies by opening a protective umbrella over them. That is a somewhat dubious practice in terms of moral standards, for it looks much like corruption working in both ways. But from the standpoint of the system's eventual destruction the net effect clearly works in one direction [*sic!*]. At any rate, the first companies have already been founded at the initiative of the apparat, and even of people representing medium-level Party authorities, and some of those new companies are chaired by people from the top echelons of power in Poland. This way the already faltering reform got unexpected yet strong support from that side.[23]

Paszyński in this quotation puts his finger on a very dangerous process that deserves to be exposed and studied as a warning. This self-destruction of the system is taking place amid widespread corruption as the "communist ethos" of thousands of apparatchiks is obviously crumbling. The otherwise natural process of one generation replacing another is unfolding amid an unprecedented crisis that seems to have no end.

Now, in these circumstances—with the rule of law remaining as a postulate only—the privatization of the Polish economy would lead to a situation that would have as little in common with the blueprint of Polish neoliberals as the ideal of perfect competition had with the notorious Panama affair. If for no other reason than this one, Poland cannot do without public control over this process and a variety of group ownerships involving participation, self-management, and cooperative sharing are more promising eventually than the "*Nomenklatura*-led privatization."

But there are also those among the neoliberals who are openly preaching the South Korean model of dictatorship plus free market (one of them publicly asked why the General had needed to create new trade unions). They are making the fundamental mistake of failing to see that the transition in Poland from state ownership, or "nobody's property," to private ownership would be a hundred times more prone to corruption than even Third World economies are.

One could of course argue that such an infantile disease of primitive capitalism is inescapable in the initial stage, but that a dynamic and growing economy will gradually cure itself. But there is no certainty about the economy growing really strongly once it has embarked on large-scale privatization. South Korea and Spain, for example, got huge injections of foreign capital as well as the latest technology. Given conditions in Poland, it is quite likely that the inflow of foreign venture capital will be considerably more modest. The costs to society of the reconstruction, especially the costs of joblessness, may turn out to be much greater than anticipated and hardly tolerable.[24]

## One-sided receptions

Western neoliberalism (mostly of the American variety) has virtually dominated the illegal literature in Poland during recent years. I wish therefore to point out the one-sidedness of the theories that are being spread, and which is particularly remarkable in the literature concerned with economics. For want of space, I am going to indicate only two cases in point, but more could be found if necessary.

First, let me mention the theory of property rights, which, of course, is a result of the Chicago school's expansion into the questions that used to be largely ignored by neoclassical economic theory. The main notion of the theory is that of property rights as a bundle of rights or of entitlements. As particular property rights are distinguished for analytical purposes, much more can be said about different ownership systems and their effects on economic behavior and undertakings. In Poland, however, the theory of property rights is being received with a baffling lack of criticism. It is being used almost universally to demonstrate the full spectrum of ownership forms from state ownership as "nobody's" through different degrees of "incomplete" ownership (e.g., self-management property and other versions of group ownership) to the ideal of full ownership, that is, individual private ownership.[25]

Yet none—literally none—among the Polish "recipients" of that theory seems to have noticed that precisely the same interpretation of property as a cluster or bundle of rights has been used by many Western socialists to justify a mixed socialist economy. In fact, back in the 1950s a group called Socialist Union (a team of theoreticians of the British Labour Party) had this to say in its programmatic booklet:

> The third, and perhaps most serious, misconception was the belief that ownership was one indivisible right, which could be held only as a whole—either by private persons or by public authorities; an industry was either wholly in private or in public control. In fact ownership consists of a bundle of rights. These rights are not sacred; they are upheld by the state and society. They are not fixed and unalterable; they can be changed and modified to any degree that state and society desire, and indeed they are constantly changing. Nor are they indivisible. Each separate right can be limited separately and by different methods; some can be in private and some in public hands.[26]

This interpretation of ownership as a bundle of rights was put forward by the group as the foundation of its concept of a mixed socialist economy ("part private, part public, and mixed in all aspects").[27]

A Swedish school of socialism, referred to as "Functional Socialism," is not much younger as a doctrine based on a similar theory of property rights. That theory goes back to the works of two socialist thinkers of the beginning of this century, the British economist R.H. Tawney and the Swedish lawyer Osten Unden. Gunnar Adler-Karlsson in his book *Functional Socialism* developed and popularized their ideas.[28] Property, according to him, is the sum total of many functions that may be held by many owners. It is on that concept that Swedish Social Democrats based their idea of the socialization of property. Socialization in that sense implies that private holders are being docked of their functions one by one. The Swedish Social Democrats do not renounce expropriation where absolutely necessary. But they regard it as their chief line to resort to socialization through modifications or redistribution of particular property rights.

I am not trying to convert anyone to these social democratic interpretations of property rights. I only think that both the British and the Swedish authors have moved too far away from the concept of *homo oeconomicus*, dropping the neoclassical one-sided view of private benefits as the sole motive of economic behavior. But in so doing, they tended to succumb to a *dualistic* view of the "mixture" of private and state ownership, while ignoring, if not disparaging, the importance of group ownership versions. Group ownership is the issue in my other illustration of the one-sided reception of the theory.

Elemer Hankiss has recently popularized in Hungary and Poland what is known as the "tragedy of the commons" theorem. [29] Along with the "prisoner's dilemma" and the "impossibility of rational democratic choice," that theorem has been widely discussed in the West as a model of a "social trap," and has touched off a true avalanche of publications over the past twenty years or so. The theorem is disarmingly simple. Ten cows graze in a common pasture. They belong to as many owners. When one of them gets the idea of putting out two cows to graze in that pasture, he will reduce the milk yield of the other cows, but his personal gain will be much larger than his loss (the reduced milk yield from his first cow). But his marginal benefit will induce the other owners to try their luck with the same. If many of them follow the first man's example, the commons will be destroyed, the cows will perish, and eventually their owners will also go under.

Hardin's theorem was of course a grand metaphor intended as a dramatic warning of an imminent ecological disaster. Viewed thus, it served a useful function. But it has become customary to draw two conclusions from that "trap," one of which is categorical while the other offers an illusory choice. The categorical conclusion is: "The only way to avoid the tragedy of the commons in natural resources and wildlife is to end the common-property system by creating a system of private property rights." [30]

The alternative to privatization, supposedly, is external enforcement imposed by a Hobbesian Leviathan (or an absolutist version of socialism) upon different communities. Quoting this and other statements, a Bloomington (Indiana) scholar in political science, Eleanor Ostrom, says:

> What is perplexing, as well as dangerous, is that scholars are willing to propose the imposition of sweeping institutional changes without a rigorous analysis of how different combinations of institutional arrangements work in practice. The current lack of sophisticated analyses of alternative institutional arrangements is a major weakness of contemporary work in social sciences. Limiting institutional prescriptions to either "the market" [used here to mean a private market economy—TK] or "the state" means that the social scientific "medicine cabinet" contains only two nostrums. [31]

This warning deserves to be heeded closely, as it comes from an author who has long been studying behavior and institutions connected with joint ownership. She began her research in the 1960s at a Californian system of drinking water reservoirs. From there she went on to study fishing communities in Turkey, common grounds in the Swiss mountains, and jointly held farmland in the Japanese countryside. Her conclusion is that human communities are not collections of individuals passively adapting themselves to the relevant institutions, but that they themselves are adapting institutions and rules to their own needs as they are seeking to reconcile their long-term interests with current temptations. Those people are "lawmakers" who put their hands into the making of their own "micro-constitutions."

It is hardly surprising that Eleanor Ostrom's studies have aroused little interest in the United States. What is surprising, though, is that such studies have aroused little interest in the academic community of a country where non-private ownership is so important. Workers' self-management in Poland (even though it emerged as a spontaneous "grass roots" movement) was formed (*gleichschaltet*) by the state authorities as far as its legal status and internal organizational structure are concerned. This makes it a very uniform and rigid structure. As self-management bodies are constantly having to defend themselves against the bureaucratic administrations and the *nomenklatura* trying to get control of them, they cannot concentrate on their own internal structure as their prime concern. The trade unions' ill-defined status has further obscured the issue. Wage demands and other typical union functions have become mixed up with the functions that self-management bodies should perform. Self-management bodies, accordingly, have never really had the chance to work normally, or to learn by doing. The situation they are in may now be improving, but whether or not the chance will be realized depends largely on the intelligentsia, above all the research centers. The same is true, perhaps even more so, of other related versions of property.

## Some conclusions

1. Changes in ownership principles, especially a tendency toward privatization, are the new feature of economic reforms now under way in the countries of "real socialism," a new feature that is most pronounced in the Polish and Hungarian cases.

2. The dominant and, in some countries, monopolistic state sector (apart from agriculture) is heading for an uncertain future. In Poland, a strong tendency has appeared toward privatization, mostly in the form of companies. But privatization has little chance of succeeding for the time being, if for no other reason than the want of large enough capital resources and personal savings. Under the circumstances any massive purchase of stocks is very unlikely. Self-management bodies' opposition may be (and probably is) another major obstacle to privatization.

3. As for material conditions, the easiest and probably the most useful road would be the transformation of most of the state sector into a socialized sector involving different versions of non-private ownership, such as authentic self-management owned enterprises, cooperatives, employees' joint-stock companies, municipal enterprises, enterprises owned by public organizations, etc. That, of course, does not rule out privatization as a meaningful way of making some state-owned enterprises more efficient.

4. This particular road of development may stumble over another major obstacle, which is the "economic imagination" of the general public, in particular of the intelligentsia's leading circles. They tend to view the ownership issue less from a pluralistic than a dualistic vantage point, thinking in terms of either state or private ownership. As statism has clearly fallen from grace as a system, public opinion has swung excessively toward private ownership. The party daily *Trybuna Ludu* (20 February 1989) reported that "a large number of people from the power structures are moving . . . into private business," but there are hardly any press reports about those long-standing proponents of "real socialism" engaging in group ownership, such as creating cooperatives.

**Notes**

1. In this article I am dealing with problems of the mixed economy in real socialism on the basis of Polish experiences. But I believe that other countries of Central and Eastern Europe are, or will be, facing similar problems on the road to transformation. This paper is a continuation of my study "On Crucial Reform of Real Socialism," in H. Gabrisch (ed.), *Economic Reforms in Eastern Europe and the Soviet Union* (Boulder: Westview Press, 1989), and this is why I skip the issue of political conditions and framework boundaries for the transformation as well as the question of the functioning of a mixed economy with a predominance of non-private and non-state forms of property. The underlying assumption is that the economy in question would be a market economy with limited strategic planning.

2. In "What Remains of Marxism" she wrote, "Socialism has not emerged out of advanced capitalism, but has turned up in societies at stages far back in the Marxian series, while capitalism continues to flourish side by side with the new economies." J. Robinson, *Collected Economic Papers*, vol. 3, p. 158.

3. Otto Bauer, *Zwischen zwei Weltkriegen* (Prague, 1936). That book was never published in Polish.

4. Michael Ellman, "Changing Views on Central Planning 1958–1981," *The ACES Bulletin, A Publication of the Association for Comparative Economic Studies*, 35: 1 (Spring 1983).

5. P. Wiles, "Growth versus Choice," *Economic Journal* (June 1956).

6. W. Brus and T. Kowalik, "Socialism and Development," *Cambridge Journal of Economics*, 7: 3–4 (1983).

7. Here is a good illustration of that. Several years ago when the left-wing monthly *Zdanie* [Point of View] appearing in Kraków published a selection of Hayek's texts, the Hayek-Lange dispute was not mentioned at all. When a similar selection of Ludwig Mises's texts was published more recently, a telling note was appended to the contribution saying that "His [Mises's] findings concerning the question of calculation in socialist

economy were confirmed by reality in a spectacular manner (Oskar Lange, who challenged Mises on that matter, displayed more ideological commitment than analytical expertise)." *Zdanie,* 12 (1989).

8. *Przeglad Katolicki* [The Catholic Review], 28 (1987).

9. The charter says, among other things, "Private ownership of property is the practical side of the Christian principle of auxiliariness, which implies that public life should concentrate mainly in intermediate groups situated between the human individual and the state." The *Laborem Exercens* appears to belong to a different, even opposing current of social thinking.

10. A. Walicki, "Liberalism in Poland," *Critical Review* (Winter 1988).

11. The Party has a long record of about-faces. But even Wałesa shifted recently from a self-management to a property rights inclination. Right after sending a letter of support to the *Self-management Forum,* he said in the interview, "Elsewhere in the world, management is a responsibility of directors, computers. . . . Self-managing bodies could become something like public control bodies, making sure that all wheels are turning in the right direction. . . . Now we have first got to change the ownership system. I am not speaking about capitalism or any other system, but I would like to see things this way: when I enter the shipyard I should feel a little part of it belongs to me too." *Tygodnik Robotniczy* [The Workers Weekly], 6 (1989).

12. *Przeglad Katolicki* [The Catholic Review], 28 (1987).

13. O. Lange, *Dzieła* [Collected Works], vol. 2 (Warsaw, 1973), p. 472.

14. See, for instance, "For twenty years I have dabbled in designing a better economic system for Poland. But now I am against such design games . . . let all kinds of ownership forms be in the ring, all kinds of private initiative, and let them compete against one another to see which of them is the best one." "Bez pointy dyskusja," *Dwadziescia jeden,* 3 (1986), p. 13.

15. J. Lewandowski and J. Shomburg, *Uwłaszczenie jako fundament reformy społeczno-gospodarczej* [Endowment as the foundation of socioeconomic reform], report from a seminar on Transformations of the Polish Economy (Warsaw, 1988).

16. Tomasz Gruszecki, An introduction to a seminar of Association of Employees Self-management Activists, 3 February 1989.

17. Kisiel (Stefan Kisielewski), end page column in *Tygodnik Powszechny* [The Common Weekly], 22 January 1988.

18. A. Paszynski, "Drogi i bezdroza reformy" [Roads and Blind Alleys of the Reform], *Tygodnik Powszechny* [The Common Weekly] (December 11, 1988).

19. S. Kawalec, *Zarys programu prywatyzacji polskiej gospodarki* [A Program Outline on the Privatization of the Polish Economy], report submitted to seminar mentioned in note 15.

20. M. Dabrowski, *Własnosc grupowa jako jedna z dróg przeksztalcenia własnosci panstwowej* [Group ownership as one way of transformation of state ownership], report submitted to seminar mentioned in note 15.

21. P. Roman, "Przedsiebiorstwo pracownicze" [Employees' Enterprise, summary of a draft law], mimeographed.

22. Harold Lydall, *Yugoslav Socialism, Theory and Practice* (Oxford, 1984), p. 292.

23. A. Paszyński, ibid. Let me point out a trifle that is not one. In the text you will come across the word "one-sided" in an unusual meaning. It may well have been a misprint (for the Polish word for "unequivocal"), but that may as well have been the price paid for a compromise with the Catholic editors of *Tygodnik Powszechny,* a journal that is, so to say, obliged to denounce any line of human activity that is morally dubious.

24. J. Marczewski, the Nestor of Polish emigre economists, published an article called "An Economic System for Poland after Its Liberation," *Kultura,* 12 (1987). His idea of a

D-Day when "the Polish people will finally be free to choose in a truly free and democratic manner, the political, social and economic system under which it wants to live" seems rather utopian to me. But I want to make clear that Marczewski beats neoliberal economists living in Poland to a firm sense of realism, as he openly acknowledges the great problems and difficulties such as any major transformation of the system is likely to cause.

25. The best review of the pertinent literature in Polish is J. Strzelecki, Jr., "Teoria praw własnosci: geneza, podastawowe pojecia i twierdzenia" [The Theory of Property Rights: Roots, Main Concepts and Contentions], mimeographed (Warsaw, 1984).

26. Socialist Union, *Twentieth Century Socialism, The Economy of Tomorrow* (London, 1956), p. 126.

27. Ibid.

28. G. Adler-Karlsson, *Functional Socialism, A Swedish Theory for Democratic Socialization* (Stockholm, 1967), p. 20. There is also a Canadian edition edited by Abraham Rotstein.

29. E. Hankiss, *Pułapki społeczne* [The Social Traps] (Warsaw, 1987). The author of the theorem is Garrett Hardin, "The Tragedy of the Commons," *Science*, 162 (December 1966).

30. R.J. Smith, "Resolving the Tragedy of the Commons by Creating Private Property Rights in Wildlife," *CATO Journal*, 1: 2 (1981); quoted after E. Ostrom, Institutional Arrangements and the Commons Dilemma, mimeographed by Indiana University, March 1987, p 7.

31. E. Ostrom, "How Inexorable is the 'Tragedy of the Commons'? Institutional Arrangements for Changing the Structure of Social Dilemmas," mimeographed by Indiana University, April 1986, pp. 9–10.

# Does Yugoslavia's Self-Management System Promote Income Equality?

## Henryk Flakierski

For some time I have been investigating the relationship(s) between the degree of decentralization of the economic system and inequality of pay in Eastern Europe.[1] My recent work addresses the nature of this relationship in two Eastern European countries, Poland and Hungary,[2] and the present paper is drawn from a study of the same question in Yugoslavia. In this study I examine the relationship between the self-management system of Yugoslavia and the income distribution pattern in that country. Let me begin with a few comments about the nature of the distributional pattern in Yugoslavia.[3]

(1) The Yugoslav distributional pattern is characterized by low levels of skill differentials and high levels of interbranch and interfirm differentials. This implies that the dispersion of pay is substantial within each occupational group and stratum but very weak between occupational groups and strata. In spite of the high levels of interbranch and interfirm differentials, however, the overall relative dispersion of pay is quite egalitarian, due to the fact that the low skill differentials counteract the high interbranch and interfirm differentials.

The distributional pattern of pay differentials indicates that increases in the inequality of pay between branches and firms do not necessarily increase the stratification of society, if the pay differences between skills and occupations do not increase. This is the case because an increase in interbranch differentials will raise the dispersion of pay *within* each occupational group and stratum but not *between* them.

The possibility of increasing the relative dispersion of pay without an increase in stratification of society affords the state an additional degree of freedom in its distributional strategy. The state can, if it so desires, increase the inequality of

The author is at the Department of Economics and Social Science, York University.

pay without exacerbating conflicts between strata. However, substantial differences in earnings for the same job, skill, and occupation in different branches and enterprises create political pressure to reduce those differences by administrative measures. Experience has shown that workers in Yugoslavia do not accept substantial differences in pay between enterprises as fair and require remuneration more or less equal to that prevailing in the best working enterprises. Thus, great differences in pay for the same job lead to a general rise in earnings in excess of labor productivity.

(2) The Yugoslav system, from the point of view of the equality of pay, has not done badly. The general picture of pay inequalities is not worse, and in fact in many cases is even better, than in other socialist countries. The Yugoslav experience suggests that a decentralized economic system can have smaller inequalities of pay than a more centralized economy.

(3) Examined from the "incentives" point of view, however, the Yugoslav system of pay contains the worst possible elements. Employees receive high rewards in prosperous enterprises to which they have contributed very little, since in most cases the higher incomes result from monopolistic practices of all kinds. At the same time, the pay system in place rewards very little the contributions that employees have actually made. Indeed, better work and higher skills receive a very small premium.

**Skill differentials and
Yugoslav self-management**

Let us now turn our attention to those features of the distribution pattern that can be attributed to the economic system itself. We begin with a systematic analysis of interskill differentials. Can we detect a link here between the nature of those differentials and some general systemic features?

It is claimed by many advocates of participatory industrial democracy that, in an environment where workers identify themselves with the firm due to their direct participation in decision making, smaller skill differentials will not diminish work effort, responsibility, and the desire for advancement in one's career. There is considerably less reliance upon personal incentives in a participatory work environment.

The adherents of industrial democracy (like the traditional left in general) question the effectiveness of wage differentials and close supervision for motivating workers effort. According to some scholars in this field, especially industrial psychologists and sociologists,[4] work effort has three dimensions: duration, intensity, and quality. The worker has ultimate control over the second and third of these. But material incentives and organizational controls are external to the worker, and in practice even elaborate external incentives can fail to stimulate top productive performance. A participatory work environment, according to such writers as Vanek, Espinosa, and Zimbalist, enhances the probability that the worker will internalize the goals of the enterprise. Once the process of goal internalization begins, sources of effort untapped by external incentives are progressively opened and the potential comes closer to being realized.[5]

A similar view is expressed by Williamson. He argues that market relations presume and legitimize a calculating mentality. Unless this is offset by some form of social control, *quid pro quo* relations (payment for effort) invite individualistic, free-riding exploitation of flaws in the management system.[6] Even capitalist firms, argues Williamson, introduce certain forms of social control to induce social obligation and in this way to modify the calculating mentality. Other examples of social control cited by many authors include mores encouraging hard work and respect and adherence to authority. The seniority system is yet another device to create a long-term relationship and sense of obligation between workers and firms. Successful social control instruments, according to Carter, "create an expectation of long-run fair and reciprocal obligation, and lessen the need for precise short-run accounting of individual behavior."[7]

Although most participatory enterprises do still maintain skill differentials (since goal internalization is a long and gradual process), inequality of remuneration and reliance upon personal incentives are significantly reduced in a self-managed environment, according to the proponents of industrial democracy. The examples of Maoist China, the Yugoslav firms, enterprises in Chile during the Allende government, and the Mondragon cooperatives (where skill differentials are much smaller than in the rest of Spanish industry) are used to argue that worker-created structures are more equal than those imposed by the capitalist system; and further, that equalization of wages does not reduce motivation, because it creates worker solidarity, whereas very large differentials divide the work force and foster internal rivalries.

The evidence that self-managed enterprises in general, and those in Yugoslavia in particular, have smaller differentials than capitalist firms is very strong. But can we link this with the specific nature of self-management in Yugoslavia? A cautionary note is in order here. Although formally, social control devices are probably easier to introduce under self-management, whether or not they are successful depends to a large degree on the genuineness of participation in general, and particularly where issues of personal income distribution are concerned. A sea of ink has been used to describe how very often self-management in Yugoslavia has degenerated into a mere formality, whereby the collective rubber stamps the decision of the power elite, usually composed of the top management and the trade union and party bosses.

All the evidence from sociological research indicates that the majority of semiskilled and unskilled manual workers in Yugoslav industry does not participate in the activity of the workers' councils, and that they behave as traditional wage laborers. Considering that these two skill groups represent the majority of manual workers, and that they account for 70–80 percent of workers' council membership, the scope of participation is sharply reduced. Indeed, even the participation of skilled workers in the decision-making process of the firm is far from impressive. A survey conducted by Obradović for twenty industrial enterprises in four republics over a period of three years indicates that the managerial staff plays a decisive role in the decision-making process, especially when technical, organizational, or market-oriented issues are discussed.[8] According to this survey, members of the executive group take up 80 percent of the total time spent in the discussions of the workers' council; they provide 70 percent of all explanations; and 75 percent of all proposals that are accepted were offered by members of this group. What is more, the above-cited study and other surveys also report a very high correlation between the hierarchical status of the individual in the firm and his level of participation in the workers' council; the higher one's position on the executive ladder, the more intensive is his participation.

It is to be expected that managers would play a major role in decisions about technical matters, marketing, and cooperation inside and outside the firm, since these require competence and expertise. But, surprisingly, even in matters of income distribution and working conditions, where we would expect the most intensive worker participation in decision making, the situation is not what one might predict. Seventy percent of all employees (mostly the unskilled and semi-skilled), according to Obradović's study, participate very little or not at all in discussions about income distribution and related matters. It is enough to say that of all the proposals accepted in this area, 86 percent were made by managers, who comprise no more than 8 percent of the total workforce.[9]

Although it is not our aim to give a full analysis of the reasons why the real status of the workers in decision making is so weak, a brief description of a few points of view is very suggestive.

(1) Social power, according to the distinguished Yugoslav sociologist Županov,[10] is distributed hierarchically in favor of the leading personnel, with workers having the least power. From this point of view, the situation is not essentially different from the existing industrial organization in the West. The reason why social power has not changed in the Yugoslav firm is linked with the fact that, as hierarchical organization has survived, so has hierarchical subordination. The key position of management in the communication process and in coordination has not been affected by the introduction of the formal structure of self-management. Management has retained the strategic position in dealing with external demands and environmental pressures stemming from technological and market forces. Although formally managers are not granted entrepreneurial prerogatives (this authority belongs to the workers' council), in reality they are better equipped to carry out these functions. Županov's conclusions in this matter are worth quoting:

> Even the most radical changes in the formal institutional blueprint do not assure an effective participation of employees, for they do not necessarily redress the power imbalance between management and employees which is

inherent in industrial organizations everywhere. In other words, they do not overcome the power barrier to successful participation.[11]

(2) The existing model of self-management organization is composed of two different structures which are not quite compatible: a hierarchical one functioning in the daily work process, and a nonhierarchical one functioning only sometimes. But each of these structures is based on a different definition of the producer's role, and on different organizational principles.

(3) Self-managed firms cannot be fully autonomous in a market environment. Inside the enterprise the workers are formally autonomous and equal, but in the market situation they are dependent and unequal. The fact that factors outside the control of the workers' council (the possibility of financing investment from credit, the market price, the demand for goods on the market, prices of inputs, etc.) become more important for the success of the firm than the workers' own efforts reduces worker interest in what is going on in the enterprise. As a result, the issues that are discussed and decided on in the workers' council are secondary. This means that genuine self-management in a single unit is not really possible. Only in a broader framework can it make sense, namely if workers are able to control the surplus on a national scale via a vertically integrated central workers' council.[12]

(4) Even under the best of circumstances, full-scale council democracy, where decisions are taken by general vote, can work efficiently only in rather small groups, because there is a limit to the capacity to process information. As Williamson points out, "Everything cannot be communicated to everyone and joint decisions reached without preempting valuable time that could be productively used for other purposes. Since the number of linkages in all channel networks goes up as the square of the number of members, peer group size is perforce restricted."[13] It is possible that this informational constraint is not as strong as Williamson describes, but there is no question that the larger the size of the collective, and the less transparent and simple the information structure, the more difficult it is to make decisions on a broad democratic basis. The attempt in Yugoslavia in the 1970s to break the larger firms into small units of associated labor (BOALS) was intended to make self-management more meaningful; but this, as we know, comes into collision with the technical requirements of coordination and planning. The dismemberment of firms into small units, and the introduction of market exchange between the associated labor units in the larger firm, proved costly and inefficient, especially where economies of scale play an important role. A retreat from this fragmentation is under way. New proposals suggest that the independence of BOALS should be limited, and especially that commercial trading between them should cease.[14]

Whatever the reasons for the weak status of workers in enterprise decision making, the relatively small skill differentials in the Yugoslav economy can be linked with its self-management only if we assume that the majority of employees participate effectively in the decisions on distribution of personal income. If, however, this is not the case, we must look for other explanations. We would suggest that egalitarian socialist ideology has played an important role in establishing low skill differentials, independently of the self-management system.

Studies done by some Yugoslav economists and sociologists[15] indicate that egalitarianism is the dominant value shared by those employed in industry. For workers, equality and equity rank highest of all values, while self-management and solidarity rank very low among both workers and managers. But managers, by contrast with workers, give very little value to equality, stressing instead personal freedom, payment according to work, etc., which of course is not unexpected for this social stratum.

In view of the overwhelming superiority of management (especially top management) in the enterprise decision-making process, including decisions about income distribution, the question arises as to how the egalitarian ethos of the majority of workers is translated into egalitarian skill differentials, despite management opposition.

Obradović's survey indicated that members of the League of Communists participate very actively in the decision-making process of the workers' council on all subjects, and especially intensively on matters of personal income distribution. This is not surprising, considering that the majority of executives and many experts are party members.

Although on most issues the League of Communists, especially its secretary in the firm, sides with the top management (there being a strong connection between the political and technological structures in the enterprise) in matters of income distribution and relations with the outside world, the party elite's view differs in many instances from that of the managerial elite. The party sides with the values of the majority of workers and exerts influence on the managers and trade unions in support of an egalitarian pay structure. These matters are thus determined more by political aims and motives than by economic ones. The influence of the League of Communists on the income distribution in the enterprise is therefore a sort of ''indirect'' state intervention.

The egalitarian tendency to level off skill differentials was reinforced by the economic crisis in the 1980s, when real personal income declined substantially. By the end of the 1970s, some republics (notably Serbia) had established guidelines[16] for average skill differentials in order to protect low paid groups from economic crisis and falling real incomes; but these were soon abolished because the actual dispersion of skill differentials was even lower than the prescribed guidelines. A decline of the total sum available for distribution in the enterprises[17] has forced a compromise in favor of the lower and average paid workers.[18] It is difficult not to agree here with Bićanić when he claims that the economic crisis in Yugoslavia has made the problem of distribution more acute and has strengthened egalitarian tendencies—as he calls it, the perception of equal stomachs.[19]

To conclude this part of our analysis, the egalitarian tendency is not specific to the Yugoslav self-management system. It was, after all, well pronounced before self-management was fully established in the period 1945–65. What is more, egalitarian skill differentials were and are in evidence in other socialist countries.

## Interbranch pay differentials
## and Yugoslav self-management

We shall now investigate the link between interbranch and interfirm pay differentials and the Yugoslav economic system. The point of departure for our analysis will be an overview and critique of different theories as to why interbranch and interfirm differentials in Yugoslavia are as large as they are, a question that has been widely debated in economic literature, both in the West and in Eastern Europe. We can distinguish three main schools of thought about the nature of income distribution in Yugoslavia: the labor school, the capital school,[20] and the property rights school. Following a brief description of each, we shall offer a critical appraisal.

### *The labor school*

The labor school of wage determination applies the neoclassical static equilibrium analysis of capitalism to the Yugoslav firm, to show that specific differentials are created in the framework of self-management.[21] Adherents of this school claim that the differences in wages in different enterprises and branches are linked with the logic of self-management, and that they are too large to be explained by economic policy alone. This school of thought, like the others under review, assumes that a firm under labor management will maximize income per worker, in contradistinction to the capitalist firm, where the objective function is the size of profit.

The labor school also assumes that there is no labor market under Yugoslav self-management, hence labor mobility is restricted. As a result, differences in the marginal product of labor will not be equalized, and certain firms will have permanent gains which will not be transferred to other enterprises.

According to Estrin, a prominent figure in the labor school, in a capitalist economy, an increase or decrease of marginal product leads to the hiring or firing of workers, so that labor is attracted from firms with low, and to firms with higher, values of marginal product. This process of reallocation continues until efficiency is restored in the labor market. But in a self-managed firm, Estrin argues, an increase in the price of its products automatically leads to increased earnings, since a lack of labor mobility prevents entry into high-earning enterprises. As a result, wages and marginal products of labor are not equalized in different uses, and the more "successful" firms permanently enjoy higher wages.

Because a lack of labor mobility prevents an efficient allocation of labor, Pareto's optimum cannot be achieved. Assuming a suboptimal allocation of labor, it follows that, if a proper reallocation of labor between firms were to take place, the level of output could be increased. Furthermore, a more efficient allocation of labor would reduce interfirm differentials. On this point in particular, Ward was probably the first in the labor school to use neoclassical tools to argue that interfirm differences in income in Yugoslavia are a result of an inefficient allocation of labor.

The fact that labor is not mobile and is inefficiently allocated points to the conclusion that under self-management firms employ less labor than they would under more developed labor market conditions. The gist of the argument is as follows: Given that the objective function of the self-management firm is the maximization of income per worker, the marginal product of labor must be equal not to the wage rate ($w$), as in a capitalist firm, but to income per worker ($y$). Assuming the law of diminishing returns, it follows then that workers' income in a socialist firm must be larger than capitalist wages ($y>w$) in an identical capitalist firm where profit is positive. A self-managed firm will therefore employ fewer workers and use a more capital-intensive method than its capitalist counterpart. Hence the model predicts high rates of unemployment and a labor-saving tendency under self-management.[22]

## The capital school

The capital school, represented by Vanek, Jovičić, Milenkovitch, and Staellers,[23] links the differences in incomes and high capital-labor ratios in Yugoslavia not with the imperfections of the labor market or with the specific property rights of the Yugoslav firm, but rather with the imperfections of the capital market. According to this intellectual tradition, maldistribution of income, which is a signal that the Pareto optimum has not been reached, is strictly linked with inefficient allocation of resources.

Within the framework of the capital school, inefficiencies in income distribution are explained by the low price of capital, resulting in its rationing, which allows enterprises with privileged access to credit to acquire a quasi rent which is distributed to workers as wages. A lack of capital mobility prevents equalization of price for that factor of production and does not allow the efficient allocation of assets; this in turn produces a quasi rent which is the difference between the marginal product and the cost of capital. Workers appropriate this difference from the capital allocated to their firm by the planners. Better access to capital, in one form or another, creates this kind of monopoly quasi rent, and is mostly manifested in firms and branches with high capital-labor ratios ($K/L$).[24] The greater the share of capital in the formation of net output, the greater the possibility of earning such a quasi rent. If enterprises were to be charged a price on capital reflecting scarcity (a price equal to the marginal productivity of capital), the quasi rent would disappear, and the extra differentiation of wages among firms and branches for the same skill profession would disappear along with it. A low cost of capital (below the marginal productivity) not only creates unequal distribution of incomes, due to variation of rent in different industries, but is bound to produce unnaturally high capital-labor ratios and, consequently, small potential to increase employment in the firms.

According to Vanek, this tendency for excessive capital intensity is exacerbated by some specific state policies intended to prevent excessive income inequalities. The social agreements requiring that branches and firms with higher-than-average incomes should save a higher percentage than those with lower-than-average incomes are, even if well intended, counterproductive. The end result of such intervention is a further increase in the capital intensity of the economy. This is so because, in a situation where there is no control over the particular capital intensities, firms with larger savings will install more labor-saving equipment, which will further increase labor productivity and incomes, setting the stage for further capital-intensive accumulation. This cumulative process is succinctly described by Vanek: "rich enterprises will grow richer, the poor ones and the unemployed will be left behind."[25] (A similar point is made by S. Popov, another proponent of the capital school in Yugoslavia.)

Vanek sees the process of self-financing of investment as one of the major stumbling blocks hindering the remedy of the shortcomings of the Yugoslav economy in general, and the maldistribution of wages in particular.[26] Under a usufructus property regime,[27] self-financing prevents the equalization of marginal productivities of capital in different uses, because the time preferences of working collectives vary significantly. He advocates a switch from internal to external funding, to a pure rental process of investment which, together with a proper price for capital and more developed capital markets, would permit an efficient allocation of capital under the existing property relations.

External funding, according to Vanek, is philosophically and ideologically more in tune with the property relations in Yugoslavia—with the usufructus regime—simply because the capital stock cannot be traced to those individuals who have created it. In reality all Yugoslavs have created this capital; therefore the interest and rents from such capital should belong to society as a whole. In Yugoslavia, however, workers earn and consume rent on alienated labor other than their own, and at the same time they collectively save funds which they cannot recuperate. Economic power in Yugoslavia, Vanek complains, depends, to a degree, on the amount of capital that organizations have at their disposal, and not only on their labor potential. He considers self-financing of investment an aberration in the labor-managed economy, something that is inconsistent with its very nature and should be abolished.[28]

A variant of the capital school is the so-called *capital price school* whose major proponents are Bajt, Horvat, Mihailović, and Popov.[29] They attribute inefficiencies in the allocation of resources to capital shortages, inefficient capital-rationing procedures, and low or negative real interest rates. The capital price school is quite popular in Yugoslavia, probably because it does not link short-comings of the allocation of resources with the very core of the system—that is to say, with self-management *per se*.

## The property rights school

The third stream[30]—the property rights school—holds that one of the characteristics of property relations in Yugoslavia is a lack of individual property rights, which in turn works as a hindrance to the mobility of both labor and capital. A worker in a Yugoslav enterprise, unlike some other forms of cooperative (e.g., Mondragon),[31] cannot take away the proportion of funds that he has accumulated as part of the enterprise's capital stock when he leaves his job. He enjoys the benefits of investment funds in the form of a larger personal income, better working conditions, and so forth, but only as long as he stays with the firm. The same is true regarding workers' investment in collective consumption services. They enjoy the benefits of kindergartens, hospitals, cafeterias, housing, etc., only as long as they are with the firm.

The longer a worker stays with the firm, the larger is the return on his investment; the larger is the proportion of nonpecuniary benefits in the total income, and therefore the stronger is his determination to stay with the firm. Those who remain in the firm and those who join it, even if they make very little contribution to the investment fund, take over the benefits of those who invested their income in the enterprise for a prolonged period.[32] For all these reasons, workers are not inclined to change jobs and lose their benefits.

Since workers' income and nonpecuniary benefits depend not only on their own effort, but also on how much capital was accumulated in previous years, moving to another enterprise may bring a reduction in one's personal income and benefits if the new enterprise has accumulated less capital than the previous one.[33] Under these circumstances, the likelihood of a worker switching from one enterprise to another would be greatly enhanced if some compensation for the loss of his investment in nonowned assets were to be awarded to him. This compensation would go beyond just higher pay; the worker would also be able to consider to what extent the proposed employment promised a superior income stream over his planned employment period.

For comparative purposes it should be emphasized here that the property rights school, like those we have already discussed, does not deny that low mobility of labor and capital is the reason why the pay for the same job varies in different branches and enterprises. But, in contradistinction to the others, it identifies as the most important cause of that low mobility, and the consequent interbranch differentials, the specific property regime in Yugoslavia, rather than the maximand of Yugoslav firms (as argued by the labor school) or specific imperfections of the capital markets—self-financing and the wrong price of capital.

Having said that, however, we should stress that like the others, the property rights school, especially as represented by the Furubotn-Pejović version, is well embedded in the neoclassical tradition. All of them link the inability to equalize marginal productivities of labor and capital, and hence to achieve Pareto optimum, with the imperfections of the market. They differ when it comes to explanations. The property rights school blames these problems mainly on the lack of individual property rights in Yugoslavia, whereas for the others this is only one of the factors, and not the most important one, explaining interbranch differentials.

According to the property rights school, the lack of individual property rights, which deprives the worker of the possibility to take away his or her reinvested funds when he leaves the firm, not only creates specific interbranch differentials, but also substantially reduces the incentive to save in a Yugoslav firm. Under these circumstances it only stands to reason that younger members are usually more inclined to reinvest than either their older colleagues nearing the age of retirement or those who do not want to stay in the firm for a long time. This situation is reinforced by the fact that pensions in Yugoslavia are linked to the size of personal income in the last five years before retirement and do not reflect the income generated by the worker over the years, including his contribution to the reinvestment fund.

**Critical appraisal**

The three schools reviewed above, although they take different approaches to the causes of interbranch differentials, have something in common: they link those differentials with the nature of the Yugoslav self-management system. They all argue, directly or indirectly, that the absence of both labor and capital markets is a defining feature of the Yugoslav self-management system and limits the mobility of both factors of production. The use of neoclassical general equilibrium tools allows the adherents of the various schools to prove that under these circumstances interbranch and interfirm differentials are bound to be specific; that certain industries and firms will pay higher wages than others for the same occupation or job.

But the question to be raised here is this: Are these differentials specific to the Yugoslav type of self-management? We can convincingly argue that the phenomenon of substantial differences in wages for the same occupation, job, etc., is not specific to the Yugoslav self-management system, but rather to any market economy,[34] whether it is self-managed or not. What is more, in Yugoslavia certain nonsystemic factors are also at work that contribute to the existence of such differences. Let us elaborate on these points.

In the neoclassical world, the argument goes, wages provide incentives for labor mobility. Shifts in product demand lead to transitory wage differentials, reflecting current differences in labor productivity. These differentials, however, are not destined to last for long. Wage equilibrium for the same job or occupation is bound to be reached. The "transitory" wage differentials initiate a flow of workers from low-productivity/low-wage sectors to high-productivity/high-wage sectors, a flow that will, in the long run, ensure the equalization of productivity and wages among branches and firms for the same job or occupation. In this "ideal" world, wage differentials associated with a specific industry are bound to disappear sooner or later, together with unemployment, precisely because wages adjust themselves until the demand for workers equals supply. This equalization brings, in effect, a clearing in the labor market. It is worth emphasizing here that in this line of reasoning unemployment is linked with wage dispersion; or, to put it in different terms, unemployment results when wages are above the marginal productivity of labor.

If there is a shortcoming with this line of reasoning, it is that the reality defies it. We know all too well that in reality interbranch differentials in the developed capitalist countries are anything but transitory. On the contrary, they have a tendency to persist for long periods of time.

A brief survey of the relevant literature testifies to the validity of this point. Kruger and Summers, Dickens and Katz, among others,[35] have accumulated impressive evidence showing that in the United States the impact of industry affiliation on wage differentials is not just significant but very large indeed. Available figures from 1984 indicate wide-ranging differentials from a high of 38 percent above the mean in the petroleum industry to a low of 37 percent below the mean in private household services. Sizable wage differentials for the same job were found in September 1985 in Cleveland,[36] where a key-entry operator's wages ranged from $160 to $480 per week.

The data also indicate a similarity in the wage structures of various developed capitalist countries and a remarkable stability of those structures over time. Moreover, the differences are not characteristic only of very specific jobs or occupations, but are evident in all jobs and professions. Certain industries pay higher wages not only to their highly skilled employees, but to clerks and unskilled workers as well, whereas others pay everybody low wages. As a result, in all industries the relative differences in wages for various skills and occupations or between men and women are more or less the same and show very little tendency to change over the long run.

Bringing together the findings from our statistical analysis of the wage structure in Yugoslavia and findings on wage differences in capitalist countries, we can conclude that in both cases wages for the same job or occupation tend to differ a great deal by branch and enterprise. In other words, such wage differentials are as widespread a phenomenon in capitalist countries as they are in Yugoslavia. This would suggest that the competitive neoclassical approach cannot satisfactorily explain interbranch differentials either in Yugoslavia or in capitalist countries.

It seems to us that the neoclassical analysis overlooks the fact that any system in which remuneration is linked in one way or another with the actual economic results of the enterprise, measured by profitability or net output, or for that matter by any other economic indicator such as market share, is bound to create differences in wages for the same occupation in different branches and enterprises. The mere fact that labor productivity and market conditions are different for different branches and enterprises practically guarantees that wage differentials cannot be equalized as the neoclassical textbook analysis would have us believe.

Be that as it may, the fact that substantial differentials in pay for the same job or occupation persist in Yugoslavia and in many capitalist countries raises the question: What contributes to these differentials? Two theoretical approaches to this question demand our attention: the efficiency wage theory and the fair wage theory.

## *The efficiency wage*

The premise of the efficiency wage concept is that labor exchange is open-ended. Particular work activities and work intensity are not specified in the labor contract. These aspects of labor activity are determined by the ability of the employer to exercise authority over the employees. In many cases, firms may deliberately set wages above the market clearing level in order to encourage greater work effort, and to reduce turnover, which is disruptive to the operation of the firm. But these are not the only reasons for higher wages. They also attract superior applicants, allow the firm to retain the workers it has, and, most importantly, they provide the necessary incentive to workers in key positions to perform better. Overall, the efficiency wage theory holds that firms, in some respects, are not wage takers but wage makers, because wages are not something externally given to them, but rather are controlled by the firm as a determining factor contributing to higher productivity. We can deduce from this that the relationship between wages and productivity is a reciprocal one: high productivity determines high wages and high wages determine high productivity. This in turn implies that over some range, increases in wages may very well raise the profits of a firm,[37] because it is reasonable to expect that in some firms costs will increase less than the increase in productivity.[38]

## *The fair wage*

Advocates of the fair wage theory share some of the views expressed by the efficiency wage theory school, but raise objections to some other aspects of their theory. For instance, they share the view that high wages in some industries affect productivity positively without reducing profits. They also accept the argument that high wages paid to induce effort and discipline are usually above the clearing wage. On the other hand, fair wage theory advocates find that the efficiency wage theory does not explain the fact that all employees in the high wage industries are paid relatively higher wages, even in those jobs where efficiency wage elements are not important. While it may be understandable that a skilled machine operator receives a wage premium, it is not so clear why clerks and unskilled workers in the highly paid industries receive such premiums. The adherents of the fair wage concept[39] therefore propose an amendment to the efficiency wage concept, namely that all workers in certain industries are paid high wages because this is considered fair.

This last point brings into focus another important concern. Which firms and industries are able to pay relatively high wages and what are the factors determining an industry's ability to pay high wages? The predominant view shared by both schools mentioned above is that high wages are usually paid in industries that manifest the following characteristics: they have substantial market power; are made up of large firms with large establishments; have high union density; have high capital-labor ratios; and employ fewer women. At the other end of the pay spectrum, of course, are those industries with the opposite characteristics. It is striking that the characteristics of industries paying high and low wages (except for density of unionization) also apply to Yugoslav firms.

However, the mere fact that interbranch differentials for the same occupations do exist both in Yugoslavia and in the developed capitalist countries does not entirely invalidate the claim made by the previously reviewed schools, and the labor school in particular, that Yugoslavia is, after all, specific in this matter, as long as it can be proven that those differentials are visibly larger in Yugoslavia than in the developed capitalist countries. This is exactly what Estrin, one of the prominent representatives of the labor school, tried to prove, with little success. He used the coefficient of variation measure for international comparisons of interbranch differentials. This measure, however, is not without reproach, mainly because the size of this coefficient depends on the number of branches in the sample and the weight of different industrial branches, not to mention the exact definitions of branches. Needless to say, these factors differ significantly between Yugoslavia and the Western economies. But, even overlooking, for the sake of argument, the questionable usefulness of the coefficient of variation for international comparisons, available statistical data for the United States presented by Estrin himself do not indicate any substantial differences in interbranch differentials measured by this tool between that country and Yugoslavia. In fact Estrin's data indicate that the United States has a coefficient of variation at least as high as Yugoslavia's, if not higher.[40]

Reflecting on the issues and arguments raised in the previous pages, we can conclude that the self-management system in Yugoslavia is probably not the main cause of substantial interbranch differentials. Our analysis points to the fact that this phenomenon is rather linked with the Yugoslav decentralized coordinating mechanism—the market—as well as with other factors not linked, at least not directly, with the economic system itself.

More precisely, our analysis suggests that in Yugoslavia, more than in many other countries, some distributional phenomena are not entirely systemically determined. We can point out at once a few aspects of the distributional pattern that cannot be linked with systemic characteristics.

For example, state economic policies in the field of distribution, which are not in conformity with the requirement or logic of the system, cannot be attributed to systemic inadequacies alone. It is practically impossible for anyone to determine unambiguously which elements of state policy can be attributed to the logic of the system and which are alien to it. The arbitrariness in this matter is very evident when the state decides to redistribute income, as is the case in Yugoslavia. The self-management reward system, in an environment of imperfect competition, sometimes allows gains in net personal incomes which are unrelated to the overall effort and performance of a particular enterprise. There is then an ideological and practical effort by the state to skim the unjustified incomes via taxes and other monetary and fiscal tools.[41] But, given the very nature of the system, no objective criteria can be worked out to separate justified from unjustified income without undermining the self-management market system itself. Thus, in practice, exhortations that enterprises should be rewarded according to their contributions in terms of labor can mean only an arbitrary use of the tax system. The state authorities are the final judge in deciding which incomes are earned and which are not.

The specific and important role of the state in this matter must, however, be seen in conjunction with a multitude of sociopolitical factors, many of which are not quantifiable, which have played some role in determining the dispersion of wages. It must be emphasized here that the economic and social policies of the Yugoslav state are strongly shaped by regional diversity, underdevelopment, and the need to protect the communist party's monopoly on power. In addition, ideology and certain strong biases held by the communist regime have strongly influenced economic policies. As is the case in other East European socialist countries, the elite in power has a strong mistrust and fear of uncontrolled market forces; a fascination with bigness; a bias in favor of material production; and a fear that if nonlabor income is allowed it will lead to capitalism.

The reluctance of the state to modify the property relations even slightly is another example of deep-rooted ideological concerns and fears. The major fear of the authorities is that incomes from property will create a class of rentiers and increase the stratification of society. The experience of the capitalist world, from its very early stages, justifies this fear. Income from property is more unequally distributed and tends to be more concentrated in comparison with income from employment, and thus adds a new dimension to social stratification. Furthermore, the implementation of property rights requires, in one form or another, the creation of a genuine capital market in which firms can participate directly. There is, however, no historical experience of the creation of an institutionalized genuine market within the framework of public ownership. The most relevant case at hand is the Yugoslav experience after 1965, when investment allocation was decentralized and enterprises were encouraged to use banks—which were supposedly independent of the state—as a sort of capital market. But the results of this arrangement were disappointing.

A further expression of ideology and strong bias against the market is the state's far-reaching intervention in product markets. In Yugoslavia, product markets and specialty markets of factors of production are seriously limited by state intervention. These barriers and limits are much more extensive than in the most developed capitalist countries with the highest levels of state intervention. Even in the 1965–72 period, the heyday of liberalism, when the scope of market forces was substantially broader and before the so-called social agreements were introduced, approximately 50 percent to 60 percent of all prices in industry were directly or indirectly controlled by the federal, republican, or local authorities.[42]

As far as income distribution is concerned, the state has always had some control over the wage differentials. Formally, in accordance with the theoretical construct of a market self-managed economy, the state plays no role in establishing either interskill or interbranch differentials. The only parameter of distribution is the federal minimum wage; the rest is left to the discretion of the enterprises on a micro level and to the market on a macro level. But in reality this is far from the truth. The state has intervened both directly and indirectly in the distributional pattern. With the exception of the laissez-faire period between 1965 and 1970, when most restrictions on income distribution were abolished, the state, indirectly through its price policies, has affected (not always by design) the interbranch and interfirm differentials by granting certain industries privileges in the form of subsidies, credit, and tax exemptions. A good case in point is the direct intervention by the state in 1972 in both interskill and interbranch differentials in order to curb dispersion of wages. The right of the enterprises to distribute income was substantially reduced. Although some of the restrictions, especially on skill differentials, were abolished after 1975, social contracts on prices, income distribution, and other economic parameters have influenced the interbranch and interfirm differentials ever since. Although a lack of real coordination of the enormous number of social contracts made it impossible to implement any desired objectives on a national scale as far as interbranch differentials are concerned (even if such an objective could be formulated clearly, which is not always the case), state intervention in this field is not neutral. By granting certain branches and enterprises special treatment for whatever reason, the state *nolens volens* affects the wage differentials of those entities.

Not without importance in this matter is the lobbying power of particular branches and firms to achieve concessions from the state in the form of subsidies, tax exemptions, favorable credit conditions, etc. Those concessions are very often more important for the economic performance of the enterprise than its own "internal" effort.

Regional diversity has also played some role in shaping the overall interbranch differentials. As our statistical analysis indicates, interbranch differentials are larger in underdeveloped regions than in the more developed ones. This phenomenon can probably be explained by the logic of underdevelopment; a greater scarcity of skilled manpower and a greater abundance of unskilled workers will *ceteris paribus* produce larger pay differentials in preferential branches and firms than will be the case in the more developed regions. In any case, the regional element adds some new dimension to the inequality of pay.

Whatever the reasons for large interbranch and interfirm differentials, they have serious negative consequences, because they lead to a situation in which what you do is not as important as where you do it. The level of wages for a particular job depends more on what region, branch, or firm you work in than on your qualifications, skills, and responsibilities. There can be no doubt that this does not accord with the sacred principle of distribution according to work.

## Notes

1. I should like to thank the members of the economics department of the University of Belgrade for their hospitality and their help in collecting materials during my visits to Yugoslavia in March 1985 and May 1987. I also gained greatly from consultations with colleagues at the Institute of Economics in Zagreb. Special thanks are due to Professor R. Stojanović for arranging my trip to Yugoslavia and numerous meetings with other scholars. I was also privileged to participate in a seminar on Economic Problems in the Communist Countries, led by professors W. Brus, M. Kaser, and F. Seton. Their comments on my working paper on Yugoslavia helped me a great deal. Last, but not least, thanks to the Canada Council. Without their generous financial assistance this project could not have been undertaken. All of these contributions helped to make this study possible. Needless to say, none of the above-mentioned people or institutions is in any way responsible for the views I have expressed, or for errors my analyses may contain.

2. H. Flakierski, *Economic Reform and Income Distribution: A Case Study of Hungary and Poland* (Armonk: M.E. Sharpe, 1986); and idem, *The Economic System and Income Distribution in Yugoslavia* (Armonk: M.E. Sharpe, 1989).

3. This summary is based on a statistical analysis of (a) the overall dispersion of wages in Yugoslavia and its republics in general; (b) skill differentials for the federation as a whole and for republics; (c) interbranch differentials for the federation as a whole and for the republics. The reader may obtain these data from the author on request.

4. See V.H. Vroom, "The Nature of the Relationship between Motivation and Performance," in V.H. Vroom and E.L. Deci, eds., *Management and Motivation* (New York: Penguin, 1977); idem, "Industrial Social Psychology," in ibid., pp. 392–415; H. Leibenstein, "Allocative Efficiency vs. X-Efficiency," *American Economic Review*, June 1966.

5. See for more detail J. Vanek, *The General Theory of Labour Managed Economies* (Ithaca: Cornell University Press, 1970); J.C. Espinosa and A.S. Zimbalist, *Economic Democracy. Workers Participation in Chilean Industry 1970–1973* (New York: Academic Press, 1978).

6. See for more detail O.E. Williamson, *Market and Hierarchies* (New York: The Free Press, 1975).

7. M.R. Carter, "Revisionist Lessons from the Peruvian Experience with Cooperative Agricultural Production," in D.C. Jones and Jan Svejnar, eds., *Advances in the Economic*

*Analysis of Participatory and Labour Managed Firms*, vol. 1 (London: JAI Press, 1985), pp. 179–95.

8. See for more detail J. Obradović, "Distribution of Participation in the Process of Decision Making on Problems Related to the Economic Activity of the Company," in *Participation and Self-Management*. Report of First International Sociological Conference on Participation and Self-Management (Zagreb, 1972), vol. 2. pp. 136–64.

9. See for more detail ibid., Tables 18, 19, 20, 21.

10. J. Županov, "Employees' Participation and Social Power in Industry," in *Participation and Self-Management* (Zagreb, 1972), vol. 1, pp. 33–41; J. Županov and A.S. Tennenbaum, "The Distribution of Control in Some Yugoslav Industrial Organizations," in A.S. Tennenbaum, ed., *Control and Organization* (New York: McGraw-Hill, 1966).

11. Županov, "Employees' Participation," p. 40.

12. This point of view is expressed by R. Supek, "Two Types of Self-Managing Organization and Technological Progress," in *Participation and Self-Management*, vol. 1, pp. 150–74; a similar view is expressed by B. Fleas, "Yugoslavian Experience of Workers' Self-Management," in *Participation and Self-Management*, vol. 6 (1973).

13. Williamson, *Markets and Hierarchies*, p. 46.

14. See for more detail B. Horvat, "Two Widespread Ideological Deviations in Contemporary Yugoslav Society," in *Eastern European Economics*, Fall 1984.

15. J. Županov, "Egalitarizam i Industrijalizam," in *Naše Teme*, 1970, no. 2; S. Bolčić, "The Value System of Participatory Economy," in *Participation and Self-Management*, vol. 2, pp. 97–122; I. Bićanić, "Nejednakosti i lićini dohoci" [Inequalities and personal income], in *Ekonomska Politika*, no. 1718 (1985), pp. 24–26.

16. I was informed during my visit to Yugoslavia that some kind of guidelines were introduced, relating different categories of skill to unskilled labor, but were later abolished.

17. The share of personal income after taxation as a ratio of the total income of the enterprises declined from 46 percent in 1976 to 30 percent in 1982. In five years of crisis, 1979–1984, the state drastically reduced the share of net personal income in the total earned income of the enterprises. As a result much less was left to distribute between the employees. See M. Jovićić and B. Cerović, "Raspodela lićnih dohodaka i proizvodni rad" [The distribution of personal income and productive labor], in *Raspodela prema radu. Protivurečnosti i perspektive* [Distribution according to work. Contradictions and perspectives] (Belgrade, 1983).

18. According to official statistics real personal income in 1979–84 declined by nearly 35 percent.

19. Bićanić, "Nejednakosti i lićnih dohoci."

20. This distinction between the labor and capital schools was first made by S. Estrin and W. Barlett in "The Effects of Enterprise Self-Management in Yugoslavia: An Empirical Survey," in D.C. Jones and J. Svejnar, eds., *Participatory and Self-Managed Firms: Evaluating Economic Performance* (Lexington: Lexington Books, 1982).

21. This stream of thought is represented by Benjamin Ward ("The Firm in Illyria—Market Socialism," *American Economic Review*, no. 4 [1958]), J. E. Mead ("The Theory of Labour-Managed Firms and of Profit Sharing," *Economic Journal*, no. 81 [1972]), H. Wachtel ("Workers' Management and Inter-Industry Wage Differentials in Yugoslavia," *Journal of Political Economy*, vol. 3, no. 80 [1972], pp. 540–60), and particularly by S. Estrin (*Self-Management: Economic Theory and Yugoslav Practice* [Cambridge: Cambridge University Press, 1983]). A good presentation of the labor school view can be found in an article by Estrin and Jan Svejnar, "Explanations of Earnings in Yugoslavia: The Capital and Labor Schools Compared," *Economic Analysis and Workers' Management*, vol. 19, no. 1 (1985), pp. 1–12.

22. A very strong critique of the labor school in general and of Ward in particular will be found in three articles by Horvat published in 1986. See B. Horvat, "Farewell to the Illyrian Firm," *Economic Analysis and Workers' Management*, no. 1 (1986), pp. 23–29; idem, "The Theory of the Worker Managed Firm Revisited," *Journal of Comparative Economics*, no. 10 (1986), pp. 9–25; and idem, "The Illyrian Firm: An Alternative View. A rejoinder," *Economic Analysis and Workers' Management*, no. 4 (1986), pp. 411–16. In the Western literature S. Rosefielde and W. Pfouts have taken issue with Ward's Illyrian model. See "The Firm in Illyia: Market Syndicalism Reconsidered," *Journal of Comparative Economics*, no. 10 (1986), pp. 160–70. See also Joan Robinson's polemic with Domar, "The Soviet Collective Farm as a Producer: Comment," *American Economic Review*, no. 57 (1967), pp. 222–23.

23. See J. Vanek, "The Yugoslav Economy Viewed through the Theory of Labor-Management," *World Development*, no. 9 (1973), pp. 39–56; J. Vanek and M. Jovičić, "The Capital Market and Income Distribution in Yugoslavia," *Quarterly Journal of Economics*, no. 89 (1989), pp. 432–43; D.C. Milenkovitch, *Plan and Market in Yugoslav Economic Thought* (New Haven: Yale University Press, 1971); R. Staellerts, "The Effects of Capital Intensity on Income in Yugoslav Industry," *Economic Analysis and Workers' Management*, no. 15 (1981), pp. 501–16.

24. This point is very strongly emphasized by S. Popov in "Intersectorial Relations of Personal Incomes," *Yugoslav Survey*, May 1972, pp. 63–80. She tries to prove that there is a very strong correlation between firms with high $K/L$ ratios (usually large by any indicator of concentration) and their size of personal income.

25. See Vanek, "Yugoslav Economy Viewed through the Theory of Labor-Management."

26. Other factors are the underdeveloped capital market, arbitrary limits on interest rates, and some of the social agreements.

27. This terminology to describe the property relations in the firm was first used by Vanek. See J. Vanek, "Identifying the Participatory Economy," in B. Horvat, M. Marković, and Rudi Supek, eds., *Self-Governing Socialism ~ Reader*, vol. 2 (White Plains: M.E. Sharpe, 1975), which tries to distinguish between ownership of capital assets and the right to enjoy the fruits of material goods that are in their ownership in the traditional sense of the word. In this context it is worthwhile to mention A. Bajt's concept of the nature of capital in the Yugoslav system. Bajt distinguished ownership of capital from ownership of the particular physical means of production. Society is the owner of capital but the owner of the physical means of production is the collective of the firm. See Bajt, "Social Ownership—Collective and Individual," in ibid.

28. Many economists both in the West and Yugoslavia question Vanek's assertion that self-financing is at the root of maldistribution and the disincentive to save collectively and that exclusive external financing is the panacea for remedying those shortcomings. See B. Gui, "Limits of External Financing: A Model and Application to Labour-Managed Firms," in Jones and Svejnar, eds., *Advances in the Economic Analysis of Participatory and Labour Managed Firms;* J.P. Bonin, "Labour Management and Capital Maintenance: Investment Decision in the Socialist Labour Managed Firm," in ibid.; M. Kamusić, "Economic Efficiency and Workers' Self-Management," in M.J. Brockmeyer, ed., *Yugoslav Workers' Self-Management* (Dordrecht: Reidel, 1970).

29. See A. Bajt, "Društvena svojina—Kolektivna i individualna" [Social ownership—Collective and individual], *Gledišta*, vol. 9, no. 4, pp. 531–44; B. Horvat, *Towards a Theory of a Planned Economy* (White Plains: M.E. Sharpe, 1964); K. Mihailović, *Ekonomska stvarnost Jugoslavije* [The Economic Reality of Yugoslavia] (Belgrade: Ekonomika, 1982); S. Popov "Intersectoral Relations of Personal Income," *Yugoslav Survey*, May 1972.

30. The most popular version in Western academic circles is given by Furobotn and Pejovich. See E.G. Furubotn and S. Pejovich, "Property Rights and the Behaviour of the Firm in a Socialist State: The Example of Yugoslavia," *Zeitschrift für National-Ekonomie*, no. 30 (1970), pp. 431–54; idem, "Property Rights, Economic Decentralization, and the Evolution of the Yugoslav Firm, 1965–1972," *Journal of Law and Economics*, October 1973; S. Pejovich, "The Firm, Monetary Policy and Property Rights in a Planned Economy," *Western Economic Journal*, September 1969, pp. 193–200.

31. Yugoslavs do not call the socialized enterprise a cooperative, but an "organization of associated labor." The intent here is to distinguish the Yugoslav firm from the cooperative form as far as property rights are concerned. Members of the Yugoslav enterprise do not have individual control over their invested capital as is the case with a cooperative.

32. It is difficult not to agree with Peter Wiles when he claims that the typical supporter of reinvesting will be the skilled and influential middle-aged worker with a family and a satisfactory house and possibly active membership on the workers' council. The typical voter for more personal income will be the uninfluential, the mobile workers, etc.

33. See for more detail H. Lydall, *Yugoslav Socialism: Theory and Practice* (Oxford: Clarendon Press, 1984), pp. 215–18.

34. Command economies also have substantial interbranch differentials, but they are established by the center in accordance with its preferences. What is more, the differentials are in most cases and most of the time smaller than in market-oriented systems.

35. For more detail see A. Kruger and S. Summers, "Efficiency Wages and the Inter-Industry Wage Structure" (mimeo, Harvard, 1986). See also idem, "Reflection on the Inter-Industry Wage Structure," in K. Lang and J.S. Leonard, eds., *Unemployment and the Structure of Labour Markets* (Cambridge: Basil Blackwell, 1987); W.T. Dickens and L.F. Katz, "Inter-Industry Wage Differences and Industry Characteristics," in ibid.; and K.M. Murphy and R.H. Topel, "Unemployment, Risk, and Earnings: Testing for Equalizing Wage Differences in the Labor Market," in ibid.

36. U.S. Department of Labor, Bureau of Labor Statistics, 1985.

37. A full survey of efficiency wage theories can be found in L.F. Katz, "Efficiency Wage Theories: A Partial Evaluation," in S. Fischer, ed., *National Bureau of Economic Research Macroeconomics Annual 1986* (Cambridge: MIT Press, 1986).

38. Kalecki can be considered a pioneer of the efficiency wage concept. In his seminal paper of 1943, "Political Aspects of Full Employment" (in *Selected Essays in the Dynamics of the Capitalist Economy, 1933–1970* [Cambridge: Cambridge University Press, 1971]), Kalecki claims that unemployment is necessary to maintain work discipline and work intensity on the shop floor.

39. On the fair wage concept see G.A. Akerlof and J.L. Yellen, "Fairness and Unemployment," *American Economic Review*, Papers and Proceedings, May 1988, pp. 44–49.

40. See Estrin, *Self-Management*, Appendix B, Table B4. International comparisons made by Kruger and Summers (1986), Tables 2.3 and 2.4, using a different set of econometric tools, indicate that in many Western countries, the dispersion of wages between branches is greater than in Yugoslavia.

41. Some well-known Yugoslav economists, such as Horvat, Bajt, and B. Marendić, believe that it would be possible to guarantee enterprises equal economic opportunity only if worker collectives were permitted to retain only those net incomes which are a result of their labor contribution and quality of management, and not effects linked with better capital endowment and market conditions. It should be stressed, however, that the concepts of labor contribution used here are ambiguous. In one instance the labor contribution means effort, intensity of work, education, and skill; in another it means the result of work in terms of output. See A. Bajt, "Dohodna cena kak normalna cena u našoj privredi" [Income price as a normal price in our economy], *Ekonomist*, no. 4 (1964); B. Horvat,

"Raspodjela prema radu medu kolektivima" [Distribution according to work between collectives], *Nasa stvarnosta*, no. 1 (1962), pp. 52–66; idem, "Fundamentals of a Theory of Distribution in Self-Governing Socialism," *Economic Analysis and Workers' Management*, nos. 1–2 (1976).

The dominant group of economists in Yugoslavia believes that net income of the enterprise should contain at least a part or all effects from monopoly power on the market and other forms of monopoly. See, for example, M. Korać, *Problemi teorije i prakse socijalisticke robne proizvodnje u Jugoslaviji* [Problems of theory and practice of socialist material production in Yugoslovia] (Zagreb: Globus, 1965).

42. See J. Wecławski, *System cen w Jugoslawii* [The price system in Yugoslavia] (Lublin: UMCS, 1984), p. 27, Table 4.

# An Economic Comparison of
# Poland and Spain

## Kazimierz Laski

According to Kornai (1980) and many other students of the subject, command and market economies are respectively supply-constrained and demand-constrained systems. The derived features of the respective systems are as follows.

A command economy is characterized by full employment of the factors of production, above all of the labor force, job security and an egalitarian distribution of income, and all these combined with rather low efficiency. On the other hand, high efficiency, job insecurity, and large income differentials, hand in hand with a rather high and persistent unemployment, characterize a market economy. Thus the ranking of a desirable economic system necessarily involves value judgments concerning efficiency versus ethical considerations. The purpose of the present paper is to illustrate the trade-off between full employment as a proxy for ethical considerations and efficiency, using as an example the comparative development of Poland and Spain in the period 1951–80. The period 1981–85 is not included in the main analysis because of the veritable collapse of the Polish economy in these years. Nevertheless data for that period are supplied for the sake of illustration.

According to Joan Robinson (1965), a command economy is to be treated not as a system to follow capitalism but rather as a substitute for capitalism in less-developed countries. For the latter it may play the role of a hot-house for growth. This thesis too can be tested with data derived from the development of Poland and Spain. This is the second purpose of the present paper.

A case study of any two countries can never give a definitive answer to the thesis formulated by Kornai and Robinson; it can, however, give some food for thoughts on the subject especially if both countries, as in our case, seem to

---

The author is at the Department of Economics, Johannes Kepler University, Linz, Austria.

Table 1

## GDP per Capita in Several Countries

(in current prices, in $-I)*

|  | 1980 | | 1985 | |
|---|---|---|---|---|
|  | in $-I | USA = 100 | in $-I | USA = 100 |
| United States | 11.447 | 100.0 | 16.494 | 100.0 |
| France | 10.200 | 89.1 | 12.170 | 73.8 |
| Austria | 8.625 | 75.3 | 10.876 | 66.1 |
| Italy | 7.788 | 68.0 | 10.830 | 65.7 |
| Spain | 6.353 | 55.5 | 7.589 | 46.0 |
| Greece | 5.097 | 44.5 | 5.862 | 35.7 |
| Hungary | 4.632 | 40.5 | 5.141 | 31.2 |
| Poland | 4.322 | 37.8 | 4.040 | 24.5 |
| Yugoslavia | 4.042 | 35.3 | 4.811 | 29.2 |
| Portugal | 3.832 | 33.5 | 5.573 | 33.8 |
| Turkey | — | — | 3.599 | 21.8 |
| Average of countries partici- pating in the International Comparison Project | 3.953 | | | |

*$-I = U.S.$ international. $-I equals the U.S.$ in toto but differs from it in weights attached to different groups of expenditures.

*Sources: World Comparison of Purchasing Power and Real Product for 1980* (New York: United Nations, 1986), pp. 7–8; *Purchasing Power and Real Expenditure* (OECD, 1985); *International Comparison of Gross Domestic Product in Europe 1985* (New York: United Nations, in print).

represent average countries in the groups respectively of command and market economies.

In 1950 the level of economic development as measured by the Gross Domestic Product (GDP) per head was rather higher in Poland than in Spain. In Poland this level was much higher than before the Second World War while in Spain it was lower. Hence the advantage Spain most probably had over Poland before 1939 had disappeared by 1950. For the sake of argument it will be assumed that the level of economic development in 1950 was about the same in both countries.

According to official data in the years 1951–80 the rate of growth of Gross Material Product (GMP) per head was 5.3 percent annually in Poland. It can be assumed that the rate of growth of GDP per head was about 0.3–0.4 percentage points below this level; thus, it amounted to 4.9–5.0 percent annually. The rate of growth of GDP per head in Spain was 4.7 percent annually, hence lower than in Poland. Thus in 1980 the GDP per head should have been higher in Poland than in Spain. According to the International Comparison Project (see Table 1) it was,

Table 2

**Labor and Capital Productivity in Poland and Spain, 1951–80**

|  | Poland | Spain |
|---|---|---|
| **A.** | | |
| 1. Rate of growth of GDP per capita (% p.a.) | 3.4 | 4.7 |
| 2. Rate of growth of population (% p.a.) | 1.2 | 0.8 |
| 3. Rate of growth of GDP (% p.a.) | 4.6 | 5.5 |
| 4. Rate of growth of employment (% p.a.) | 1.4 | 0.2 |
| 5. Rate of growth of GDP per employed person (% p.a.) | 3.2 | 5.3 |
| 6. (5) : (3) x 100 (%) | 70.0 | 96.0 |
| **B.** | | |
| 7. Gross fixed capital formation (GFCF) per GDP (avg. %) | 27.7 | 21.3 |
| 8. Incremental capital-output ratio (avg.) | 6.0 | 3.9 |
| 9. Increase in stocks per GFCF (avg. %) | 23.8 | 8.1 |
| **C.** | | |
| 10. Rate of growth of fixed capital (% p.a.)* | 4.4 | 4.0 |
| 11. Rate of growth of total inputs 0.6 x (4) + 0.4 x (10) (% p.a.) | 2.6 | 1.7 |
| 12. "Technical progress" (3) – (11) | 2.0 | 3.8 |
| 13. (12) : (3) x 100 (%) | 43.0 | 69.0 |

*Sources: Rocznik Statystyczny*, various editions; Banco de Bilbao, *Informe Economico 1984.*

*Author's estimate. The rate of growth of GFCF of 6.5 percent annually was reduced by 2.5 percentage points. In Greece in the period 1955–80 the rate of growth of GFCF was 7.9 percent p.a. and of fixed capital 6.2 percent p.a. Cf. *Flow and Stocks of Fixed Capital 1955–1980* (Paris: OECD, 1983), pp. 28–29. The difference between both growth rates amounted thus to 1.7 percentage points. It has been assumed that this difference was bigger in Spain because the consequences of war losses in 1955 must have been bigger in Greece than in Spain.

however, lower by 31 percent, i.e., by almost one-third. Although one should not exaggerate the exactness of such international comparisons other estimates seem to prove that the order of magnitudes should be correct (see Havlik 1983; Ehrlich 1968, 1980). A rate of growth of GDP per head in Poland consistent with the ICP data would amount to 3.4 percent annually. This means a reduction of the official rate of growth by 1.5 percentage points, which corresponds roughly with other estimates as well.

The comparison of the rate of growth of GDP per head in Poland and Spain (3.4 percent against 4.7 percent p.a.) does not support—with all due reservation—Joan Robinson's thesis presenting the command economy as an alternative to capitalism for less developed countries.

In Table 2 factors of growth are examined. On the one hand the rate of growth of employment in Poland (1.4 percent p.a.) was higher than that of the population (1.2 percent p.a.) while in Spain the situation was just the opposite (0.2 percent p.a. against 0.8 percent p.a.). On the other hand, the rate of growth of labor productivity (row 5) was higher in Spain (5.3 percent p.a.) than in Poland (3.2 percent). The ensuing rate of growth of GDP was higher in Spain than in Poland (5.5 percent p.a. against 4.6 percent p.a.) but not high enough to absorb all the reserves of the labor force. This is quite a typical situation in a market economy. Total effective demand, given the rate of growth of technical progress (as measured by changes in labor productivity), does not increase fast enough to absorb the available labor force, which leads to significant unemployment (11.2 percent in 1980). This trend started in Spain in 1973 and deepened in the years 1981–85. In that period the rate of growth of labor productivity continued to be high, although the rate of growth of GDP declined, leading to an absolute fall in employment and to a 21.5 percent rate of unemployment in 1985, the highest in Europe.

In part B of Table 2 we find that the incremental capital-output ratio amounts to 6 in Poland against 3.9 in Spain. Thus an increase of GDP per one unit requires almost two times more investment units in Poland than in Spain. The low efficiency is proven, also, by row 9. The increase in stocks amounts to about one-fourth of (GFCF) in Poland and to less than one-tenth in Spain. These tremendous increases in stocks are typical of all command economies, yet the latter remain shortage economies without true reserves.

Part C gives an estimate of the so-called total factor productivity with usual weights. The "rest factor," assumed to represent "technical progress" against simple extension of both factors of production, amounts to one-quarter of the total rate of growth of GDP in Poland and to one-half in Spain. Table 2 illustrates a much higher rate of growth of efficiency in Spain.

Table 3 shows that, given GDP per head, Poland is able to devote a smaller part of it to individual consumption. The part of GDP devoted to capital formation and government consumption (without education and health care, since they are included in individual consumption) in the year 1980 amounted to about 37 percent in Poland and to about 26 percent in Spain. Thus about 10 percent of GDP is "lost" for individual consumption. While the GDP per head in 1980 was about 31 percent lower in Poland than in Spain, individual consumption was lower by about 49 percent.

The high share of capital formation in Poland did not mean a high share of residential construction. On the contrary, the latter's share in GFCF was 20 percent in Poland against 28 percent in Spain. Thus the volume of residential construction was lower in Poland than in Spain by 34 percent. Another feature of the composition of GFCF was the high share of nonresidential construction (42 percent in Poland against 37 percent in Spain). Similar proportions in the composition of GDP and GFCF obtained in 1985.

Individual consumption per head is necessarily lower than individual consumption per one employed person because only part of the population is in the

Table 3

**Per Capita GDP and Its Main Components in Poland and Spain, 1980 and 1985**
(in current prices, in AS-I)*

| | Poland | | Spain | | Poland |
|---|---|---|---|---|---|
| | AS-I (in 1000s) | % | AS-I (in 1000s) | % | Spain = 100 |
| **1980** | | | | | |
| 1.  GDP | 66.5 | 100.0 | 96.6 | 100.0 | 68.8 |
| 2.  Capital formation | 17.6 | 26.4 | 18.9 | 19.6 | 92.8 |
| of which: | | | | | |
| a.  GFCF | 18.7 | (100.0) | 19.9 | (100.0) | 94.1 |
| of which: | | | | | |
| Nonresidential construction | 7.8 | (41.5) | 7.3 | (36.9) | 105.7 |
| Machinery and equipment | 7.2 | (38.5) | 6.9 | (34.9) | 103.9 |
| Residential construction | 3.7 | (20.0) | 5.6 | (28.2) | 66.7 |
| b.  Increase in stocks | 0.02 | 1.7 | | | 1.2 |
| c.  Exports – imports | −1.1 | −2.6 | | | 43.3 |
| 3.  Government consumption | 7.0 | 10.5 | 6.3 | 6.5 | 110.4 |
| 4.  Individual consumption | 42.0 | 63.1 | 68.6[a] | 71.0 | 61.1 |
| **1985** | | | | | |
| 1.  GDP | 67.1 | 100.0 | 126.0 | 100.0 | 53.2 |
| 2.  Capital formation | 19.6 | 29.2 | 23.2 | 18.4 | 84.7 |
| of which: | | | | | |
| 2a.  GFCF | 16.0 | (100.0) | 21.1 | (100.0) | 75.8 |
| of which: | | | | | |
| Nonresidential construction | 9.0 | (56.1) | 7.1 | (33.7) | 125.9 |
| Machinery and equipment | 4.4 | (27.7) | 6.8 | (32.1) | 65.3 |
| Residential construction | 3.6 | (22.3) | 7.2 | (34.2) | 49.5 |
| b.  Increase in stocks | 3.1 | | 0.2 | | 1,558.7 |
| c.  Exports – imports | 0.5 | | 1.9 | | 28.1 |
| 3.  Government consumption | 7.7 | 11.5 | 11.7 | 9.3 | 66.0 |
| 4.  Individual consumption | 39.9 | 59.5 | 85.5[b] | 67.8 | 46.7 |

*Sources: International Comparison of Gross Domestic Product in Europe 1980* (New York: United Nations, 1985); *Statistische Nachrichten,* no. 12, Vienna 1987.

*AS-I = Austrian Schilling international. AS-I equals in toto the AS but differs from it in weights attached to different groups of expenditures.

[a] 71.3 AS-I minus 3.8 percent because of net purchases of inlanders abroad.

[b] 91.1 AS-I minus 6.2 percent because of net purchases of inlanders abroad.

labor force and because the labor force is not always fully employed. The participation rate is much higher in Poland than in Spain (51 percent against 33 percent) and there exists no unemployment in Poland while the unemployment rate in Spain was, as already mentioned, very high (11.2 percent in 1980 and 21.5 percent in 1985). As a result individual consumption per employed person in 1980 was about 8.0 thousand zl in Poland against about 21.0 thousand zl in Spain (see Table 4). Thus, while in 1980 individual consumption per head in Poland amounted to 61 percent of the Spanish level, consumption per one employed person amounted to only 39 percent thereof. Without health care and education, financed from collective expenditures, individual consumption per one employed person in Poland was in 1980 equal to approximately only one-third of the Spanish level.

These results may seem to be quite exaggerated. Therefore in part B of Table 4 they have been confronted with average earned incomes in both countries. After deduction of taxes (including social security payments) the average earned income in 1950 was about 6 thousand zl in Poland and about 19.6 thousand zl in Spain; it amounted thus to 31 percent of the Spanish level. These figures correspond roughly to our previous results. The general proportions observed in 1980 persisted even in 1985.

As we move in Tables 3 and 4 from GDP per head to individual consumption per head and per employed person we see that the relative position of Poland in relation to Spain deteriorates from 68.8 percent to 61.1 percent and 38.7 percent (for 1980). From a certain point of view individual consumption per employed person is the most important figure because it may serve as a proxy for an average earned income. It is not a perfect proxy for many reasons but still gives us some idea about the volume of compensation for work done. One should keep in mind that GDP per head and, partly, individual consumption per head are statistical concepts, while earned income is a well-known figure playing a decisive role in the private household. The fact that earned incomes in Poland are very low in relation to those in Spain, a country which has one of the lowest earned income levels in Europe, has, and must have, a devastating effect upon the attitude of Poles toward their economic system. According to this measure they may evaluate their system as even more inefficient than it is in reality if the criterion used is individual consumption per head, not per employed person. The frustration caused by this attitude has not only political consequences but purely economic ones as well, weakening the incentives for good work.

We are now in a position to try to evaluate the trade-off between efficiency, as measured primarily by labor productivity, and losses caused by unemployment. Of course, these losses cannot be limited to economic ones only. If (in Spain in 1985) every fifth member of the labor force could not find a job—this proportion being much higher with young people—and if this situation has been persisting for years, that must constitute a deep social crisis that endangers the very base of the system. Still, it is not uninteresting to evaluate the purely

Table 4

**Individual Consumption per Capita, Labor Force, and Employment, in Poland and Spain, 1980 and 1985**
(in zlotys and pesetas, average per month)

| | Poland | Spain | | Poland |
|---|---|---|---|---|
| | in zl | in ps | in zl[f] | Spain = 100 |
| **1980 A.** | | | | |
| 1. per capita | 4,000 | 23,967 | 6,548 | 61.1 |
| 2. per labor force | 8,016[a] | 67,322[b] | 18,394 | 43.6 |
| 3. per employment | 8,016 | 75,813[c] | 20,714 | 38.7 |
| 4. (3) without individual | | | | |
| expenditures | 6,987 | 70,961 | 19,388 | 36.0 |
| **1980 B.** | | | | |
| Average earned income | | | | |
| 1. before taxation | 6,040 | 89,759 | 24,524 | |
| 2. net of taxes | 6,040 | 71,807 | 19,619 | 30.8 |
| **1985 A.** | | | | |
| 1. per capita | 14,540 | 39,303 | 31,143 | 46.7 |
| 2. per labor force | 30,166[d] | 107,974 | 85,558 | 35.3 |
| 3. per employment | 30,166 | 137,547[e] | 108,991 | 27.7 |
| 4. (3) without individual | | | | |
| expenditures | 25,551 | 126,956 | 100,599 | 25.4 |
| **1985 B.** | | | | |
| Average earned income | | | | |
| 1. before taxation | 20,005 | 149,409 | 118,391 | |
| 2. net of taxes | 20,005 | 119,527 | 94,712 | 21.1 |

*Sources: Historical Statistics 1960–1980* (Paris: OECD, 1982); Banco de Bilbao, *Informe Economico 1984*; *Rocznik Statystyczny,* various editions.

[a] Participation rate 50 percent

[b] Participation rate 36 percent

[c] Unemployment rate 11.2 percent

[d] Participation rate 48.2 percent

[e] Unemployment rate 21.5 percent

[f] According to ICP the purchasing power of 1 peseta (ps) spent on individual consumption was 0.27 zloty (zl) in 1980 and 0.792 zl in 1985.

economic consequences of unemployment. "Social" labor productivity, as measured by GDP per head, depends, given the labor productivity measured by GDP per one employed person, on two factors: first, on the relation of labor force to population (participation rate); second, on the relation of employment to labor force. The basic fact, when comparison between Poland and Spain is made, is the

Table 5

**Labor Productivity and "Social" Labor Productivity in Poland and Spain**
(in 1000 AS–I)

|  | Poland | Spain | Poland (Spain = 100) |
|---|---|---|---|
| **1980** | | | |
| 1. GDP per employed person | 133.2 | 305.6 | 43.6 |
| 2. Individual consumption per employed person | 84.1 | 217.1 | 38.7 |
| 3. GDP per capita assuming full employment | 66.5 | 108.8 | 61.1 |
| 4. GDP per capita | 66.5 | 96.6 | 68.8 |
| **1985** | | | |
| 1. GDP per employed person | 139.1 | 442.0 | 31.5 |
| 2. Individual consumption per employed person | 82.8 | 299.1 | 27.7 |
| 3. GDP per capita assuming full employment | 67.1 | 160.5 | 41.8 |
| 4. GDP per capita | 67.1 | 126.0 | 53.2 |

*Sources: World Comparison of Purchasing Power and Real Product for 1980* (New York: United Nations, 1986); *Purchasing Power and Real Expenditures* (Paris: OECD, 1985); *International Comparison of Gross Domestic Product in Europe 1985* (New York: United Nations, in print); *Rocznik Statystyczny,* various editions; *Historical Statistics 1960–1985* (Paris: OECD, 1987); Banco de Bilbao, *Informe Economico 1984.*

big difference in labor productivity (see Table 5). In 1980 the level of GDP per employed person in Poland constituted only 43.6 percent of the Spanish level. The individual consumption per employed person was still lower because the part of GDP devoted to capital formation and government consumption was higher in Poland. With this individual consumption per employed person (which as we already know can be used as a proxy for earned income), the participation rate of 51 percent in Poland was much higher than that of 35 percent in Spain, at least partly because earnings in Poland were so low. Due to the higher participation rate the differences in "social" labor productivity (measured by GDP per head) diminished. The Polish level, relative to the Spanish one, has increased from 43.6 percent to 61 percent, i.e., by 45 percent. The further improvement is caused by unemployment in Spain. Due to this factor "social" labor productivity in Poland has reached 69 percent of the Spanish level; this was an improvement by another 12 percent.

Thus, in the case of a comparison between Poland and Spain given the labor productivity per employed person, the narrowing of the difference in "social" labor productivity is more strongly influenced by the higher participation than by full employment.

The same conclusion can be drawn from data for the year 1985. The interesting point here is the relative fall of labor productivity in Poland (caused by *inter alia* the absolute reduction of labor productivity in Poland) to about 31.5 percent of the Spanish level (compared to 43.6 percent in 1980). The other is the dramatic increase of the unemployment rate in Spain to 21.5 percent (compared to 11.8 in 1980). Because the participation rates in both countries did not change substantially between 1980 and 1985 the resulting changes in "social" labor productivity were determined by these two phenomena. The relative "social" labor productivity in Poland reached 53 percent of the Spanish level (against 69 percent in 1980).

Of course, the changes between 1980 and 1985 were provoked first of all by the deep political and economic crisis in Poland. This had led to an important and rather untypical absolute fall of labor productivity. If we consider, however, the period between 1950 and 1980 we note that the labor productivity in Poland was continuously falling, as compared with Spain, because its rate of growth was smaller. And this is the decisive point if we try to project our results into the future. Whatever the other values of an economic system it has to lose in competition with another system if the latter is able to assure a higher rate of growth of labor productivity. An equal distribution of misery is not a viable alternative to an unequal distribution of wealth, as Churchill once rightly pointed out. On the other hand an unequal distribution of wealth must not include tolerance of extravagant income differentials nor must it mean leaving out in the cold the unemployed and generally less fortunate members of the society. Economic policy can attenuate a lot of evils of a capitalist system even if it is unable to eradicate them.

## Bibliography

Askanas, Benedykt, and Laski, Kazimierz. 1980. "Consumer Prices and Private Consumption in Poland and Austria," *Journal of Comparative Economic Studies,* vol. 9, no. 2.

Auer, Josef. 1987a. "Ergebnisse bilateraler Wirtschaftsvergleiche mit Polen, Ungarn und Jugoslawien für das Jahr 1985," *Statistische Nachrichten,* vol. 42, no. 12.

————. 1987b. "Wirtschaftsvergleich EG-Osterreich 1985," *Hauptergebnisse. Statistische Nachrichten,* vol. 42, no. 12.

Brus, Włodzimierz, and Kowalik, Tadeusz. 1983. "Socialism and Development," *Cambridge Journal of Economics,* vol. 7, nos. 3/4 (September/December).

Ehrlich, Eva. 1968. "Nemzetközi elemzések a magyar távlati tervezéshez"[International Analysis for Hungarian Long-Term Planning], in *Közleményei No. 2 Tervgazdasági Intezet* [Communiqué No. 2 of the Planning Institute] (Budapest, 1968).

————. 1980. "Comparative GDP Levels" *Economic Bulletin for Europe,* vol. 31, no. 2 (New York: United Nations).

Gomulka, Stanislaw. 1986. *Growth, Innovation and Reform in Eastern Europe* (London: Wheatsheaf).

Havlik, Peter. 1986. "Comparison of Real Products Between East and West, 1970–1983," *Forschungsbericht* [Research Report], No. 115 (April).
Kornai, Janos. 1980. *Economics of Shortage* (Amsterdam: North Holland).
Landau, Ludwig. 1939. *Gospodarka swiatowa. Produkcja i dochod spoleczny w liczbach* [The world economy. Production and the national income in figures] (Warsaw: Instytut Gospodarstwa Spolecznego).
Merigo, Eduardo. 1982. "Spain," in Andrea Bolta, ed., *The European Economy. Growth and Crisis* (Oxford: Oxford University Press).
Robinson, Joan. 1965. "What Remains of Marxism?" in *Collected Economic Papers,* vol. 3 (Oxford: Basil Blackwell).
Summers, Robert, and Heston, Alan. 1984. "Improved International Comparisons of Real Product and Its Composition: 1950–1980," *Income and Wealth,* no. 2 (June).
Wright, Alison. 1977. *The Spanish Economy 1959–1976* (London: Macmillan).
Zienkowski, Leszek. 1963. *Dochod narodowy Polski 1937–1960* [The national income of Poland in 1937–1960] (Warsaw: PWE).

## Statistical Sources

Banco de Bilbao, *Informe Economico 1984.*
European Economic Community, *Eurostat Review 1975–1984* (Luxembourg, 1986).
Glowny Urzad Statystyczny. *Rocznik Statystyczny* (various years).
———. *Rocznik Statystyczny Dochodu Narodowego 1986* (Warsaw, 1987).
———. *Rocznik Statystyki Miedzynarodowej 1984* (Warsaw, 1985).
———. *Rocznik Statystyki Miedzynarodowej 1987* (Warsaw, 1988).
Instituto Nacional de Estadistica, *Espana. Annuario Estadistico 1984* (Madrid, 1984).
International Monetary Fund, *International Financial Statistics*, Yearbook 1986.
Organization for Economic Cooperation and Development, *Flow and Stocks of Fixed Capital 1955–1980* (Paris, 1983).
———. *Historical Statistics 1960–1980* (Paris, 1982).
———. *Historical Statistics 1960–1985* (Paris, 1987).
———. *OECD Economic Survey*, Spain, various years.
———. *Purchasing Power Parities and Real Expenditures.*
United Nations. *International Comparison of Gross Domestic Product in Europe 1980* (New York: 1985).
———. *International Comparison of Gross Domestic Product in Europe 1985* (New York: in preparation).
———. *World Comparison of Purchasing Power and Real Product for 1980* (New York: 1986).

# The Socialist Experience in Greece

## LOUIS LEFEBER

The Greek experience under the government of the party of the Panhellenic Socialist Movement (PASOK) is so complex, and its ramifications so varied, that an exhaustive discussion cannot be undertaken within the limits of an essay: it would require a book. Furthermore, at the time of writing, the experience is not yet over. In what follows, I attempt to give only an overview of the implications of, and responses to, some of the inherited social and economic conditions and other constraints that I believe to be basic for understanding the dynamics of the successes and failures of the PASOK government.[1]

Even though questions have been raised about PASOK's concept of socialism, or the commitment of its leadership to it, Greek social and political conditions have changed for the better during the tenure of the PASOK government. But because most of these changes have been limited in scope, it is important to ask whether it would have been possible to do better than what the record indicates. Ultimately, one would like to know whether it is possible to transform progressively, or socialize, a society in a semi-industrialized country, such as Greece, that is incorporated into and depends on the mechanics of the international capitalist system. This question goes beyond the Greek experience itself. But if on whatever basis the answer is affirmative, then one must ask whether the transformation to democratic socialism is feasible by democratic means. Given the recent experience not only in Greece, but also in some Latin American and Asian countries, I believe that positive answers to both these questions require an element of faith.[2]

Although the case of Greece, as that of any country, is a special one, it is nonetheless interesting not only for its own sake, but because it in many respects

The author is at the Department of Economics, York University.

parallels the problems of other semi-industrialized and developing countries. The Greek democratic tradition—apart from the democracy of the ancient polis that long ago lost its relevance to contemporary Greece—derives more from resistance to and struggle against repression and tyranny than from extended experience of stable democratic rule. Until recently, and with the exception of relatively brief interludes, the country had been governed by various forms of dictatorships supported frequently by foreign interests. The last such dictatorial rule was imposed by a military junta in 1967 with the support of the United States government.[3] The rule of this junta, terminated by popular uprising in 1974, was brutal and destructive. Brutal dictatorships had also existed in Spain and in Brazil, but there the dictators had also made an effort to build the economy. In Greece, as in Argentina, they did not. The similarity between the recent experiences of, and the problems facing, these two countries is striking.

## Goals and purposes

Seven years after the overthrow of the last military dictatorship, in the fall of 1981, the Greek people elected the party of the Panhellenic Socialist Movement (PASOK) to form a government. The party, under the leadership of Andreas Papandreou, campaigned on a platform of democratic social change, a nonideological Swedish type rather than Marxian socialism.[4] In the 1981 elections PASOK obtained 48 percent of the popular vote and secured an overwhelming parliamentary majority of 176 of the 300 parliamentary seats. The party of the defeated government, the New Democracy (ND), obtained 36 percent of the vote and 114 parliamentary seats. The remainder of the 300 seats went to the Communist Party of Greece.[5]

Thus the required parliamentary majority for the implementation of the PASOK program was there. The underlying strength of the mandate was not commensurate: only about 50 percent of those who voted for PASOK could be thought of as socialists or committed to some form of progressive social change. The other half, mostly from the center of the political spectrum, voted for PASOK in protest against the demonstrated incompetence and corrupt practices of the ND government.

The projected noncoercive "third road to socialism" had the modernization of the Greek capitalist economy as its primary requirement. But the targets of the PASOK government were stated in Parliament by the Prime Minister as consisting of "national independence, territorial integrity, popular sovereignty and democracy, self-supporting economic and social development, a cultural revival, the revitalization of the countryside, the radical improvement of the quality of life in the towns and in the villages, social justice, and finally social liberation."[6]

The stated goals called for fundamental changes in the structure of the political, economic, and social organization of the country—the party's election slogan was *allaghee*, "change"—nonetheless at the time of the statement there was no detailed and comprehensive plan or program of action for the pursuit of the targets, even though it was recognized that for the design and implementation of the required policies new institutions were needed. Among these, democratic planning within a framework of substantial decentralization of the governmental functions was to be given a primary role.

## The background

For a proper appreciation of the size of the implied changes in the social and economic structure as envisaged by the PASOK program, and the formidable obstacles to bringing them about, one has to know something about the nature of the Greek social and economic reality. Greece is a small country of about ten million people unevenly distributed over a none too richly endowed land surface, of which at most 30 percent is cultivable. The land itself is highly fragmented. As a consequence, and in spite of the homogeneity of language and religion, the different regions made up of islands and valleys can have significant variations in local culture and traditions. About 60 percent of the population is concentrated in the two largest cities, Athens and Thessaloniki, and their surrounding regions. The per capita income is among the lowest in Europe, but in recent times there has not been any widespread destitution, except perhaps among the women of the rural poor.

   Although the differences in income distribution are significant, a clearly defined dominant class does not exist, unless it is—or was before PASOK—the military. There is, however, a tradition of centralized control that, at least until the changes instituted by the PASOK government, had often been enforced by police power. The industrial sector is small, with manufacturing making up about 20 percent of GNP. Generally, it is inefficient, and with the exception of some larger establishments, mostly small-scale. Trade and services dominate, and the economic system is a non-Schumpeterian petty merchant capitalism characterized by high rents and large profit margins on small turnover. Shopkeepers and small-scale entrepreneurs have been successful in blocking measures aimed at improving efficiency and competition in trade. Labor productivity is low, and union power is underdeveloped, except in some public services such as transportation. The banking system, also inefficient, is controlled by the government through the public ownership of the major banks, which were nationalized much before the emergence of PASOK as the governing party.

   Subject to some not easily enforceable foreign exchange controls, the Greek economy has traditionally been open. Since the accession to full membership in the European Economic Community, the economy has been limited only by EEC rules. This connection is a mixed blessing: the subsidies obtained from it are offset by the transport costs and other limitations imposed by the lack of geographic contiguity. Given the low productivity of Greek industry, the industrial export potential has remained limited. In spite of agricultural exports—fruits and vegetable products sold in competition with Italy, Spain, and other Mediterranean producers with access to EEC markets—the balance of trade (merchandise account) has been highly unfavorable.

Traditionally the source of offsetting foreign exchange earnings has been the incomes from "invisibles," that is, from services—tourism and transportation (shipping)—and from Greek emigrants' remittances. These are incomes that have depended on international economic conditions; hence they have always been outside the Greek government's direct control. Only the transfer of these incomes from abroad to Greece could be affected by domestic policies: fear of taxation and/or income redistribution could turn off the flow. This indeed had taken place already in anticipation of a PASOK victory. The imagined threat to capitalist business interests from a socialist economic program, which the PASOK government failed to dispel, brought on a capital flight, and the revenues from invisibles were retained abroad. In 1981, the last year of the government of the right wing New Democracy (ND) Party, the deficit in the balance of payments current account amounted to 6.4 percent of GNP.

Domestic real incomes had also been falling already in the preelection period. By 1981 inflation had accelerated to reach a 27 percent annual rate. This was due only partly to the increases in energy costs brought on by the second oil shock. The primary cause was the inordinate growth of the conservative government's preelection expenditures: a doubling of the public sector deficit, which was incurred in the vain effort to retain adequate public support for winning the elections.

The deficit inherited by PASOK amounted to about 16 percent of GNP. Given the competing interests, such as national defense, social services, public enterprises, and the demands for subsidies by the private sector, the question of where to cut, and by how much, was among the first political-economic problems the new government had to face immediately after the elections.

To round out the catalog of inherited problems, something has to be said, even at the risk of generalizing, about the Greeks themselves. They have a strong sense of ethnic belonging, and a loyalty to some abstract concept of "Greekness," which also permeates the diaspora. Nonetheless, in their daily existence they seem to be guided by an individualism that dominates social concern. And even though the Greeks in their private dealings are as honorable as any other people, when it comes to citizenship, be it citizen's obligation to the state or public service, relations are often corrupt.[7] To attempt to change this misdirected individualism should have been PASOK's primary task. Instead, PASOK contributed to it by, among other things, failing to introduce a socially just tax reform, by not enforcing rigorous tax collection, and by backing away from tax measures that would have affected not only the tax-evading but vocal large property owners and nonsalaried high income earners.

Combined with a concomitant and traditional lack of trust in government and government officials, corruption may be the single greatest obstacle to democratic social-political development. It is also the greatest obstacle to the development of orderly market practices, because the competitive advantage obtained by tax evaders and suborners of public officials forces even those entrepreneurs who would prefer not to be corrupt to follow suit.

Although nominally Greece has been a free enterprise market economy, the state has always played a dominant role in resource allocation. Investors have always had to go through a tortuous process of bureaucratic licensing procedures. Furthermore, in the Greek economy almost everybody—labor and enterprise—has had a claim on some form of government subsidy unrelated to efficiency or productivity increase. The main source of subsidies has been the government budget, but given the corruption in paying and collecting taxes, and the fact that the direct and indirect subsidies have been all-pervasive, it is not quite possible to disentangle who subsidizes whom. One can say with certainty, however, that wage and salary earners, that is, those income recipients whose taxes are deducted at the source, have carried a disproportionate tax burden. Although not legally exempted, as a matter of established practice farmers have never been taxed, and the professional classes and merchants have been notorious tax evaders by means of underreporting their incomes.[8]

Under such conditions, what degrees of freedom were left to PASOK for implementing its program? The answer is, not many. Nonetheless, in spite of these grievous initial conditions, the government started out with a number of measures, some of which have importantly and lastingly affected the Greek social and political reality.

## International relations

The most important successes of the PASOK government were related to the area of international affairs. If the question were put to the Greek electorate, there is no doubt that it would overwhelmingly approve of PASOK's handling of international relations, even though it has not exactly followed the lines suggested by the preelection party platform.[9] Greece has neither quit NATO nor the EEC, as was PASOK's declared intention. Nor has it terminated its standing agreement with the United States for its maintenance and use of military bases in Greece.[10] But through a new and occasionally even aggressive assertion of the independence of its stance in NATO and EEC councils, the PASOK government signaled that the status of being a client state had ended. Furthermore, the government, with the leadership of Andreas Papandreou, undertook the creation of an opening toward the socialist bloc. Over right-wing protest, Parliament voted measures for recognizing the legitimacy of the left-wing resistance to the German invaders through such measures as the provision of pensions to the survivors, and by reinstating the civil war exiles, many of whom had taken refuge in countries of the socialist bloc, as members in good standing of civil society.[11] A good neighbor policy was actively pursued toward the socialist countries of the

Balkans and Central Europe, which was recently extended to include Albania. An agreement among Greece, Bulgaria, Rumania, and Yugoslavia for a nuclear-free Balkans was initiated by the Greek government.

Considering the point of departure, a traditional client state of Western powers and one of the poorest members in the European Community, these were important achievements. The left in and outside PASOK was vocally dissatisfied with the unfulfilled commitments to quit NATO and the EEC, and with the lack of aggressive moves toward the elimination of the U.S. bases. But in spite of popular resentment of the perceived U.S. support for the 1967 military putsch, the junta, and right-wing governments, this dissatisfaction was not shared by a significant segment of the electorate.

The PASOK government, and the people at large, came to recognize the potential vulnerability of the nation's domestic stability, economy, and territorial integrity, particularly in the Eastern Aegean. Accordingly, even though national defense and the maintenance of military preparedness were expensive (between 6 and 7 percent of the Gross Domestic Product), they were given much attention both for domestic and international reasons. From the beginning, the PASOK government—with the memory of the last military dictatorship very much alive—was sensitive to the possibility of a cool reception from the military to a socialist government. Furthermore, even though Greece is part of the NATO alliance, it considers itself more threatened by Turkey, its Eastern NATO partner, than by its communist neighbors in the North. There is reason behind the paradox: the Soviet Union has adhered to its Yalta commitment not to interfere in Greek domestic affairs, whereas the Turks—apart from the old enmities— have revealed an aggressive interest in the exploration and exploitation of the mineral wealth of certain parts of the Aegean continental shelves that are located under seas traditionally claimed by Greece.[12] Thus, for Greece, the NATO affiliation has been an umbrella toward the East rather than the North.

As to the EEC affiliation, at this time, and for the foreseeable future, it would be difficult to see what viable alternatives might exist. Although the PASOK government has established and maintained good relationships with the Arab countries and the PLO, and Greece could be thought of as a leading participant in some indefinite future Eastern Mediterranean Market, the unstable political conditions within the region would, at this time, make the economic viability of such an association highly doubtful.[13] The socialist bloc, too, has little to offer in terms of trading opportunities and other economic benefits.

Given the close ties to the international economy and dependence on the service sector for foreign exchange earnings, Greece has had no viable alternative to EEC membership. And when it comes to national defense, a neutral, nonallied position would leave Greece without protection against territorial encroachment from the East; hence, there is reason for caution in the handling of matters relating to EEC and NATO affiliations, and the status of foreign military bases.

## Advances and failures on the domestic front

In domestic development the problems caused by the inherited conditions were much more difficult to cope with. The fact that previous governments—including the military junta—routinely placed the blame for any of their failures on the specific conditions inherited by them does not change the fact that the distorted and deeply embedded political-economic conditions carried over from past administrations could not have been readily corrected or eliminated in the short run. But it is also true that the political will and unity of purpose in the PASOK leadership were inadequate to overcome the adverse initial conditions.

Even so, there was notable progress in certain areas that are important for social transformation. The government used its parliamentary strength to change the legal status of women, whose human, civil, and economic rights had traditionally been subject to those of men.[14] Programs for increasing and extending various forms of social services were initiated, in particular social security, public health and medical care, and education. Measures were introduced to increase welfare in the agricultural sector and to extend social services to the rural population, including the hitherto much neglected rural women. But for various reasons, among which the government's failure to restructure the organization of the delivery of the services was primary, performance—particularly in medical services and education—did not meet expectations. Accessibility undoubtedly increased, but the quality of the services did not improve, and in some cases it diminished.[15] At the same time, the social services in general, and the social security system in particular, became the heaviest contributors to the public deficit. Nonetheless, the people's claim to such services was greatly strengthened, and barring the return of another dictatorship, these rights will not be readily denied in the future by any democratically elected government.[16]

Soon after the elections, and in spite of the inflationary conditions, the government declared a 40 percent increase in minimum wages. Indexation was introduced and laws were passed for the protection of workers in employment, and for narrowing the salary differentials of those on the public payroll. It was expected that in response to the improvement of social services—increasing "social wages"—the pressures for higher wages would be mitigated. The pressures continued, however, partly because the ongoing inflation, in spite of partial indexation, wiped out a significant portion of the initial gains in real incomes, and partly because the original expectations by the lower income groups for rapid increases in their living standards greatly exceeded what could be delivered under the prevailing circumstances.[17]

In the election platform, decentralization—political, economic, and bureaucratic—had been considered one of the cornerstones of democratization. Nonetheless, moves toward decentralization were slow and limited. Neither the government nor the party recognized that there can be no political, administrative, or economic decentralization without first creating the institutions for replacing the centralized chains of command. As a consequence, any move toward the introduction of democratic planning had to come to naught. The allocation of some of the funds available for use in the regional administrative units (nomarchies) was decentralized, but the prefects (nomarchs) are still appointed from the center, even though some or most members of their supporting councils—marginal in their functions—are now locally elected. The continuity of the monolithic character of the central administration was somewhat diminished—at the cost of creating considerable initial confusion—by the abrupt elimination of the position of "general director" in the ministries, the highest rank in the permanent civil service. But by concentrating the power of appointments and authorization of expenditures—even those that had already been budgeted—in the hands of a ministerial triumvirate, the PASOK government maintained, and even augmented, the tradition of centralized control.

One of the primary problems of the PASOK government was the sagging economy and the design of policies for its revitalization. From the beginning administrative measures and legislation were introduced to provide incentives for, and encouragement of, new investment. With much delay, a five-year plan was prepared for mapping out resource allocation and regionalization in accordance with the announced goals of the government.[18] But because of lack of forceful leadership on the domestic economic front, inherited bureaucratic cumbersomeness of the licensing procedures, and investors' hesitation to cooperate with the socialist government, the rate of progress was disappointing.

The above social and economic programs, some of them very expensive to both the private and the public sectors, were initiated under inflationary conditions. Nonetheless, in spite of the costs, and by cutting the size of certain other budgetary items, the rate of inflation moderated, and by 1983 the government deficit was reduced to less than 12 percent of GNP. But the problem of complex bureaucratic procedures and universal subsidies remained. In the beginning the PASOK government, while considering a gradual rationalization of the system, shied away from instituting rapid changes because of a fear of unpredictable economic and political upheavals, which could have been brought on by a potential worsening of the unemployment already very much in evidence and growing in 1981 and 1982. Such fears may not have been baseless: the idea of rationalization of the subsidy system threatened the short-term interests of both labor and capital. And the streamlining of the administrative mechanism ran counter to the interests of the in any case inefficient civil service.

Two inherited problems were particularly difficult to deal with: the time-honored practice of less-than-cost pricing by, and concomitant subsidies to, inefficient public enterprises, and the liquidation or reconstruction of the privately owned, virtually bankrupt firms called "problematic enterprises."

Although the deficit of the public enterprises was a heavy burden on the fisc, the rationalization of the management of, and the price structure for, public services was not effectively undertaken. Both in government and among the

public there was, on grounds of ill-defined populist ideology, a widespread sentiment—not unique to Greece—in favor of "cheap" public services, even though
the burden of the subsidies needed for maintaining the services fell primarily on
the tax-paying wage and salary earners, while the benefits accrued in large
measure to producers and other members of the higher income classes. In terms
of its economic impact, cost pricing would eliminate the indirect subsidies to
consumers and producers, and its introduction—as in other parts of the world—
could have adverse implications for social stability. Furthermore, price increases
for public services under inflationary conditions do contribute to the already
prevailing pressures on the price level. Nonetheless, the efficiency of the public
enterprises could have been improved through technical and managerial reorganization. But the PASOK government, as in all matters requiring structural
change, moved slowly and cautiously with the restructuring of the public enterprises.

As to the inherited practice of satisfying the ever increasing borrowing
needs of the "problematic enterprises," it resulted in the necessity of subsidiz-
ing, beyond the enterprises, the commercial banking system itself. Many of the
problem firms, particularly the larger ones with significant employment levels,
would have collapsed without the government's direct and indirect subsidies and other forms of intervention. In the end, in order to resolve the employment and other political-economic problems, the government took over
the management of thirty-nine of the most important ailing firms.[19]

The subsidy system, of course, contributed to the growth of excess demand
over and above what the Greek economy could satisfy through its productive
capacity. Over time the Greek economy satisfied this excess demand by means
of a deficit on the international trade account, that is to say, through imports in
excess of exports. As pointed out above, this deficit has always been sizable, but
traditionally it had been offset in large measure by foreign exchange earnings
from "invisibles," such as tourism, shipping, and emigrants' remittances. But
with the protracted recession abroad, the offsetting item, that is, the surplus from
invisibles, significantly declined between 1975 and 1985 while the deficit on
trade account remained and, in fact, grew. The choice confronting the PASOK
government was to restrain demand to cut imports, or to accept the continued
accumulation of foreign debts. The choice, more by default than by conscious
decision, was made in favor of the latter. As a consequence, the inherited foreign
indebtedness continued to grow from about an initial 8 billion U.S. dollars in
1981 to about 15 billion in 1985, and to almost 21 billion in 1987.[20]

**Problems of economic reconstruction**

PASOK inherited an economy that was already in great difficulty. For this reason, it was evident from the start that its program for social transformation could
not be undertaken without rebuilding the economy. But given the inefficiency of

domestic industry, the international recession, and the consequent need to rely on foreign borrowing, the task of rebuilding could not have been undertaken without the solid support of all sectors of the economy. The reality is that neither capital nor the bureaucracy was in a mood to cooperate. And after the initial enthusiasm had passed, support from labor also declined, albeit for reasons different from those of the capitalists and bureaucrats.

From the beginning the PASOK government was facing extreme hostility from the right, the manifestations of which went much beyond the limits of loyal opposition.[21] This political hostility undoubtedly added fuel to the already palpable distrust by the traditional bureaucracy and by private entrepreneurs. The former resented PASOK's declared intention to shrink its size and limit its power: in response, its members dragged their feet in implementing policy.[22] This was further reinforced by the PASOK government's practice of frequently circumventing regular service channels through the use of "outsiders," that is, nonadministrative personnel employed in the various ministerial secretariats.

The capitalists, in turn, were alienated by PASOK's platform commitment to improve social justice. They did not want to lose their paternalistic control over labor. Contrary to the principles of free enterprise, they particularly feared measures that would have forced them either to become efficient producers or to get out of the market, that is, policies that would be taken for granted in market economies, such as Thatcher's England or Reagan's America. Given their established ways of working with borrowed funds instead of risk capital, they also feared the end of easy credit and subsidies for their unprofitable and inefficient enterprises, which hitherto they could obtain without regard for their contribution to productivity and the health of the national economy. Motivated by fears and resentments, the capitalists and entrepreneurs withheld their investable funds from the market. They moved and kept capital abroad, and let the economy settle into a state of inertia.

In the matter of rapid progress toward rebuilding the economy, the government had only limited means at its disposal. The state could not assume, or substitute for, the functions of the alienated capitalists, because it had neither the entrepreneurial nor the managerial capacity to take control of the economy. Whatever initial potential there may have been for generating such functions, it was further weakened by legislation limiting the salary levels in public employment: the state could not compete with the private sector or foreign employers for the best technical, administrative, and managerial talents. There was no ready means for substituting for private-sector management and entrepreneurship. Early on it should have been possible to bring around the younger, more progressive, and enterprising entrepreneurial talent amply available in Greece, by means of a rapid reorganization and simplification of investment licensing and credit provisions. This would have required the streamlining and depoliticization of the bureaucracy, the transformation of the credit system from the practice of traditional money lending into modern banking organization, and the provision of technical assistance to new industrialists. But moves in this direction came late, and even then slowly and not very effectively.

Paradoxically, in order to rebuild the economy, the socialist government would have had to start out with policies for establishing what earlier capitalist governments had failed to do. Had PASOK inherited a healthy economy with a reasonable balance between the various sectoral demands and supplies, with no unprofitable enterprises maintained by subsidies, and with wages in a sustainable relationship to productivity, that is, if the conservative ND government had behaved according to the rules of capitalist market organization, then PASOK— assuming that they could have defeated the ND under such conditions—would have had no difficulty with starting its social programs, including the correction of the market distribution of income according to its preconceptions of social justice. But the conservatives had not governed according to their own free market principles: they left behind a plundered and distorted economy where investment and productivity had been permitted to fall well in advance of the arrival of the socialists, and where profits and funds borrowed from Greek banks at negative real interest rates had frequently been taken abroad to earn high real returns.

It was left to the incoming socialist government to cope with the imbalances, the distorted markets, the inflation, and the deteriorating balance of payments. As a consequence, PASOK was confronted with an immediate and very difficult problem, one that has recently plagued several democratic governments attempting to reconstruct their ailing economies inherited from right-wing or dictatorial regimes. The policies for reconstruction are particularly painful for governments concerned with social justice, because part of the process consists of measures that necessarily cause at least a temporary lowering of the living standards of labor and other lower income groups. Even the elimination of subsidies and other forms of protection for unproductive private enterprises, that is, measures that penalize inefficient capitalist owners, cause at least transitional unemployment and/or dislocation of labor. The control of inflation, the attainment of a sustainable foreign balance, the elimination of excessive government deficits, and the correction of all other structural distortions, have short- or medium-term effects that adversely affect the welfare of the lower income groups.

The requirements of economic reconstruction are similar, whether it is undertaken in a capitalist or a socialist economy. The important difference consists in the distribution of the burden of, and the benefits from, the effort. In free-market economies the major part of the burden has traditionally been permitted to fall on labor and the lower income groups, while the benefits have accrued primarily to the capitalist owners. In contrast, socialist ethics require that the burden of adjustment on the lower income groups be mitigated by whatever measures are available to that end, and that a fair share of the long-run benefits accrue to them. But even then, as Kornai has pointed out, conflicts between the demands for efficiency and the ethical principles of socialism are inevitable.[23] This is the case even if the concept of efficiency is broadened to include those humanistic elements that do not form part of it in its competitive market interpretation.

After the first enthusiasm that greeted PASOK's victory—or the defeat of the right—labor soon realized that its expectations for rapid increases in its welfare would not be satisfied. The benefits from the initial labor legislation for increased job protection, the initial wage increases, and the promise of increased welfare from improving social services did not mitigate demands for further increases in money wages. Labor did not recognize the relationship between productivity and sustainable wage levels. This was the consequence of PASOK's failure to encourage the growth of an independent and responsible democratic socialist labor organization that could have been brought into political decision making. In reality, the PASOK government alienated those elements in the labor movement that could have been most helpful in building an independent democratic socialist labor organization. Only through such an organization could labor have been convinced, through dialogue and moral suasion, of the reasons for particular policies and the need for restraint.

But equally important is that labor's understandable impatience for attaining a higher level of current welfare was in conflict with its long-run interests. In a society where the working classes have never had adequate political representation, the value of future satisfaction would naturally be heavily discounted. After years of frustration, and with the exaggerated expectations fostered by PASOK during its opposition to the ND government, followed by PASOK's victory at the polls, the urge to satisfy long-delayed demands for higher living standards became dominant.

The inadequacy of a PASOK labor organization left control of the labor movement partly with the well-organized Communist Party, and partly with various syndicates, unions, and associations concerned only with the welfare of their own members. Well-to-do unions, such as that of the bank employees, secured additional benefits for themselves by means of repeated strikes at the expense of the economy, the popularity of the government, and the less protected lower income groups. There was also a tendency to exploit the laws for workers' protection enacted under the PASOK government in ways that lowered work discipline and productivity.

Given the frustration of the initial unreasonably high expectations and the inadequacy of the PASOK labor policies, it is not surprising that labor was not keen to restrain its wage demands or maintain a higher level of discipline in the workplace. But the dissatisfaction did not reach its full extent during PASOK's first term in power, because the unpopular policies—the bitter medicine—for correcting the inherited distortions in the economy, had not been introduced, at least not in adequate measure.

PASOK was reelected in 1985 with an absolute parliamentary majority, albeit with significantly reduced strength. The preparations for these elections were accompanied by large increases in government spending that led, in turn, to a rekindling of the same inflationary pressures PASOK had to cope with after its 1981 victory over the incumbent ND government. The balance of payments deficit was getting out of hand, while the conditions for borrowing abroad to cover the imbalance had become increasingly tight. At that point there was no alternative to instituting a series of corrective policies.

A few months after the elections the government declared a stabilization program that was based mostly on income policies without any significant effort to bring about structural changes. The set of policies also contained devaluation, ostensibly for improving the competitiveness of Greek industry, but primarily to satisfy the lenders' traditional demand for first "putting the house in order." The devaluation was accompanied by wage, but not price, controls. The result was a massive redistribution of incomes in favor of employers and profit earners without any of the hoped-for productivity effects. The burden of the austerity measures fell almost totally on labor. When it protested, it was expelled from the party. Two years later labor demonstrated the full measure of its anger by joining the conservative right in the municipal elections. PASOK suffered defeat in some of the largest cities of the country, including Athens, Piraeus, and Thessaloniki.

**The sources of failures**

What should, or could, PASOK have done to reconstruct the economy so as to attain a measure of efficiency without provoking the anger of the working classes? As discussed above, the failure to provide adequate leadership in the labor movement was an important omission that had adverse consequences. But this was only a manifestation of a characteristic feature of PASOK: it remained, as has been pointed out at various times, a movement that failed to turn into a party either in the ideological or the organizational sense. The unity of purpose that prevailed during the fight against the dictatorship, and was maintained during the years of parliamentary opposition to the ruling conservatives, diminished with the electoral victory of 1981. Instead of developing a unified party organization for the pursuit of the party's goals, PASOK became a conglomeration of rival interest groups under the shared umbrella of the power and popularity of the undisputed leader of PASOK, Andreas Papandreou, the Prime Minister.

Had there been an effective party organization and political will, the PASOK government could have taken advantage of its enormous initial popular support to introduce certain necessary changes right at the beginning—such as tax reform and decentralization—which in the long run would have led to more rapid social and economic progress. Part of the explanation of its failure to do so may be that the party leadership and the government were inexperienced: with the exception of the Prime Minister, the ministers and high-level administrators had no previous governmental, or professional political-administrative, experience. This may also explain why some of the senior ministers of the PASOK government had a fundamental misconception about the nature of economic policy-making. The solution of economic problems is a political and not simply a technocratic matter. The political costs of economic policies that ultimately necessitated the stabilization program and determined the form of its implementation demonstrate the consequences of their misconception.

But it can also be argued that the government may have underestimated the political maturity of the electorate. At the time of the electoral victory in 1981, the people were ready for responsible change and would have been prepared to sacrifice for a better future. The proof of this was the massive protest vote by the nonsocialist center in favor of PASOK, which was a clear signal of a desire for change. But the delay in tax reform, in legislation making tax evasion a criminal act, and in the rigorous enforcement of the laws, served to encourage the corrupt elements in the private and public sectors to believe that they could continue with their accustomed ways.

It was, perhaps, the desire to diminish the role of the police, or the reluctance of leaders who had suffered repression under earlier dictatorships and police regimes, that prevented the government from the use of police power in controlling corrupt practices. There is, however, a difference between tyranny and the legitimate use of the power of the state for the defense of civic morality under a democratically elected government. Tax evasion and other forms of corruption led to the creation of a second, underground economy, outside the fiscal control of the government, which became the main source of the growing inequality between the wage and salary earners whose taxes are deducted at the source, and the various classes—merchants, professionals, contractors, and farmers—that partially or totally evade taxation. The growing inequality, combined with a lack of trust in government, was the primary threat to social progress and development. It may, ultimately, motivate the electorate to bring back into power the reactionary political right, not because they want them back, but as a means—albeit a self-defeating one—for expressing their disappointment with the domestic policies of the PASOK government.

The early failures had costly economic and social consequences. The fundamental problem, however, lies elsewhere. For better or for worse, the free market imposes a certain discipline on both labor and capital. The rules of the market—as Adam Smith observed—can be defied only at one's peril. But the market has never been an instrument of social justice or democratic ideals. These demand different rules and other means of discipline. But if the discipline of the market is removed, what other forms of discipline are there that are compatible with democratic socialism and can ensure the productivity of labor and the necessary supply of capital for increasing living standards? The question remains unanswered. Yet, in the long run, increases in living standards can come only *pari passu* with increases in productivity.

It is, perhaps, because this question has remained unanswered that the nondemocratic left has so often called for a type of revolutionary change with totalitarian means for the enforcement of discipline in the organization of production. Apart from its unacceptable ethical implications, by now we know that efficiency cannot be imposed by totalitarian means. Furthermore, in countries where the government does not have the managerial capacity for taking control of the economy, as is surely the case in Greece, there is no alternative to working with the private sector.

It follows that conditions have to be created in which the private sector can and will function. The private sector is motivated by self-interest; hence the national economy has to be so structured as to eliminate potential conflicts between the private profit motive and the democratic social interest. First, civic responsibility must be enforced by eradicating private and public corruption in all its forms. Secondly, the areas open for private-sector activity need to be clearly delineated. Entrepreneurs have to be given the confidence that in those areas they are free to pursue their profit interests, subject only to well-defined and reasonable rules. Obviously, the state has a decisive role in setting and enforcing limits, and guaranteeing freedom of action within those limits.

But the state must also be a teacher. A democratic society must be made aware of the fact that democratic socialism demands a higher-order discipline than the one imposed by a capitalist market organization. If market and social justice are to coexist, capitalist employers and labor have to be persuaded that it is in their respective interests to compromise by sharing political and economic power. It is not an easy lesson to learn: the recognition of enlightened self-interest does not come readily. It is here that the teaching role of the state and the electorate's willingness to maintain trust in the government become crucially important.

## Conclusion

This leads back to the question of whether it is possible to transform progressively, or socialize by democratic means, a semi-industrialized country that is integrated into the international capitalist system. The Greek experience does not seem to provide an answer. What it does show is that an effective party organization combined with political will is a *sine qua non* for implementing a program for a democratic social-political transformation.

Political will has been exercised in the conduct of external affairs, and the goal of increasing national independence has been pursued without breaking relations with that international capitalist system on which the country depends for the protection of its economy and territorial integrity.

However, the conduct of foreign affairs does not necessarily depend on the same kind of party organization that is required for the implementation of domestic programs. Apart from its role in elections, one of the most important functions of the party must be to contribute, through organized effort, to grassroots understanding of government policies. In fact, the ultimate test of democratic leadership and party organization is public support for policies that call for sacrifice in the short run. PASOK failed to attain such support.

Equally important is the fact that corruption has not been eradicated and, hence, civic responsibility has not been developed. Yet, these are prerequisites of those social and political conditions in which capital can be induced to invest in harmony with the social interest, and labor develops that trust in government which it must have to recognize what is necessary for advancing its own welfare.

The high political cost of inadequate political will and party organization is the lesson to be learned from the Greek experience. But, in spite of it all, Greece has undergone some significant changes over the last eight years. Women are no longer the property of men. They have organized and become a democratic political force that neither PASOK nor any other party or future government can ignore. The claim for social services has been made general. And the population at large, in the past always prepared to resist repression, appears to have no respect for, or fear of, arbitrary authority. The people have acquired a palpable sense of confidence, or self-awareness, in using the ballot as a means for calling for change. One way or the other, the PASOK government will be the first to experience the consequences of this new popular self-awareness, which may very well turn into a permanent feature of the Greek polity. If so, it will be a most important legacy of the PASOK government.

## Postscript

National elections were held on June 18, 1989. The political debate during the preceding six to nine months was dominated by a series of accusations of alleged corruption in the highest levels of government. The Prime Minister, his family life very much under public scrutiny, was recovering from the aftereffects of a complex bypass and heart operation. PASOK entered the elections handicapped by its earlier failures, the tarnished image of some of its high officials, and a weakened leadership. In the event, PASOK was defeated.

The main contenders were the right-wing New Democracy (ND), PASOK, and the Electoral Coalition of the Leftist and Progressive Forces (made up of the Communist Party of Greece and other left-of-PASOK parties and groups). None obtained absolute majority. In the final count ND got 44.4 percent of the popular vote and 145 parliamentary seats, PASOK 39.1 percent and 125 seats, and the left coalition 13.1 percent and 28 seats. The remaining 2 of the total of 300 seats went, one each, to the right Democratic Renewal and the Western Trace Moslem parties.

Even though the two parties of the left taken together had the majority of the popular vote and parliamentary seats, a political stalemate developed that was resolved by the formation of an interim government jointly backed by the ND and the left coalition. They agreed on a cooperation of three months' duration, to be followed by new national elections in November 1989. The leaders of the cooperating parties were excluded from the cabinet of the interim government. Under Prime Minister Tzannis Tzannetakis—a hitherto not too prominent ND politician who was interned for his active opposition during the military dictatorship—two key ministerial posts (Interior and Justice) were allocated to extraparliamentary members of the left coalition. The other cabinet members were drawn from the right.

The mandate of the interim government was strictly circumscribed: other than routine matters of governance, it can undertake only "catharsis," the judicial investigation of the role of PASOK ministers and other high level officials in the alleged financial scandals and other forms of corruption.

One may readily concur with the view that a catharsis of Greek political life is called for. In reality, it would have to go much wider and much deeper than just cleaning up after the alleged wrongdoings of PASOK government officials. But it is most doubtful that an interim government that does not represent a national consensus can undertake it and complete it within the allotted time. The real question is whether this fellowship between the ND party and the Coalition of the Leftist and Progressive Forces was motivated by the desire to carry out a catharsis, or to destroy PASOK, given that animosity toward socialists is the one sentiment that capitalists and communists have traditionally shared, each for its own reasons. One need not excuse the failures of PASOK if one agrees with the former Prime Minister of Greece, Andreas Papandreou, that for the left to have entered into such an alliance is nothing less than a historic error.

## Notes

1. This paper was prepared for seminar presentation in March and completed for publication in December 1988, about six months before the 1989 Greek national elections. A short postscript was added and minor adjustments were made after the June 1989 elections. I owe a debt of gratitude to several colleagues who commented on earlier drafts, but I am uniquely responsible for the arguments and views contained in the paper. I have refrained from presenting quantitative estimates of economic change even where the statistical information is available in Greek currency (drachma), because the complex interaction of domestic inflation and changes in foreign exchange rates during the period under discussion make it difficult to express the various macroeconomic magnitudes in constant dollars. Some of my arguments rely on direct observation that cannot be documented for lack of statistical or other quotable evidence.

2. As far as I know, there is no consistent theoretical framework for the systematic analysis of the processes of social transformation. Alec Nove's *The Economics of Feasible Socialism* (London: George Allen & Unwin, 1983) is an effort in this direction. It is more relevant, however, to the question of what may constitute "feasible socialism" than to the dynamics of reaching it.

3. See, e.g., Yiannis P. Roubatis, *Tangled Webs: The U.S. in Greece 1947–1967* (New York: Pella, 1987). The bibliography lists a useful selection of articles and books on the political history preceding the events discussed by Roubatis.

4. The platform followed the program set out in the "3rd September 1974 Manifesto" of PASOK, also known as the "Little Green Book."

5. It is also referred to as the Communist Party of the Exterior, because of its rather orthodox ideology oriented toward the USSR. In contrast, the Communist Party of the Interior, no longer in existence, had a Western orientation somewhat akin to Eurocommunism. This party failed to obtain Parliamentary representation in the elections, and gave up its independence in 1987 by forming part of a new political party organization, the United Democratic Left.

6. Prime Minister's statement to Parliament, entitled "Programmatic Declaration of the Government," 22 November 1981 (unofficial translation).

7. Until a recent legislative change introduced by the PASOK government, the anachronistic institution of a debtor's jail had been maintained while tax evasion had not been a criminal act. Corruption is not confined to the taxpayer alone. At very great cost to the fisc and private citizens, tax collectors and other officials have well-known ways of extorting money from the public at large. In some instances, corruption has been alleged to have reached high political and governmental levels.

8. According to the most recent estimates, the actual or realized GNP may be by at least 40 percent higher than the official statistic, and the corresponding revenue loss may be sufficient to cover the government budget deficit (see "The Two Wounds of the Greek Economy," *Epikerotita* [13 August 1989] [in Greek]; the author, Costas Kalivianakis, is former governor of the Bank of Attika and currently director of a research project on the "underground economy" at the Mediterranean Foundation in Athens).

9. Actually, the question has been tested by opinion polls that are, however, not in the public domain.

10. The future of the bases is still under negotiation.

11. Many exiles and their offspring decided to return. Of those who were brought up and educated abroad, quite a few found government, teaching, and research employment in Greece, and have contributed to the establishment of commercial and cultural connections with the countries of their exile.

12. The Greek government has repeatedly offered to submit the matter to adjudication by the International Court in the Hague, but the Turkish government has steadfastly refused to go along with this proposal.

13. Although the PASOK support for the PLO was viewed with hostility by the Israeli lobby in the United States, the government had *de facto* recognized the 1967 borders of Israel.

14. Legislation of women's rights was not universally popular within PASOK. But even the diehards realized the importance of women's votes, and the increasing political power of the women's organization, in which Margaret Papandreou, the Prime Minister's former wife, had a leading role. Legislation is, of course, only the first step toward the attainment of equality. Affirmative action, as a needed follow-up to legislation, has been lagging.

15. Adequate restructuring of the administrations and rationalization of the technical organizations would have increased the respective capacities of the delivery systems even with the existing facilities. But beyond that, the rate at which education and health services can be expanded depends in large measure on the rate at which additional professionals can be brought into the system. This is the case even where capital substitution for service personnel is possible. Since professional education requires long training periods, the rate of expansion is correspondingly slow. But equally important is a change in attitude by the members of the respective establishments concerning the nature and form of delivery of the services that in their traditional forms may not be compatible with social goals. The broadening of health services requires a much greater emphasis on epidemiology (prevention) than traditional medicine, whose primary focus is on individual care. And broad-based public education requires a reorientation toward disciplines that are in

line with the needs and aspirations of the population at large. Such changes are not necessarily welcomed and may even be sabotaged by the professionals of the service establishments, as in fact has been the case in Greece.

16. According to a recently published study by Efthalia Kalogeropoulou ("Election Promises and Government Performance in Greece: PASOK's Fulfillment of its 1981 Election Pledges," *European Journal of Political Research*, 17: 3 [May 1989]), "while [the PASOK government] did not totally transform Greek society, it did promise a number of reforms, the majority of which were carried out on the political level." This conclusion was based on a comparison of the structure of state expenditures under the preceding ND government and the first term of the PASOK government. The policy changes followed the ideological differences between the two parties: "law and order for ND, welfare for PASOK."

17. Average earnings in manufacturing changed in real terms as follows: in 1982, +10.4 percent; 1983, –0.7 percent; 1984, +6.6 percent; 1985, +0.4 percent; 1986, –9.4 percent; 1987, –5.5 percent. In overall terms, the share of wages and salaries in nonagricultural incomes was reported to have increased from about 58 percent in 1981 to about 62 percent in 1987 (Bank of Greece). But these figures are based on official income estimates that exclude unreported incomes (see note 8 above).

18. *Greece: The Five-year Economic and Social Development Plan. 1983–87* (summary), edited by the Center of Planning and Economic Research (Athens, 1984).

19. The "problematic enterprises" originally became unprofitable in large measure because of the owners' policy of operating with highly unfavorable debt/equity ratios. The debt increases were made possible under previous governments by the easy availability of preferential low interest credit, obtained ostensibly for investment and modernization, but frequently as a means for moving capital abroad.

The takeover of the 39 firms by the government resulted in the protection of about 10,000 jobs, but at a very large cost to the government and the economy in general. This is a cost over and above the enormous accumulation of mostly nonperforming loans owed to the banks, which continues to grow at an alarming rate (see, e.g., *Greece's Weekly*, 8 August 1988).

Arguably, it would have been preferable for both labor and capital to liquidate these ailing firms. Then the funds could have been used for retraining workers and creating new, state-of-the-art industrial employment through a vigorous investment program. Lacking trust, both labor and capital were strongly opposed to any such solution.

20. Of these amounts the share of the public sector's foreign indebtedness was about 66 percent in 1981, 75 percent in 1985, and 85 percent in 1987 (Bank of Greece).

21. For example, according to a statement to Parliament by the Prime Minister, certain elected representatives of the right (whose names he withheld from the public but offered to reveal to the leader of the right-wing opposition) were alleged to have approached foreign bankers with the suggestion that foreign credit should be denied to Greece under the PASOK government.

22. Contrary to declared intention, the size of public-sector employment continued to grow significantly under PASOK management.

23. For problems of reconstruction in socialist economies, see J. Kornai, *Contradictions and Dilemmas* (Budapest: Corvina/MIT Press, 1985). The parallels between the difficulties encountered in socialist bloc countries and in democratic countries attempting a social transformation while tied into the capitalist world economy are striking.

# The "Depoliticization of the Economy" or the "Democratization of Politics"?

## Leo Panitch

### I

The way we see the dilemmas of socialism today depends very much upon our own experience of the history of socialism in this century.[1] We pose the questions that arise out of our experience: those who have lived under Eastern European "actually existing socialism," under the tutelage of Communist single-party rule and central planning bureaucracies, tend to see the dilemmas of socialism very differently than those of us in the West whose experience with socialist politics relates primarily to the practices and failures of social democracy. In the former case, the question that is still most commonly posed is: how did we get from Marx to Stalin? In the latter case, the question that is rather more relevant is how did we get from Kier Hardie to Margaret Thatcher?

Of course, we live in a common world, and no one can ignore the lessons that broader experiences teach. In the West today, discussions of the dilemmas of socialism have been forced to confront not only the Thatcherite promulgation of market freedom as the solution to the West's ills, but also the popularity of the idea of "market socialism" in the East. Are the failures of the socialist project in this century, East *and* West, perhaps commonly grounded in a failure to come to terms with the value of markets? Alec Nove's *The Economics of Feasible Socialism*[2] has had a considerable impact on discussions of socialist dilemmas in the West, and Nove's concern to demonstrate that a socialist market is necessary for pluralism as well as efficiency has been seen by many as central to finding a way out of the impasse of socialist politics in the countries of advanced capitalism as well as being of obvious relevance to the crisis of the Communist societies.

The author is at the Department of Political Science, York University.

It is not the intention of this paper to undertake a full discussion of the case for market socialism. This paper shall concern itself rather with the limits and possibilities of attempts that have been made recently to transform Western social democratic parties into viable forces for socialist renewal. But it may be a useful starting point, for a discussion bringing together intellectuals from Eastern Europe with intellectuals in the West to discuss the dilemmas of socialism, to clear the ground for my discussion by asking at the outset whether the projection of the retrieval of the market does indeed help to establish the conditions for a democratic socialism in the West and enhance its desirability and credibility.

There are some, of course, who insist that a market socialism is no socialism at all. I would prefer to remain agnostic on this question. After all, Nove's model does envision the social ownership of all the major means of production and designates as state corporations, subject to central planning and administration, not only banks and other credit institutions but also all those sectors that operate in large, interrelated units or have a monopoly position. Even with regard to the socialized enterprises that would have "full autonomy" as well as cooperatives and small-scale private enterprises (that would exist only "subject to clearly defined limits"), central planning would have "the vital task of setting the ground rules for the autonomous and free sectors, with reserve powers of intervention when things got out of balance, or socially undesirable developments were seen to occur." Major investments and the share of GNP going to investment would be also centrally determined: this is obviously no "unplanned economy." Nove makes it clear that he expects that most final and intermediate goods and services will be bought and sold, but insofar as he explicitly designates that the management of the autonomous enterprises will be responsible to the workforce and establishes that a broader "democratic vote could decide the boundary between the commercial or market sectors and those where goods and services could be provided free," this seems to put effective restrictions on the extent to which this "market socialism" would be market determined, even if it could be said to be "commodified."

It would seem churlish, therefore, to dismiss Nove's market socialism out of hand. But the question remains: to what extent does the market socialist model actually help us in the West? Unfortunately, not very much. Indeed, Nove's argument on how a transition to his market socialism might be effected in the West is extremely thin. Apart from the sweeping denunciations of the "extreme left," and his attack on import and exchange controls and traditional nationalization as a recipe for driving the center into the arms of the right, which occupy most of his discussion, his own proposals are remarkably slight. "The biggest obstacle of all" to "a gradual shift in economic power away from big business" are "trade unions pursuing the narrow sectional interests of their members." But while he advocates limits on wage increases, he is at the same time opposed to price controls, import restrictions, and material allocation. He advocates a new approach to nationalization, whereby the nationalized firms would operate on "normal commercial criteria" where competitive conditions exist, and where specific firms rather than whole industries are removed from the private sector. Industrial and service cooperatives would also be encouraged insofar as they operate in a competitive environment. Both nationalized industries and private corporations would have to introduce "elements of workers' participation into the management structures," a turn of phrase he apparently considers less vague than the "totally undefined workers' control" he attacks the "Marxist utopians" for advocating, since he provides absolutely no further elaboration of what this means except to say that there is much to be learned from West German *Mitbestimmung*.

In light of much careful argument in the rest of the book, one cannot but be appalled at the slightness of Nove's chapter on the West. It would seem as though the existence of a market in the Western capitalist countries makes irrelevant for Nove the need for a serious discussion of how a social democratic reform program would lead on to anything like Nove's model of socialism; and of why the bourgeoisie would come to acquiesce in the social ownership and control of the means of production even if its political administration were conceived of as democratic and its economic dynamic as competitive. What is even worse, the connection posited between markets and pluralism seems to render irrelevant any discussion of the changes that would be necessary in the existing political organizations of the Left that would lead them to undertake a project of socialist change; or any discussion of how western political institutions would need to change if they are eventually to compose a democratic socialist state.

It would indeed appear that W. Brus's old critical comment on market socialism speaks as much to the problems of socialists in the West as it does to those in the East: "it is not 'depoliticization of the economy' but the 'democratization of politics' that is the correct direction for the process of socialization of nationalized means of production, . . . the problem of socialization turns into the question of the democratic evolution of the state, of the political system."[3] One of the difficulties associated with the advocacy of market socialism in the West is that it leads people away from addressing the difficult problems of political structures, especially of social democratic parties, and their relation to the capitalist state. Without attention paid to these problems, no socialist renewal—even if the goal is some sort of market socialism—is possible. Recent experience in the West certainly tells us this, as we shall now see.

## II

For some twenty to thirty years after World War II, socialism, as ideology, as program, as organizational practice, had been to all intents and purposes effectively sidelined from the agendas of social democratic parties throughout Western Europe. The Keynesian and corporatist policy framework that governed social democratic practice led to the marginalization of any vision of an alternative future other than that offered by the inherent trends of "actually existing capitalism" in the conjuncture of its greatest period of social mobility and growth, and in its welfare statist dimensions. It was inevitable that internal party life would be significantly affected thereby. When the socialist vision becomes transmuted into actually existing capitalism, there is little place for, and less need for, a party-based "counter-hegemonic" community. The activity of party branches continues to serve an instrumental function in electoral terms and in playing their allotted role at party conferences, but they lose what *raison d'être* they had as centers of education and mobilization toward an alternate way of life. Individual membership in absolute terms and as a percentage of the total electorate was for such reasons likely to stagnate, if not fall, and this was in fact the trend for all social democratic parties in Europe in the postwar era (with the single exception of the West German SPD, whose achievement in any case was that of managing to keep its membership abreast of the increasing size of the German electorate).[4]

Although the student radicalism and industrial militancy of the late 1960s led to a sharp turn by activists to extra-parliamentary forms of activity, the reverberations were bound to be felt in the parliamentary socialist parties as well. This entailed, first of all, a revival within these parties of a socialist discourse within which issues were discussed (or, more often, debated) and solutions, even reformist ones, advanced. The language of "class," of "capital," of "exploitation," of "crisis," of "struggle," of "imperialism," of "transformation," while never entirely extirpated from these parties, had certainly become marginalized within them in the decades after World War II. By the early 1970s it was again within constant earshot at party meetings and conferences. Even the term "social democracy" was often used pejoratively, and one suddenly found even many of the most jaded leaders now calling themselves "democratic socialists." But more than language was involved: there was a programmatic turn as well, in which the questions of taking capital away from Capital through major extensions of public or workers' ownership (or at least through radical measures of investment planning and industrial democracy) and the pursuance of a foreign policy independent of the United States, came onto the agendas of some of these parties.

The question remained, of course, of whether socialism could be placed back on the agenda, not only of these parties, but in the broader political arena. It certainly cannot be claimed that there was a ready-made groundswell of socialist electoral opinion just waiting to be tapped: it needed to be created in the interplay between party discourse and popular experience. The eventual victories in the early 1980s of the French, Greek, and Swedish parties on the basis of the most radical programs put before their electorates at least since the 1940s certainly invalidated simplistic claims, so commonly heard even on the left today, that parties which advanced such a program were inherently inelectable. But if a socialist alternative not only was to avoid conjuring up a negative electoral reaction, but was to produce the popular support needed to sustain a socialist government's radical thrust, this depended on a sea change in the organizational and ideological practices of the parliamentary socialist parties themselves. They had to become unified around the socialist alternative; they had to find the means to be effective vehicles for a transformation and mobilization of popular attitudes; they had to develop mechanisms to ensure that their leadership not only mouthed a socialist discourse the activists wanted to hear at party meetings, but shared a commitment to radical change and maintained such a commitment even when subject to the conservatizing pressures of office.

It was a tall order indeed. The programmatic changes that occurred in a number of social democratic parties in the 1970s were obviously developed with some awareness of these questions, such as the emphasis placed on industrial democracy alongside nationalization and investment controls, or on the decentralized socialization of capital through trade union administered wage earners' funds. These policies were conceived with a view to popularizing a socialist alternative via obviating its association with the authoritarian practices of Eastern European "actually existing socialism" as well as the bureaucratic practices of state-owned enterprises in the West. But this was itself a small first step. For even to make this credible and popular, fundamental organizational changes within the social democratic parties themselves were necessary to make them effective vehicles for a democratic socialist alternative.

The restructuring of the old socialist parties that produced the new *Parti Socialiste* certainly yielded a new program and a new discourse. François Mitterand declared flatly that the PS constituted a radical break with the "errors of the past," that it had "nothing in common with the corrupt compromises of a Schmidt or a Callaghan, let alone a Mollet."[5] It also was based on a new organizational structure, ostensibly "the most pluralistic" of all the French parties, whereby it gave representation on its *Comité Directeur* to the various groups in the party according to the proportion of the vote their platforms obtained at the biennial national party congress. Yet, less visible but more significant was the underlying—and unchallenged—reality of the organizational structure of the PS, which was to have an enormous effect after Mitterand's and the Socialists' victories in 1981. As Raymond Cayrol observed as early as 1978 regarding Mitterand's dominance of the party organization through his personal *cabinet:*

> It is the case of a party whose cement is still largely provided by loyalty to the line taken by its first Secretary, and the organization of the national headquarters eloquently institutionizes his indisputable preeminence at every level. There is, to be sure, a double circuit of legitimacy within the socialist apparat. But in the day-to-day affairs of the party it is the one which is based on François Mitterand's trust that appears to be dominant.[6]

Once established in office, it soon became clear that everything now hinged on the man in the Elysée. By 1983, with the Government having already shifted gears to a virtually monetarist economic policy and having shown itself entirely uninterested in the "autogestion" that was to have made the nationalizations undertaken in the first months popularly based, Raymond Cayrol could write:

> [T]he PS has not been able to elaborate an adequate role for itself which would ensure a certain autonomy from the government and provide it with the capacity to initiate vis-à-vis the government. . . . Rarely has presidentialism and the asserted primacy of the executive been so consecrated as under a left government. This phenomenon constitutes an obstacle for the emergence of a pluralist debate within the party and within the governing institutions—all roads appear to lead to l'Elysée.

Cayrol concluded that in lieu of any "dialectical relation between the action of the party's rank and file and that of the political action at the top . . . [the] PS seems to have voluntarily trapped itself in the State." [7]

A similar situation had developed in the course of PASOK's short "march to power" in Greece. After the downfall of the Junta, PASOK emerged on the basis of an alliance among the various resistance organizations and the old cadre of the socialist party with a decidedly radical orientation. Its goals were no less than a "structural reorientation of Greek society" and "the creation of a polity free of the control or influence of the economic oligarchy." Its program included the complete nationalization of the powerful private financial sector as well as withdrawal from NATO, since behind "NATO and the American bases there are the multinational monopolies and their local subsidiaries." All this was seen as the prerequisite for the realization of "national independence, popular sovereignty, social liberation, and political democracy." PASOK constantly criticized social democracy and even on occasion insisted that Marxism was the party's "method of social analysis." But although it promised a mass democratic and participatory party structure that would distinguish it from the centralism of the traditional left and the clientalism of the bourgeois parties, PASOK in fact evolved in a decidedly autocratic fashion under Andreas Papandreou's leadership. The rapid and conservative policy reorientation the Papandreou government underwent after its election in 1981, especially in economic policy, was preceded by unsavory intraparty developments during the short march to power that were marked by a series of major expulsions of those radical sections of the party that questioned Papandreou's personalized form of control over the party. A very knowledgeable Greek student of PASOK's internal development has written:

> While in its founding Document the Movement undertook to make "the principle of democratic procedure" its living organizational practice, during the seven years following 1974, PASOK became a prime example of an undemocratic, even authoritarian organization. Controlling intra-party opposition

by administrative means, Papandreou established a centralized organization in which everything revolved around the omnipotent leader and his inner circle.

Michalis Spourdalakis has gone on to document the effect of this on the Greek state itself.

> PASOK's presence in the edifice of Greek state power has promoted a general tendency towards authoritarianism in the central state apparatus. . . . PASOK has systematically exempted the military, the diplomatic service and the Justice department from parliamentary or public scrutiny. This is especially troubling since Papandreou's Government has surpassed its immediate predecessor in the scale of state coercion in certain areas. The heavy-handed policing of strikes, the increased surveillance of places where young people congregate, the cracking down on punks and the constant harassment of gays, are some striking examples of this depressing picture.[8]

No such picture of the Swedish state under social democracy can be drawn, and this must serve as a reminder, as Spourdalakis properly avers, that "political parties are portraits in miniature of the societies which they have chosen for their social project." Nevertheless, it is important to note that the new "middle way" to socialism that the wage earners' funds proclaimed entailed no significant or political mobilization of the SAP's and the labor movement's supporters such as would have made its realization a possibility in the face of an increasingly alarmed and conservative Swedish capital. The wage earners' fund proposal, which emanated from the trade unions, was always looked upon with intense suspicion by the party leadership. They were content to refer the critical details of the proposals to a series of commissions, which in the period between the infrequent (triennial) party conferences managed to water down the content, so that by the time they were actually introduced by the SAP government elected in 1982, they amounted to little more than a forced savings scheme providing a pool of capital for an unreconstructed corporate sector and a quid pro quo to wage restraint. To its credit, and by virtue of the continuing absorptive capacities of the public sector and the training schemes of the Labor Market Board, the government has kept unemployment relatively low. But the orientation of recent economic policy toward "the renewal of the private sector as the engine of the economy" involving tax incentives for capital, a tighter money supply, and a wage freeze, has left the unions again vociferously complaining of an income and wealth distribution to the benefit of capital in the face of a stock market boom, while real earnings have declined by 10 percent over the past decade. In the run up to the 1987 party congress (the last was in 1984), there was again grumbling, especially in the youth wing of the party, that the party had lost its vision, amid complaints that "terrible class differences are returning to Sweden."[9] The final word on the aspirations that so many socialists had placed on a hegemonic social democratic party in Sweden being the locus of an attempted transition to socialism may be given to the powerful Minister of Labor, Anne Leijon, who in response to a question on whether the party has a socialist strategy any longer, spelled out the SAP's philosophy clearly:

> We are social democrats. The democratic part of it is as important as the social part. Over 90 percent of enterprises are in private hands and they will remain at that. On the other hand we think that public services are important. So we will distribute services in a public way rather than through insurance companies. We feel the economy is not democratic enough and we will find new ways of extending industrial democracy. We have wage earner funds but not the kind Meidner proposed. We have a mixed economy and we will continue to have this.[10]

It is important to stress that it was not only business's vociferous opposition that determined this outcome. The sorry fate of the wage earners' funds as a means of socializing capital had much to do with the fact that there is in Sweden as elsewhere,

> the unfortunate general pattern of labour politics ... the failure to develop a political capacity anywhere in the labour movement, least of all in the party, as seen in the latter's typical incapacity to work through problems of policy implementation when framing electoral programs. Such are the objective, organizational roots of labour government's hasty retreats from electoral commitments, servility toward Treasury advice and ultimate sacrifice of class interests on the altar of "the national interest."[11]

A no less severe problem lay in the incapacity of the labor movement, including the party, to act as the kind of politicizing agent that was necessary to generate much popular enthusiasm for the funds as a means of socializing capital. Despite the opening the fund proposals seemed to provide for such politicization, the continuing predominance in the party of its statist and technocratic wing, part of which threatened to leave the party over the fund proposals in their earlier radical incarnation, rendered this promise inoperative.

It is against this comparative background that I want to turn to my main focus of attention: the attempt to change the British Labour Party. For here alone the enormous problem that the other left turns in social democracy failed to address seriously was readdressed. It was the problem Robert Michels had quite properly identified at the beginning of the century: the tendency to oligarchy in mass socialist parties. The issue, as he noted, pertained to these parties particularly, not because nonsocialist parties were not elitist and undemocratic in their structure, but because such characteristics were entirely consistent with their role as defenders of the social order. For parties of social change, the conservatizing effects and demobilizing effects of a leadership that was able to use the party's resources to distance itself from the pressure of socialist activists and the mechanisms of democratic control established in the party's mass organization was entirely another—and far more serious—matter.[12] But in many ways the real issue inevitably went beyond the question of intra-party democracy to the question of the *nature of democracy* in the state. As Max Weber had discerned more clearly than his pupil Michels, it was through the embrace of the state, an embrace consistent with but having far greater effect than elitism in the party, that the democratic socialist thrust of the mass working-class party came to naught: "in the long run," he wrote, "it is not Social Democracy which conquers the town of the state but it is the state which conquers the party."[13]

This bears enormous importance for understanding what the attempt to change the Labour Party was all about and why it produced such a reaction throughout the British establishment—a reaction far more deeply felt and far more hysterically sounded (including by Labour's own parliamentary elite) than that produced by Thatcherism's assault on the Keynesian/welfare state. To be sure, and contrary to much myth-making about it by its opponents, the project of those who sought to change the party remained "reformist." It did not seek to "smash the state," least of all parliament; it continued to put its faith in representative democracy and the electoral road to socialism. But its reformism, by being pointed now to a structural reform of the mode of representation, took on a dramatically novel aspect.

## III

The Labour Party, which had always been keen to present itself as the linchpin of political stability as well as reform in Britain, generated a new radical opposition out of the contradictions in its own practices in government and their effects on its constituencies in the 1960s and 1970s. A new Labour left began taking shape long before Thatcherism had established its strength, and indeed with some perceptive anticipation of the looming possibility of such a turn to the right; and it gradually set itself the task of transforming the ideology and organization of the Labour Party as the critical means of transforming British state and society. As the sorry experience of the 1964–70 Labour government was reinforced by that experience's tragic repetition from 1974–79, including the inauguration of monetarism in 1976, the Labour Party turned inward on itself to fight a battle over the very meaning of socialism and democracy and posed the question, as it had never been posed with such force before in the party's history, of whether a social democratic working-class party like Labour could be adapted to become a party directed toward socialist mobilization and change. The challenge of the new Labour left to the party's ancient structures and practices was prosecuted in an often unclear and sometimes actually confused and certainly incomplete fashion. It was also burdened with occasional but on the whole minor "entrist" allies, such as Militant, who reflected some of the more troubling aspects, and the most easily challengeable by the forces representing the status quo, of a committed but sectarian practice. Nevertheless, the new Labour left was moving—haltingly, stumbling, taking two steps forward and one back as must inevitably be the case when one is traversing new terrain under enemy fire—toward a new conception of socialist party politics, one that pointed beyond the stale and decaying practices, not only of the traditional parliamentarism of social democracy, but also of the Leninism of the vanguard parties and the alliances between the elites of various parties that was designated as "popular frontism" by the Communist parties.

The source of the attempt to change the Labour Party is not difficult to trace. It lay in the effects that the Labour governments of 1964–70 had not only on socialists but on Labour's supporters more broadly. Recent evidence has confirmed that a new generation of working-class voters who had become voters in the 1960s were more class conscious than those voters who had first entered the electorate before 1929, but less class conscious than those who had become voters over the subsequent thirty years. These new voters largely opted for Labour in the mid-1960s. But it was the same new working-class voters, who, in great numbers, deserted the Labour Party in the 1970 election, more than canceling out a lesser flow to Labour from among middle-class individuals. In that election the Labour Party suffered a decline in electoral support

> by ten times the amount we would have expected on the basis of changes in social structure. It was in that election that Labour first lost a large proportion of voters from among social groups which had previously supported the party. The loss in Labour voters from among these groups indeed continued after that date, but at very much slower rate . . . when we consider the kind of people who actually reacted against the Labour government of 1966–70 . . . the largest swings away from Labour voting occurred in the solidly working-class strata.[14]

It would thus appear that the critical period for understanding the electoral realignments that gripped the attention of psephologists with the rise of Thatcherism occurred in fact under the Wilson government of 1966–70. It was only in 1970 that a substantial portion of the working-class vote deserted Labour for the first time, with manual workers' support falling from 69 percent in 1966 to 58 percent in 1970 (where it stayed through 1974, and then fell further in 1979 to 50 percent after another experience of Labour government). As Mark Frankland has put it:

> The Parliament elected in 1966 provided the first Labour majority in fifteen years that was large enough to have a chance to build upon the achievements of 1945–50. The Parliament of 1966 thus provided the first opportunity for young voters to become disillusioned with the prospects for a socialist Britain. The same election will also have provided the first opportunity in fifteen years for the party to prove to potential supporters from middle-class backgrounds

that it was content to govern a mixed society. The latter objective was the one Harold Wilson espoused. Paradoxically, his very success in achieving this objective may have been what cost the party so much support among members of the working class. Young voters may have ceased to see any class difference between the parties during this period, and so became responsive to appeals that were not class-based.[15]

Of course, the Wilson government had no "success" in *actually* governing a "mixed society." Indeed, the proof it provided that it was content to do no more than try to do so, *and the fact that it failed so miserably in the attempt* was no doubt its—and Labour's subsequent—electoral undoing. From this point on, Labour had to prove *anew* that conscious class identity in politics, at least as reflected in support for a mass party associated with the labor movement, was relevant to a large part of its own constituency. And it was hardly surprising that a great many of the activists who stayed with the party through this debacle (and even more who subsequently joined it in the 1970s) insisted that Labour could only recover if it adopted a broad range of policies of direct and manifest benefit to working people and also *provided a new popular socialist practice so as to make it a relevant basis for political identification and distinguished itself from the other parties thereby.*

There was a marked change through the 1970s on the part of the "1968 generation" in their attitude to working within the Labour Party and the broader labor movement. If there was one common ideological theme that constantly resurfaced among the new activists once they joined the party, it was their strong opposition to what David Blunkett identified as "the belief in paternalistic, parliamentary change" within the Labour Party:

> We have to persuade those who are still living in the 1950s and 1960s that the way forward is to commit people from the bottom up in a jigsaw—that doesn't ignore national and international parameters, but relates to them. This can make it possible to mobilise people in every sense of the word at the local level, in their work, their community activity, and their commitment to the collective approach. . . . This can only be done from the local level, because you do have to fire people's imagination and commitment. They do have to have an alternative vision of the world, if you are going to overcome the obstacles. The idea that legislative paternalism is going to be successful has been discredited so many times that it is amazing that anyone in Parliament still believes it.[16]

This orientation to politics laid the basis for the more visible "municipal socialism" of the 1980s, the central orientation of which, as a recent book on the experience of the Greater London Council has articulated it, was to use the resources of the state "to extend effective democracy beyond the political franchise to increase democratic control over the economy and economic policy." The object of the exercise was for political leaders—even, indeed especially, from within the state—not just to respond to voter expectations, but to center their political practice around "raising expectations, encouraging people to make demands to organize and to have confidence in their dealings with the government they pay rates and taxes for. . . ." This was "an end in itself, as well as a way of working on economic policy" and it was premised on the notion that "where popular initiative and control grew, there was far more change than elsewhere." The role of political leadership, as articulated by these new activists, was to create a constituency that would in turn pressure *them* to produce more effective policy: "If that pressure had increased, if in a sense that constituency had turned on them and forced them to be much more responsive, then many of them would have felt they had succeeded." [17] It is crucial to understand this orientation to politics on the part of the activists who composed the new Labour left if we are to understand what the attempt to change the Labour Party was all about at the national level. A myth has grown up, sponsored in large part by Labour's parliamentary elite itself, that the internal party disputes over the accountability of MPs represented nothing other than a battle conducted within a "hermetically sealed train" by orthodox socialists wholly unconcerned with the issue of developing popular support outside the party. The truth is actually otherwise. It was the new activists who recognized, on the basis of the experience with the Labour governments of the 1960s and 1970s, that the traditional loyalties underlying Labour support were fraying severely and that the only way to remedy this was not to attempt to reassert the old "parliamentary paternalism" of a social democratic welfare state in crisis but to turn the party into an agency of social and political mobilization. To be able to practice the kind of politics that eventually yielded fruit in the new municipal socialism in the early 1980s, these activists had to engage in considerable intra-party conflict against the old guard at the local level. Their determination to see this through was a sign of their seriousness, of a recognition that a change of leadership was a condition of effecting the new kind of politics. A similar consideration determined the practice of the new Labour left at the national level.

By the early 1970s the politics of the new local activists were still relatively inchoate and they had not yet thrown up any nationally recognized leaders or distinct organizational space within the party. If there is a single departure one can point to that more than any other signaled the clear initiation of the project of the new Labour left, it lies in a series of speeches made by Tony Benn in the early 1970s.

Benn's starting point in these speeches was the extra-parliamentary militancy of so many new activists at the time and the meaning it bore for democracy. He was convinced that this had been triggered not only by the heightened expectations produced by the rising incomes and collective bargaining strength of the postwar capitalist boom but also by higher levels of education and training that had improved people's analytical capacities and by the mass media revolution that gave people an unprecedented mass of information about current affairs and exposure to alternative analyses of events. He repeatedly pointed to

> the thousands of ... pressure groups or action groups [that] have come into existence: community associations, amenity groups, shop steward's movements, consumer societies, educational campaigns, organizations to help the old, the homeless, the sick, the poor or under-developed societies, militant communal organizations, student power, noise abatement societies.

He saw in them "a most important expression of human activity based on issues rather than traditional political loyalties, and [they] are often seen as more attractive, relevant and effective by new citizens than working through the party system." But he recognized at the same time that this was only one side of the picture. A decade later, some of those commentators who discerned in Thatcher a new authoritarian populism would insistently criticize the new Labour left and Benn himself for failing to recognize its appeal. But as early as 1970 Benn in fact had anticipated them. He warned of an

> alternative philosophy of government, now emerging everywhere on the right, [taking] as the starting point of its analysis that modern society depends on good management and that the costs of breakdowns in the system is so great that they really cannot be tolerated and that legislation to enforce greater and more effective discipline must now take priority over other issues. The new citizen is to be won over to an acceptance of this by promising him greater freedom from government, just as big business is to be promised lower taxes and less intervention and thus to be retained as a rich and powerful ally. But this new freedom to be enjoyed by big business means that it can then control the new citizen at the very same time as government reduces its protection for him.[18]

This was a most serious reaction, Benn contended, to a situation where people were showing that by banding together collectively in a myriad of new organizations with clear objectives they could win surprising victories on given issues against large and centralized corporations and governments that were increasingly vulnerable to dislocations. The focus of decision-making power still remained in place in these "lumbering monoliths," however, and the perpetuation of their power, increasingly enveloped with a philosophy of less state regulation of the economy but more discipline over an obstreperous citizenry, remained at the same time also intimately bound up with the traditional structures of parliamentarism:

> If the people have so much potential power why do those who enjoy privileges seem to be able to hold on to them so easily? The awful truth is this: that it is outdated concepts of parliamentary democracy accepted by too many political leaders in Parliament and on Local Authorities, which have been a major

obstacle. . . . For too many modern political leaders have inherited an aristocratic view of parliament and their role in it. . . . This philosophy explains why
political leaders often seem to be telling us two things: *first*—"there is nothing
you have to do except vote for us"; and *second*—"If you do vote for us, we can
solve you your problems." Both these statements are absolutely and demon-
strably false. . . . A real leader will actually welcome the chance to give way to
the forces that he has encouraged and mobilized by a process of education and
persuasion. Legislation is thus the last process in a campaign for change. . . .
The people must be helped to understand that they will make little progress
unless they are more politically self-reliant and are prepared to organize with
others, nearest to them where they work and where they live, to achieve that
they want.[19]

Benn's central point was that if the Labour Party reacted defensively or with
hostility to the new organizational activism that had emerged outside the party,
the party would become obsolescent. "I see it as our business so to reconstruct
the Labour Party so that a Labour government will never *rule* again but will try
to create the conditions under which it is able to act as the natural partner of a
people, who really mean something more than we thought they did, when they
ask for self-government." If most of the recent progressive forces had developed
outside the party, this had much to do with the fact that the party's "internal
democracy is also riddled with the same aristocratic ideas as deface our national
democracy." He articulated at this time many of the dimensions of reform that
later became so familiar: the selection process for parliamentary candidates, the
electoral base of the Leader and Deputy Leader, the accountability of Cabinet
members, MPs, local Labour Groups and Councillors, and trade union delegations. It was "not on narrow and legalistic constitutional grounds" that these
issues had to be taken up, but in terms of their contribution to fostering a much
broader and profound change in the party's orientation.

Tony Benn had by the early 1970s convinced himself, and certainly convinced many of those who came into the party after having rejected it in the
1960s, that "the public will become very interested if they think we are ready to
criticize ourselves and really want to make ourselves and British politics more
democratic," and if the party initiated "a period of intense public discussion
about the nature of Parliamentary democracy and the nature of Party democracy.
. . . If it is thought they are too difficult, or too dangerous or too divisive to
embark on this debate I fear we shall miss a great opportunity." If the party just
devoted itself to "more research to produce detailed policies which will win back
public confidence in our capacity to run a modified capitalism," it would entirely
mistake the reasons it lost the 1970 election. This defeat was very largely bound
up, in his view, with the party's concentration "*on the role of Government to the
exclusion of the part that the people themselves could play in solving their own
problems.*" When Benn coined the phrase in 1972, "a fundamental shift in the
balance of wealth and power in favour of working people and their families," he

was in his own mind putting the stress on power and meant by it much more than a shift in power from capital to the state. With a characteristic optimism that inspired many new activists but maddened many others, Benn believed that the debate he was calling for "is more likely to unite than divide the party—helping it to see its way forward to a new broader interpretation of modern popular democratic socialism." But he admitted that whether he was right or wrong in this judgment would depend on whether the themes the new Labour left was trying to develop would "command general support in the movement." And he warned that if the party did not face the issue of democracy directly it would find itself in a situation where other less salient differences within the party and the unions would emerge and further weaken people's confidence in the Labour Party, and "the trend to the right would continue."[20]

It is one thing for socialists to define and articulate a project for socialist renewal; it is another thing to construct such a project and realize it. And, in the latter respect, the evolution and the fate of the new Labour left inevitably needs to be understood in terms of the dialectic between its goals and the resistance it faced.

The parliamentary leadership discovered after 1970 that they no longer had the same unchallenged initiative in policy formation within the party as they had in the early 1960s, but they certainly retained the veto power that went with the continuing independence of the parliamentary party and the strength of its appeal to party unity on narrow electoralist grounds. Harold Lever, who was to play an important role in the 1970s in articulating the "realistic" policy posture of the parliamentary leadership in the face of the radical policies being advanced by NEC and the conference, perhaps expressed the Parliamentary leadership's philosophy most clearly:

> Clause four or no clause four, Labour's leadership plainly believes in a mixed economy ... [it] knows as well as any businessman that an engine which runs on profit cannot be made to run faster without extra fuel. ... For their part, businessmen should show less sensitivity and more sense. It is time they realized that a ringing political slogan is often used as a sop to party diehards or as an anaesthetic while doctrinal surgery is being carried out.[21]

It was precisely for this reason that it was the bringing the question of the adequacy of the vehicle, not just the adequacy of the policy, onto the Labour Party's agenda that stamped the new Labour left with a truly original and strategically salient mark.

Given the extent of the underlying crisis, the imperative condition for the success of the new Labour left's strategy was to win over the party quickly so that an outwardlooking mobilization could be inaugurated. Where this was accomplished in local parties or in the unions, significant changes in the representative role of local councilors and union officials were registered, although their policies and mobilizing capacities were inevitably highly constrained insofar as a transformation of the party at the national level did not take place. But such a rapid turnabout in the orientation of the parliamentary party was simply not in the cards. The intransigence of the "parliamentary paternalists" could not defeat the new Labour left, but it could turn its struggle inward and thus deny its potential for effecting the broader strategy it had articulated. The problem is simply stated. The new Labour left, with substantial and growing support in the extra-parliamentary party, was trying to get its leadership to develop a socialist strategy, in terms not only of program but of mobilization. But the preponderant part of the leadership was not interested in developing a socialist strategy; it did not believe in it; it considered it irrelevant, or actually harmful, to the Labour Party's and to Britain's problems. Roy Jenkins told the party conference in the early 1970s that "socialism is just a slogan." One local councilor (later an MP closely associated with Benn) retorted that this missed the very point that the new activists were trying to make: there was "a crying need" for the party "to translate the abstractions of economic control into concepts that people can understand . . . and to translate them in such a way that makes them not just moonshine, but something which is eminently and imminently practical." [22] The dilemma for the new Labour left, however, was how it could turn the party into a socialist party without purging itself of its leadership—without lopping off its own head, so to speak.

It took the whole decade of the 1970s, including the formation of the internal party pressure group, the Campaign for Labour Party Democracy, until the matter was brought to a head at the party conference. Constituency delegates were traditionally an "amorphous mass" at party conferences and trade union delegates generally met only with their own delegations to decide how they would cast their bloc votes. By 1979, the CLPD had effected a dramatic change in this pattern both by lobbying constituencies in advance of the conference in relation to the resolutions on democratizing the party, and by bringing union and constituency delegates together at massive meetings on the eve of the conference, to plan tactics to get those resolutions on the agenda, and to secure their passage in the face of opposition from the platform. There is no doubt that most activists saw the constitutional reforms in instrumental terms: taking the election of the leader and deputy leader out of the exclusive hands of MPs and passing it to the party conference would, they expected, mean that Tony Benn would take the leadership; requiring a competitive reselection process for MPs in their constituencies would at least force MPs generally to be more mindful of their activist political goals. But the increasing sense of urgency with which they organized to accomplish this reflected their recognition that the issue of the autonomy of parliamentarians was not just about whether they were free to make decisions inside the state. It was at the same time about the autonomy the Labour leadership's vaunted position of "government" at the pinnacle of the state gave them from the task of renewing class identity and undertaking socialist mobilization in the face of an ever more visible and explicit right-wing populist threat.

Although it scarcely seems credible today, it was only some eight years ago that there was a widespread impression inside Britain and out, and ranging over the whole political spectrum, that something approaching a fundamental transformation of the Labour Party was in train. The CLPD's organizing efforts and the parliamentary leadership's cynical manipulations of union loyalties to obtain their support for years of wage restraint finally yielded sufficient support for the constitutional reforms to have them carried through at party conferences in 1980 and 1981.

To be sure, many observers on the left were generally more sober regarding what had transpired in the Labour Party. They recognized that most social democratic parties (and many bourgeois parties) elected their leaders at conferences and required a competitive reselection process for sitting parliamentarians. What mattered was whether the inauguration of these reforms in the Labour Party would sustain the momentum of the new Labour left so that its much broader strategic perspective, as we have outlined it above, would become dominant in the party. This was still to be tested in Benn's campaign for the deputy leadership under the new electoral college in 1981: the fate of further proposals for constitutional reform being advanced to open space for enhanced women's and blacks' representation in the party; in the national party's degree of support for the new experiments in municipal socialism; above all, in the kind of leadership they provided for extra-parliamentary struggles against Thatcherism.

Yet the deep intransigence of the bulk of the party leadership continued. And this proved to be the determining factor in ensuring that the intra-party debate on democracy (which was itself unstoppable) produced not unity but continuing division and abrasiveness on all sides. It had taken over ten years of struggle by the Labour left to effect two quite moderate constitutional changes. By this time Thatcher was in power and was effecting a counterrevolution against the welfare state. And by this time as well, before the ink was even dry on Labour's constitutional changes, a counterrevolution was in effect in the party led by those still convinced that reproducing Labour's traditional image as an alternative parliamentary "team" was the way to restore its ever more severe electoral problems. The balance in the party had temporarily shifted far enough to the left to yield the new Labour left a momentary victory. But it had not shifted far enough to sustain their momentum in the face of both of these counterrevolutions.

Right through the intra-party struggle on the constitutional reforms, until early 1981, Labour had run well ahead of Thatcher in the opinion polls. This, together with the elections in France and Greece of parties whose programs were even more radical than Labour's, and the new Labour left's taking control of the Greater London Council, emboldened the forces for change in the party. But a combination of factors rapidly undermined such confidence. The SPD's emergence as the first media-created party in Britain's history showed immediate potential for capturing a sizable portion of Labour's vote. The Falklands war established, on the basis of a recrudescent chauvinism (tragically connived in by Foot himself) Thatcher's image as Britannia incarnate; and the international capitalist recession, as well as domestic austerity policies, had the effect of reducing inflation, thereby raising the real wages of those sectors of the working class not immediately touched by the massive rise in unemployment. It suddenly became clear that Thatcherism might not be a temporary interregnum. The new Labour left had long understood that only a long-term campaign of mobilization and education to refashion and reconstruct working-class and socialist identities could restore securely Labour's electoral base. But they had also expected that this might still be accomplished through scraping back into state office as Labour had done in 1974 (and was still doing at the local level in the 1980s) and using state resources to empower popular forces. What now became all too clear was that the new Labour left's balancing act—between changing a party fundamentally while relying on an antigovernment vote to sustain in the meanwhile the viability of the party's claim to office—was no longer sustainable itself. The choice between a long-term campaign and immediate, even if unstable, electoral viability became a stark one after 1981. The attempt to change the Labour Party at that point ran up against the most intractable barrier that stands in the way of changing an electoralist party: that is, that trying to change it in as fundamental a way as the new Labour left proposed involves continual—not temporary— disunity within it, and a visibly disunified party cannot win elections. And winning elections appeared ever more important if only as a defensive mechanism against the depredations of Thatcherism.

Yet such was the severity of Labour's failure over the previous decades in government as well as in sustaining the party as a counter-hegemonic community, that despite the marginalization of the left at the national level before the 1983 election campaign, and even more so under Kinnock's leadership thereafter, Labour's parliamentary team has failed miserably to restore Labour's electoral fortunes. The one accomplishment that can be claimed is that voiced by Austin Mitchell, MP, after the 1987 election campaign: "The Labour Party has now moved back to the middle ground. . . . It is not the Labour Party of 1981. It has reverted to the historic mould." [23]

The trouble with this, of course, was that it closed off the possibility of constructing out of the current crisis anything resembling a *socialist* alternative to Thatcherism within the given party system. Conference commitments on unilateralism remained intact, but they sat uncomfortably with a renewed commitment to NATO and increased expenditure on conventional defense within it. Kinnock's attack on the use of Marxist rhetoric did not mean that he was abandoning rhetoric himself, but reasserting the primacy of social democratic rhetoric in the hope of recovering the good old pre-Thatcherite days when the use of such rhetoric was so familiar it was invisible. Nevertheless, the strength and depth of the socialist mobilization in the party that preceded this was such that there has been no smooth passage to presenting a unified face to the electorate through the rhetorical swamp of social democratic verbiage. In the world of the 1980s there was no clear road back to the nostrums of Atlanticism in foreign policy and Keynesianism and corporatism in domestic policy. It was in good part because of this that the challenge from the left was far more profound and still has deeper resonance in the party than anything that went before. Under these circumstances, the exorcism of the left could be a one-off event, and this made the leadership's strategy not a little problematic. For the danger in a strategy that depended on the Labour leadership proving it was worthy to govern by its attacks on the left was that there can never really be sufficient proof that will make the strategy credible. Despite the expulsions that preceded the 1983 election, despite such unimpeachably respectable figures as Dennis Healey and Peter Shore presiding over the daily press conferences at party headquarters during the campaign, Mrs. Thatcher was still able to make a leading theme of her campaign the choice this "historic election" offered between "two totally different ways of life," with the prize to be fought for being "no less than the chance to banish from our land the dark, divisive clouds of Marxist Socialism." And David Steele could still allege that Labour was "drawing its inspiration from the decaying bones of Karl Marx in Highgate Cemetery." Given what transpired in the party after 1983, the Labour leadership hoped that continuing McCarthyism of this sort would sound unfair. Yet, despite Kinnock's attack on Militant and the Miners' union leadership, *The Times* immediately turned its attack on the party's women and black activists, and blamed Kinnock for not barring their way into the party.[24]

The tendency in the British media to blatant distortion of the socialist Left, in all its diversity, is based on the most crude presumptions of what the term "Marxism" is attached to in the eyes of those who subscribe to such ideas in the party. Indeed, it is probably not even in the broadest terms accurate to identify most of the women and black activists as Marxists at all. But this very crudity derives from an *a priori* passion finally to write finis, albeit some two decades later than it was supposed to happen, to the "end of (socialist) ideology." This passion is not much less strong among those in the Labour Party who long for an end to Thatcherism than it is in the opinion *The Times* represents. For instance, the right-wing Solidarity Group of MPs labeled as "Stalinist" a Campaign group (formed around Benn after 1981) of MPs' questionnaire that asked whether candidates favored recorded votes for PLP elections and meetings; party conference control over PLP rules; election of the shadow cabinet by the electoral college that elects the leader; black sections in the constituencies; a strengthened role for the women's conference of the party; inclusion of at least one woman and one black on all constituency short lists for parliamentary candidates; withdrawal from the Common Market; and expulsion of people giving any support to the Militant Tendency.[25] That a questionnaire designed to reveal the political positions of candidates for party office should have been construed as Stalinist, of all things, presumably implying some ultra-centralist organizational practice rather than the antithesis of it (as is patently the case), is worthy of Ronald Reagan's designation of the Contras in Nicaragua as "freedom fighters." But it is the function of such political rhetoric, not its accuracy, that counts. The function of the rhetoric hinges on establishing the illegitimacy of the very attempt to change the Labour Party on the basis of the political principles that the left had *actually* taken up in the 1970s, that is, denying the complete autonomy of parliamentarians between elections, advancing the common ownership of the means of production as a relevant goal, and conceiving of strategic questions in terms of class and popular struggles. The notion that these principles are inherently totalitarian, or the claim that they are catechisms of a dead church, can only be taken seriously if they are seen for what they really are: ideological aids in the struggle to consolidate the old parliamentarist mold.

If the new Labour left was "unrealistic," as has so often been alleged, it was mainly in that it severely *underestimated* the sheer breadth and depth of the parliamentary leadership's commitment to the old parliamentarism and the sheer weight of conventional wisdom and bourgeois opinion they could call to their side in defense of it. It also *overestimated* the commitment of the left union leadership to the new Labour left's struggle and the staying power of the collective instrumentalism of industrial militancy under conditions of capitalist restructuring, mass unemployment, and state reaction. In the face of this, as is so often the case in history, some of the new Labour left's original activists, and even more of the commentators who watched from the sidelines, initially with some sympathy, became themselves dispirited and confused about what had been the point of the thing all along. Many of them succumbed to the illusion that Labour's electoral disintegration was caused by the intra-party debate, forgetting that this debate was itself but a symptom of the failures of parliamentary paternalism.

At the 1988 Labour Party conference, Neil Kinnock pledged "to run the market economy better than the Tories." Is this a victory for the idea of market socialism? Hardly. It represents, as is common in social democratic parties today (now that the attempt at socialist renewal has been defeated within them), a craven attempt to revive the old social democracy by engaging in policy debate on the terrain set by the Right in the advanced capitalist societies. It may well be that in the West, no less than in Eastern Europe, the forces of socialist renewal face implacable problems in any attempt to transform the traditional parties of the Left and will have to address themselves to building new political organizations. There will be enough popular struggles, both East and West, on which to build. As for now, one thing is surely clear. Perry Anderson was quite correct to say some years ago, in a comment on Alec Nove's book, that only a "politics of feasible socialism" could rescue the "economics of feasible socialism" from the realm of utopian thought.[26] Socialists, even if they are also economists, will have to contribute to that aspect of socialist renewal that concerns the democratization of politics if the blockages to such renewal are ever to be overcome.

# Notes

1. This paper was originally presented as a lecture given to York University's "Workshop in Political Economy," January 26, 1988. This lecture drew extensively on my paper, "Socialist Renewal and the Labour Party," subsequently published in *The Socialist Register 1988*. Cf., especially for the comments on Alec Nove, my article in *The Socialist Register 1985/6*.
2. Alec Nove, *The Economics of Feasible Socialism* (London, 1983). The subsequent quotations are derived from pp. 200–20, 160–75.
3. Quoted in G. Hodgson, *The Democratic Economy* (London, 1984), p. 165.
4. See S. Bertolini, "The Membership of Mass Parties: The Social Democratic Experience, 1889–1978," in H. Daalder and P. Mair, *Western European Party Systems: Continuity and Change* (London, 1983), pp. 185–91.
5. R.W. Johnson, *The Long March of the French Left* (New York, 1981), p. 159.
6. R. Cayrol, cited in Johnson, p. 158.
7. R. Cayrol, "The Crisis of the French Socialist Party," *New Political Science*, 12, Summer 1983, pp. 11, 16.
8. M. Spourdalakis, "The Greek Experience," *The Socialist Register 1985/6*, pp. 151–52.
9. See P. Walters, "Distribution Decline: Swedish Social Democrats and the Crisis of the Welfare State," *Government and Opposition*, 20:3 (Summer 1985), pp. 356–57; and R. Stanbridge, "Palme Faces Workers' Revolt," *The Guardian* (20 January 1986).
10. Verbal reply to author at the Labour Market Adjustment Conference, York University, Toronto, 11 December 1986.
11. W. Higgins, "Political Unionism and the Corporatist Thesis," *Economic and Industrial Democracy*, 6:3 (August 1985), pp. 361, 371–72.
12. R. Michels, *Political Parties* [1915] (New York, 1972). It is worth noting that one of the very few Marxists of the time who took Michels's "iron law" seriously enough to engage with it was Bukharin. See his comments on Michels's "very interesting book" in N. Bukharin, *Historical Materialism: A System of Sociology* [1921] (Ann Arbor, 1969).
13. M. Weber, *Gesammelte Aufsätze zur Soziologie und Sozialpolitik* (Tübingen, 1924), p. 409.
14. M. Franklin, *The Decline in Class Voting in Britain* (Oxford, 1985), pp. 153, 161.
15. Ibid., p. 174.
16. Interview with David Blunkett in M. Boddy and C. Fudge, *Local Socialism* (London, 1984), pp. 244–45.
17. M. Mackintosh and H. Wainwright, *A Taste of Power: The Politics of Local Economics* (London, 1987), p. 399.
18. T. Benn, *The New Politics: A Socialist Reconnaissance*, Fabian Tract 402 (September 1970), pp. 8–9, 12.
19. *Speeches by Tony Benn* (Nottingham, 1974), pp. 277–79.
20. See *Speeches*, pp. 275, 281, 285, 287–88; and *The New Politics*, p. 28.
21. Quoted in *The Observer* (3 April 1966).
22. *Labour Party Conference Report* (1971), p. 236.
23. Quoted in *Tribune* (11 September 1987).
24. *The Times* (10 December 1985).
25. "Whips refuse 'Stalinist' questions," *The Times* (21 October 1985).
26. P. Anderson, *In The Tracks of Historical Materialism* (Chicago, 1984), p. 103.

# Socialism as a Living Idea

## THOMAS T. SEKINE

### I

This paper is devoted to a theory, not a case study, of socialism. It is therefore all the more desirable to begin with a clear idea or concept of socialism, but such a thing is not readily available. Most authors are content merely to refer to that "familiar notion" of socialism with many shades of meaning and diverse implications, without bothering to specify in which particular sense or senses their use of the term ought to be interpreted. This is not a satisfactory point of departure, as it entails confusion at a later stage of the argument. I wish to minimize such confusion by stating at the outset that modern socialism is the antithesis of capitalism.[1] This proposition, although commonplace, teaches us the fundamental lesson that one must first have a clear and definite idea of capitalism in order to meaningfully talk of its reversal: socialism.

But that was precisely Marx's argument when he criticized the utopian socialists and warned his followers against resorting to pipe dreams of a liberated society before they undertook an in-depth study of capitalism, i.e., before they came to grips with the inner law of motion (or logic) of capitalism. Only when one got that side of the story straight, as Marx reasoned, could one hope to radically criticize capitalism beyond which lay socialism. It was in this spirit that Marx produced his monumental work *Capital*, the content of which defined capitalism as the dialectic of capital.

Capitalism is a synthetic concept in the sense that it cannot be defined, as in dictionaries, with formal-descriptive statements. It can only be defined (i.e., specified or determined) as a self-contained logical system which I call the

The author is at the Department of Economics, York University.

dialectic of capital.[2] Formal-descriptive definition is useful for simpler concepts in an axiomatic (or similarly constructed) system such as geometry where, for instance, a circle is adequately specified as "a closed plane curve every point of which is equidistant from a fixed point within the curve." When applied to a more complex concept, however, this kind of definition conjures up only a vague impression. Thus, for example, the Merriam-Webster dictionary defines capitalism as "an economic system characterized by private or corporation ownership of capital goods, by investments that are determined by private decision rather than by state control, and by prices, production, and the distribution of goods that are determined mainly in a free market." Other leading dictionaries give us similar descriptions. While perfectly adequate for the proper usage of the term in English, these characterizations are not meant to be scientific. It clearly devolves on economists to bring forward a more precise definition of the term. Yet what they do is usually not much more than to emphasize: (a) the private ownership of the means of production; (b) the conversion of labor power into a commodity; (c) the globalization of the commodity economy; (d) the limitlessness of the accumulation of wealth, etc., as the leading characteristic(s) of a capitalist economy. Any one of these is, of course, perfectly correct but only to the extent that it reflects an aspect of the working of the inner logic (or the dialectic) of capital. In other words, the synthetic concept of capitalism cannot be fully grasped unless and until the dialectic of capital is laid bare.

If Marx, rejecting the fantasies of the utopians, left the first (if unfinished) outline of the dialectic of capital in his monumental economic work, surely his followers should have carried on with the work of completing and polishing it. For that would have given them a more accurate and deeper understanding of what makes capitalism, and hence their idea of socialism as its antithesis would have been less haphazard and arbitrary. But that point was lost on many of them who, in their activist impatience, left the completion of the dialectic to "petty bourgeois" intellectuals and rushed on to the revolutionary battlefront with an utter poverty in their philosophy. The result was the creation of a monstrous "socialism" in many parts of the world with disappointing and demoralizing track records.

But for this outcome another factor, quite apart from revolutionary impatience, is also responsible. Marx's approach, although perfectly correct in itself, holds its own peculiar danger. If, following his advice, one forgets about blueprints of future society and concentrates on economics, that is to say, on the analysis of capitalism, then in strange ways one gets trapped. For the more one studies economics the more "capitalist" one becomes. The reason is that the synthetic concept of capitalism can be revealed only from within, i.e., only by letting capital expose itself. Only capital, from its own vantage point, can tell us what capitalism is all about. If one refuses to let it speak or tries to put words in its mouth, insisting on looking at capitalism from without, as, for instance, from the point of view of the revolutionary proletariat, one ends with assuming the position of the blind man touching an arbitrary part of the elephant. In the dialectic of capital the teller of the story (the subject) is capital itself, and not "we" the human beings.[3]

This means that economics is always in essence "liberal." It is "economistic" and full of "the market mentality" as Polanyi and his followers have exposed. One can even say that classical political economy was successful only when it was liberal (and expressed the soul of capital) but it came to grief as soon as some Ricardians got overly interested in socialism and tried to repudiate liberalism. One may also say of Marx that as a great economist he wrote a book on capital (or commodities) not a book on labor (or production). The reason why a large number of naïve Marxists have discovered the early philosophical Marx to be more congenial than the late "economistic" Marx is easily accounted for by this fact. The point is that even when one wants to abolish capitalism one still has to let capital tell what that capitalism is all about. One depends on capital's own full story, not on a half-story one might wish to attribute to it. In other words, even the most ardent socialist cannot reach true socialism so long as he keeps criticizing capitalism on its many apparent failings. He reaches true socialism only when he criticizes capitalism at its best, i.e., in its perfect operation as viewed by capital. Socialist political struggles have often proved to be nonstarters because they concentrate their attack on failings of capitalism which capital itself is willing to correct, at least to some extent, within its own frame of reference.

The difficulty of criticizing capitalism in economic terms, i.e., by using the language of capital itself, has led many Marxists to abandon economics in favor of historical materialism (or the materialistic conception of history). Now this latter has the advantage of impressing on us the relative view of capitalism. Since capitalism is only one of the many modes of production destined to be replaced by something else, historical materialism does not seem to give capitalism any privileged position in the first instance. Yet it also says that capitalism is the last class-antagonistic society with which the prehistory of mankind comes to an end. What does this mean? If one sees in it only an eschatological message that beyond the revolutionary Armageddon lies the green pasture of a socialist paradise (in which man is finally delivered from poverty, greed, and repression), what one actually gets is the Kampuchean terror of the killing fields. There is a considerable danger in the perverse application of the Judeo-Christian theology to matters of social progress, especially when the application occurs unconsciously.[4] If one takes a more secular approach and admits the privileged status of capitalism as the "referent" in the light of which alone all other societies may be correctly understood, is one not liable once again to fall back on economic determinism or economism? It is this tendency that Uno warned against by calling it the commodity-economic (rather than materialistic) conception of history.[5]

In the idea that capitalism has so far been the most developed form of human society lies all the danger. But that is not all that Marx says of capitalism. He also describes it as "upside-down," or inverted, in the sense that under capitalism human beings are not in control of themselves, but act as if hypnotized by their own creation: capital.[6] One truly understands the upside-down character of capitalism by coming to grips with the logic of capital, that dehumanizing logic which, once it catches on, pervades the world until much of direct human contact or community is obliterated. Capitalism is upside-down because it suppresses concrete human beings replacing them with the abstract-universal *homo economicus*. In Polanyi's language the "disembedding" of the economy from society occurs under capitalism to make the "economic" aspect of human activity formally independent from other aspects. Capitalism constitutes the referent society, not so much because it achieves the most advanced level of economic life, as because it is upside-down, anomalous, and unnatural.

According to the late Professor Tamanoi[7] Marx's attention in the last several years of his life was diverted from the study of the logic of capital to the examination of historical and ethnographic literature pertaining to nonmarket or marketless economies. If this was indeed the case, it is easy to see why. Having understood the upside-down character of capitalist society, Marx was naturally led to inquire into the operation of some right-side-up societies. In fact in 1878, five years before Marx's death and with Marx's endorsement, Engels alluded to precisely that kind of inquiry and introduced the idea of political economy in the broad sense (PEBS), as opposed to political economy in the narrow sense (PENS).

## II

Since Engels did not elaborate much on the scope of PEBS as opposed to PENS, I shall adopt, for the purpose at hand, the simple distinction that PENS concentrates on the commodity economy, i.e., economic life primarily organized by the principles of the self-regulating market, while PEBS studies other economies as well. But here we must be truly careful. Every economist agrees that the scope of PENS is limited, and that a broadening of the scope of economics is both desirable and necessary. But the problem lies in the usual method of placing PENS right at the center and then gradually taking into account hitherto neglected questions as one extends the radius of concentric circles, as it were. Tamanoi firmly rejected that approach which retains PENS as the centerpiece, naming it the method of concentric expansion of PENS into PEBS. He called for a much more radical departure from PENS since this latter is necessarily "capitalist" and upside-down.

By far the most unsatisfactory feature of PENS or conventional economics, according to Tamanoi, is that its concept of production is much too narrow. Typically, "production" is understood as a technical process occurring in a time-reversible space; it is viewed as a mechanical and physicalistic phenomenon.[8]

Economics regards industrial production, especially the factory-based variety, as production *par excellence*, not agricultural production that occurs in the bosom of nature. The distinctive nature of agriculture is ignored, as it is absorbed into the abstract category of the primary and extractive "industry" together with mining. This "industrial" view of production is perfectly congenial to the capitalist to whom everything is an exchange of one set of things for another. Just as one basket of goods is exchanged for another in the marketplace, inputs are exchanged for outputs in a technical transformation called production. Such a false analogy seems thoroughly reassuring to the capitalist sensibility, and in particular to neoclassical economics. One should first be liberated from such a bias in order to arrive at a meaningful PEBS.

What about adopting an agricultural, rather than the industrial, view of production? In that context nature immediately ceases to be the material "object" confronting us humans, the "subject"; it does not present itself as mere "matter" to be conquered and appropriated by man but as the matrix of life on which all human activities depend. Nature coevolves with man in intimate symbiosis. In this perspective man does not unilaterally "make" things; instead things "grow" in nature if man nurtures and cares for them. The whole idea of production changes and becomes ecologically more benign.

In Diagram 1 I try to illustrate the relationship between the conventional view of production *(T)* and the broader coevolutionary view of it *(N)*. Here *(T)* is a technical input-output relation which is viewed as occurring in a time-reversible space. Today's outputs are tomorrow's inputs; today's inputs are tomorrow's outputs, where today and tomorrow refer to appropriate time $t$ and $t + 1$. This technological view of production overlooks, or deliberately neglects, the fact that the process of "producing" something in this sense is at the same time also the process of destroying some natural order (organic unity of things) or other. This fact is represented in the diagram by the vertical arrow pointing downward and cutting through the *T*-process. It may be viewed as the negative side of production in which "entropy"[9] is increased, or it may be simply described as the production of waste.

The production of waste harms (spoils or defiles) nature. Hence for the production of use-values to be sustainable, it must allow for time, real time, for nature to heal (cleanse or renew itself). The time needed here is real, not empty and reversible Newtonian, time. Science and technology cannot unilaterally shorten or eliminate the self-healing time of nature. Nature has its own rhythm and cadence, and sets the pace to what we humans do, not the other way round. This part of the story I have represented by *(N)*. Since the technical production of use-values *(T)* spoils and defiles nature, the disposal of incremental entropy becomes mandatory. The self-cleansing and renewing power of nature accomplishes this *over time*, so as to make the ingestion of low entropy possible for the next round of use-value production. Thus only when *(T)* is embedded in *(N)* is the whole process of production sustainable. A technology

Diagram 1

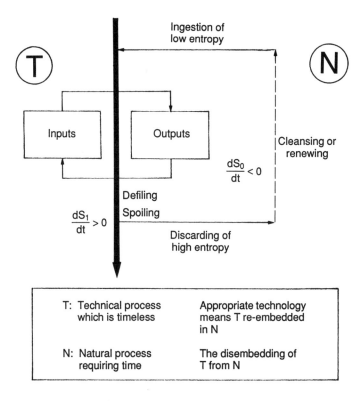

| | |
|---|---|
| T: Technical process which is timeless | Appropriate technology means T re-embedded in N |
| N: Natural process requiring time | The disembedding of T from N |

geared for sustainable production will be called "appropriate."

Originally, industry in the sense of manufacturing arose from agriculture, and branched out of it. Many things were manufactured on the farm by peasant wives in the first instance. But when capitalism began, agriculture and manufacturing tended to be separated. Capitalism, of course, did not come into being peacefully, naturally or evolutionarily, as liberal ideologues wish to believe. Nor did people gradually awaken to the advantage of commerce and industry and make a rational and willing choice to leave the country for cities. Merchants first made inroads into the farmland as putters-out. Then many peasants were forcibly driven out of their homesteads by the authorities of the mercantilist age. The formation of the labor market was deliberately contrived as the Industrial Revolution progressed, giving rise to the "age of machines."[10]

By this time, industry had acquired a self-propelled momentum. Instead of operating as a humble adjunct of agriculture, industry now sought to subordinate it. For example, liberal England imported food and agricultural raw materials from abroad, rather than producing them at home. Even though its lifeline still depended on agriculture, capitalism ideologically denied the primacy of agriculture and pretended to ignore it.[11] But precisely for this reason capitalism came to grief when it could no longer solve the agricultural problem on a world scale in the 1930s. I agree with Polanyi that capitalism proper ended at this point.[12]

Capitalism is upside-down and unnatural not only because it renders human beings into economic men or even "economic animals" but also because it ignores agriculture on which it continues to depend. Capitalism tends to evade specifically agricultural issues. It expects agriculture to operate like any factory-based industry. When this proves impossible it drives agriculture out of the country, substituting foreign trade for it. This is exactly what the nineteenth-century England did as it developed as the factory of Europe. But clearly there is a limit to this way of solving the problem. When capitalism could no longer shift agriculture outside its system, the crunch came and broke up the system; and this is what happened in the 1930s.

Capitalism was then paralyzed by a crippling depression. In fact capitalism died in the Great Depression of the 1930s. But most people did not realize this because after World War II, when fascism was defeated and bolshevism localized, the free-enterprise managerial system (sometimes also called the mixed economy) which appeared to preserve much of the capitalist virtue was reinstated. For a while it looked as though the agricultural problem was settled. This was due to the application of petro-technology. The advent of petroleum was quite as revolutionary in technological terms as the Industrial Revolution itself. Quite apart from the fact that petroleum, unlike coal, made the utilization of internal combustion engines possible and thus revolutionized the transportation of use-values, it also drastically reduced the dependence of industry on agriculture.

This point can be explained by using Diagram 2.[13] Here production is divided into three sectors: agriculture, mining, and manufacturing. Agriculture supplies food $(f)$ to consumers, and supplies raw materials $(a)$ to manufacturing, which then supplies products based on them $(a')$ to consumers. Mining also supplies raw materials $(b)$ to manufacturing, which then supplies products based on them $(b')$ to consumers. Manufacturing supplies means of production $(c_a)$ to agriculture (fertilizers, agricultural implements, etc.) and means of production $(c_b)$ to mining (shovels, pumps, etc.). Finally, manufacturing produces its own means of production $(c)$.

Now what the Industrial Revolution did was to substantially increase the supply of manufactured goods $a'$, $b'$, $c_a$, $c_b$, and $c$. This was made possible essentially because of the shift of the primary energy source from firewood to coal, which was a reduction of $a$ and increase of $b$. But the growth capacity of manufacturing still depended crucially on $a$. Although productivity in mining could be made to depend on manufacturing productivities to a great extent, productivity in agriculture could not be so easily raised. It was precisely this

Diagram 2

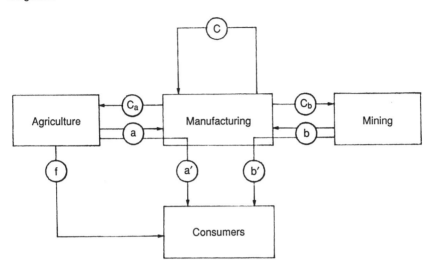

restriction that the advent of petroleum and the petrochemical industry removed. In fact this event all but abolished the dependence of industry on agriculture *a*, and reduced agriculture to almost exclusively a food producer. What did that mean? It meant that the disembedding of industry from agriculture had become much more radical and decisive. Backed by petro-technology, industry now began to dominate both agriculture and consumers, i.e., to subordinate both nature and society to its requirements. An extreme form of industrial society thus emerged.

## III

This extreme form of industrial society can no longer be described as "capitalistic." Capitalism is based on self-regulating markets and the anarchic production of commodities. Under capitalism resources are allocated more or less satisfactorily by the price mechanism of the market, and the cost of adjusting production *ex post* to market signals is not excessive. It is true that the application of this principle was increasingly in doubt since the advent of the steel industry late in the nineteenth century. But as long as coal remained the prime source of energy, the role of the government was more military than economic (and no total war requiring national mobilization was fought before 1914). Only after World War II has the mixed economy been fully established, so that a balance between the private and the public sectors has become the key issue of economic administration. The market and the state both take part in the allocation of resources and in the choice of industrial technology.

The transition from the market-based, nineteenth-century capitalism to the overtly or covertly planned industrial state of today has been subtle and often overlooked. Marxists in particular seem unwilling to admit to the quiet exit or passing away of capitalism. Yet it is essential to understand that present-day industrial society is much more reactionary and sinister than capitalism proper, since the disembedding of technology *(T)* from ecology *(N)* has now become practically measureless because of petroleum. Within the strictly capitalist context the extent of disembedding, though ideologically espoused, did not in reality exceed certain limits because of the dependence of industry on agriculture. The main problems of industry therefore were poverty and exploitation, the problems that the old-school socialists addressed. But from today's industrial society such problems are shifted away to the Third World where they assume different forms and significance. Poverty and exploitation of the nineteenth-century variety that plagued industrial nations and were all too familiar to socialists up until the 1930s have practically disappeared. At least they no longer constitute the main problems of industrial society. The real problem that it faces at present is the threat to life caused by the ravages of disembedded technology. All other problems can be viewed as derivative thereof.

Socialism that fails to recognize this fact and continues to adapt the nineteenth-century strategies of class struggles and revolutions to today's urgent context sadly lags behind the times, and cannot hope to appeal to the masses. Socialism must turn from "red" to "green" in order to respond to the changed structure of society. To some extent there are some such signs already, but they tend to appear more frequently under popular pressure than in light of mature theoretical reflections.[14] This also parallels the trend in today's Marxist literature which invariably repudiates "economism" in favor of some blind "voluntarism." A critique of economism is, of course, fundamental but it must be carried out in the proper theoretical context of Uno's "dialectic of capital" and Tamanoi's "economy of the living system." These two are the major theoretical references, the first being the most developed form of PENS and the second, together with Polanyi's writings, the most penetrating explorations into the still largely virgin soil of PEBS.[15]

Tamanoi calls the world of agriculture embedded in nature a living system in contrast to the nonliving system, or the world of industry, which transforms dead objects into dead objects. Capitalism gave birth to the nonliving system and ideologically supported it, but at the same time carefully avoided the total destruction of the living system. If socialists fail to learn this crucial lesson the fault does not lie on the part of Marx. According to the dialectic of capital of which he was the first author, the contradiction or tension between value and use-value is systemic to capitalism. Capitalism is the more perfect the more effectively value overcomes restrictions imposed by use-values, where value means capital's indifference to the use-value specificity or diversity of commodities.[16] The upside-down character of capitalist society, or the disembedding of economy from society, arises to the extent that value subsumes use-values. It is the application of the commodity-economic principle to real economic life that constitutes capitalism. This essential message, however, comes out far more clearly in Polanyi, who emphasized the "double movement," than in the writings of many orthodox Marxists.[17]

To bring capitalism into being, labor and land must be divorced (i.e., the direct producers must be denied access to the natural productivity of land); for as long as they are one, they give no room for capital to intervene. Only when land becomes empty and labor power "free in the double sense," does capital acquire the control of both original factors of production. Labor power becomes available as a commodity, and landowners must depend on tenant-capitalists to exploit the natural fertility of land. Yet the control by capital of the two factors of production is never complete. An excessive exploitation of labor is resisted by factory legislations, trade unions, and socialist movement. These are all part of the "double movement" that Polanyi talks about. There are also laws, customs, and lease contracts to protect land from unrestrained capitalist devastation, which perhaps began earlier than Polanyi's "protection of society." Especially noteworthy in the present context is the role of landed property vis-à-vis capital in the conservation and maintenance of the natural environment. Contrary to popular misconception, land is not freely traded in a purely capitalist society. For, if so, landlords and capitalists could not constitute different classes, and the logic of capital would not consistently work through. This point is well established by the theory of the "teleological coexistence" of capital and landed property in the dialectic of capital.[18]

The British landlords were for a long time bound by the legal device of strict settlement and viewed themselves as the stewards of their ancestral lands. Only the Agricultural Holdings Act of 1908 permitted tenant farmers to freely plant and dispose of the products elsewhere, provided that they returned to the soil the equivalent of the nutrients that the products had taken away from it (Section 26).[19] In other parts of the world, agriculture did not necessarily reproduce the British example. But in one way or another the idea that land constituted the source of life and had to be cared for with due respect remained as the strongest bastion against the ravages of the market economy.[20] Precisely for this reason Ricardo, speaking for capital, could regard land as "indestructible." In fact the topsoil was quite as fragile then as it is now. Yet the landlords under capitalism could be depended upon to preserve it with such punctility that capital could assume land itself to be indestructible or self-maintaining. The reason why capitalism insisted on assigning private proprietorships to what had previously been left as village commons was not only to transform peasants into industrial workers but also to circumvent the "tragedy of the commons" that might develop under the market system.[21]

Yet to capital the presence of landed property as the protector of land (which, of course, is a generic term including all terrestrial, aquatic, and atmospheric resources) was an onerous restriction, the liberation from which was sought in the switching of domestic agriculture for international trade. As Britain grew to be the factory of Europe and of the world, "commercial" agriculture developed in the outlying areas: Eastern Europe, North America, India, Australia, Latin America, etc. This led to the decline and decadence of the traditional landowning class at the center of the capitalist empire, and the concomitant loss of its responsibility as the steward of natural resources. Commercial agriculture in the periphery frankly adopted the "mining mentality"[22] and resorted to large-scale farms, mechanization, and chemicalization. By the turn of the century all the preparations were made for the present-day agribusiness, except that prior to the advent of petroleum, mechanized farming and the transportation of agricultural products were still under severe constraints. The major problem that this change eventually entailed was the worldwide agricultural crisis. Its first protracted manifestation from 1875 to 1895 weighed heavily on the capitalism of the time but was luckily overcome before becoming fatal. But the second one, which arose in the aftermath of World War I and which blended with the Great Depression of the 1930s, in effect terminated capitalism. The era of the Great Transformation as Polanyi calls it ushered in at that point present-day industrial society.

Only the advent of the petroleum age can explain why agricultural depression has not recurred since World War II. This age enabled the vast reduction of agricultural population, while industry now based on synthetic fibers, plastics, and detergents on the one hand and on highly energy-consuming automobiles and appliances on the other expanded by many staggering folds. An extreme urbanization followed, and agriculture, now a dwindling part of the national product, itself became steeped in petroleum. Present-day industrial society thus built on petroleum, however, did not solve the agricultural problem. Instead, it simply transformed and magnified the agricultural problem into the general environmental problem. If capitalism had failed, unable to cope with the question of man's interface with nature, industrial society summarily "abolished" that question instead of addressing it. The disembedding of technology *(T)* from ecology *(N)* was, therefore, pushed to its logical end to the annihilation of life.

The living system has long been held in hostage in today's industrial society. But the reactionary elements in this society that work toward the suppression of life cannot be called capitalist, since the devastation of the environment is just as severe in the East as in the West. The worship of economism (if not of the market mentality) prevails just as unconscionably in the Soviet-type planned economy as in the American-style mixed economy. The "managerial revolution" has banished the capitalists and installed the "technostructure" even in the West.[23] The new industrial state is thus controlled not by capital but by the power elite co-opted from the top echelons of the bureaucracy, the military and the business managers. The term "technocrats" may be used to cover all of them as members of the ruling class. The relative strengths of the technocracy's three components differ from one case to another. But its *raison d'être* is invariably to perpetuate and promote industrial society, the primary goal of which is to complete the disembedding of technology *(T)* from ecology *(N)*, i.e., to ensure the triumph of "death" over "life." Indeed, the more successful the attainment of such a goal, the more powerful and better entrenched the technocrats are, and vice versa.

If socialism is to have any meaning in this sort of context, it must aim at breaking the technocracy's monopoly of power and subjecting it to democratic control, so as to stop further damage to the living system. For how can humanity be liberated under the condition of a constant threat to its life? The first aim of socialism, in other words, must be to liberate humanity by providing it with a sustainable economy.[24] But the sustainable economy to be constructed in the name of socialism must, of course, be so designed as to be free from poverty and oppression, from exploitation of man by man and from indifference to, and disutility of, labor. In short it must exceed the wildest expectation of the liberal utopia. How can such an economy be realistically designed, instead of merely dreamed of as "the green pasture" lying beyond this world?

## IV

A critical weakness of traditional Marxism lies in its being (perhaps unconsciously) eschatological, i.e., in its false promise of a complete solution in the wake of a tumultuous Armageddon. It expects socialism (or communism) to be realized automatically once a proletarian revolution is successfully staged. A new age dawns upon us then, so it is believed, and the rest takes care of itself. This is like invoking a divine intervention for the construction of a classless society, while limiting the application of humanly effort only to the destruction of the existing order.[25] Such a trigger-happy adventurism deserves to fail. Indeed, history has demonstrated, time and again, that the revolutionary masses easily allow themselves to be betrayed by their trusted guides who, in the eleventh hour, make their own bid for power at the expense of the masses. Marxism has no safeguard against such usurpers so long as it leaves its postrevolutionary program blank, counting as it does on the god of scientific inevitability to determine the fate of human progress. The construction of socialism, on the contrary, is a wholly human affair fraught with many stumbling blocks and pitfalls because of the finiteness of man, and no invisible hand of providence will intercede to make things easier. It is all the more so if the process begins in the aftermath of a violent revolution with the seizure of the state power by the suddenly awakened. masses. For the momentary power vacuum that violent revolution creates can let loose all the misguided passions of discontented individuals.

It is true that Marx rejected utopianism and enjoined against the blueprinting of idealistic future societies. But the real import of Marx's warnings lies in the notion that one ought to fully understand the upside-down character of capitalism first before conceiving of socialism. For otherwise one may inadvertently carry economism, the wrong legacy of capitalism, into what is supposed to be its negation, while not preserving its more positive and desirable features (even those apart from its much touted high industrial productivity). A meaningful socialism ought to be a true supersession (*Aufhebung*) of capitalism rather than its wholesale denial. One, therefore, has to comprehend what to abolish as well as what to conserve from out of capitalist experience. Only after being informed by the dialectic of capital, the most accomplished form of PENS, can one be certain of what makes up capitalism, and hence surmise what it might be like to be free from its yokes. While being necessary, however, the knowledge of the capitalist economy is by no means sufficient for the successful construction of a socialist society. This latter must be specified more concretely as the goal. Once the starting point is made clear, one must then decide on ''where to go'' by formulating in broad outlines the new economic organization in which the liberation of mankind is expected to take place.

This formulation, by its own nature, can be made only in its broadest outlines in the first instance. Since it is a tentative goal, it must be flexible enough to allow successive revisions and further specifications as it is put into practice. Yet it must be far more concrete than a mere political programme or tabulation of aspired aims. It must involve a definite design in the form of a *tableau économique*, i.e., a table of the circular flows of the economy. For only the consistency of such a table guarantees the feasibility of the desired economic organization, feasibility in the sense that no fundamental material obstacle exists in the way of its implementation. The possession of a *tableau économique* is that which distinguishes the present approach from unrestrained utopianism. But I must hasten to stress that a table of the circular flows of the economy does not imply a general equilibrium of the market. The former is prior to, and constrains, the latter, but involves no behavior hypotheses which the latter of course presupposes. A model of circular flows merely divides the economy into several sectors, and shows how goods and services flow in such a way that no sector is left permanently out of balance in accounting terms. It applies to all forms of society whether the economy is market-based or not, whereas a market equilibrium has no meaning outside capitalism, a global commodity-economy.

In designing the economic organization as outlined in Diagram 3, I have not been informed by PENS but rather sought to explore PEBS. The economic organization that, I hope, underlies a socialist society is guided by the principle of ''re-embedding'' economy in society, industry in agriculture, technology in ecology, and man in nature. It consists of three sectors: the state factories, the communities, and the cities. All goods are categorized into either ''quantitative'' (intermediate) goods *(U)* or ''qualitative'' (final consumption) goods *(F)*. Services are either labor services *(L)* or land services *(T)*. I stipulate that the communities severally own all pieces of land in society. This enables, as the diagram shows, that the communities to obtain intermediate goods *(U_1)* from the state factories in return for land-services *(T_1)*, and produce final consumption goods for themselves *(F_1)* and for the cities *(F_2)*. The cities supply labor services to the

Diagram 3

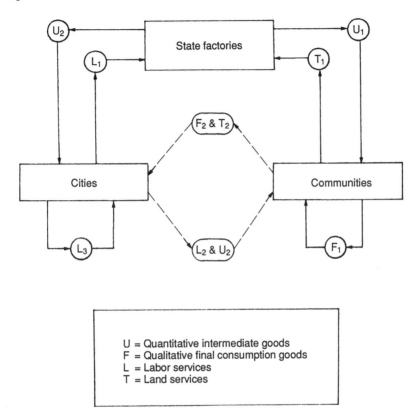

state factories $(L_1)$ and the communities $(L_2)$, in addition to consuming some $(L_3)$ for themselves. This enables the cities to obtain final consumption goods $(F_2)$ and land-services $(T_2)$ from the communities. Some intermediate goods $(U_2)$ that the state factories produce go to the communities via the cities rather than directly. This *tableau* describes the circular flows of the economy consistently, so that such an economic organization can in principle exist. In other words, appropriate rules of the game can be devised to put this idea into practice.

By the "communities" I mean localized groups of people who produce use-values "for themselves," i.e., for their own families and neighbors. According to the philosopher Nikolai Berdyaev, Christ taught men to love their neighbors, not those who lived "far off."[26] Neighbors are concrete human beings while mankind in general is an abstract idea. The love of the former is real and genuine but the love of the latter comes from an academic or ideological speculation. Feuerbach too stressed the importance of concrete human beings rather than the abstract concept of humanity. Man does not begrudge the hardest and the most unpleasant labor for his own and his loved ones' survival or enrichment of life. This kind of labor is self-motivated, and does not constitute a source of disutility. Marx's famous claim, in his commentary on the Gotha Programme, that labor under socialism should become "life's prime want" refers precisely to this kind of context. True socialism must first of all establish a place larger than the immediate family in which labor is more than a source of disutility.[27] That place is a small enough community (though much larger than the family) in which people produce their own use-values.

If use-values are produced for self-consumption inside the community, no one can be either indifferent to, or irresponsible for, the process of production. No one would produce harmful use-values, or operate a technology that spoils the community's environment. But here I talk primarily of final consumption goods which I would call "qualitative goods," since they immediately affect the quality of life. For example, food produced locally for local consumption is guaranteed to be of good quality in the sense that it is made to fit the local tastes while being free from various dangerous chemical treatments which tend to be applied to the products of cash-crop agriculture. Also, an excessive use of chemical fertilizers which eventually impoverishes the community's soil will be avoided automatically. To such qualitative goods I contrast what I call "quantitative goods" which are mostly intermediate goods for producers, and are more advantageously mass-produced in several standard types, grades, or patterns. These are goods of a very different kind, their production-process being largely mechanical and requiring little creative human participation. Such goods should be produced outside the communities, specifically in the state factories, with the application of automated and robotized processes.[28]

How large or small the community should be is a difficult question, and cannot in any case be determined abstract-formally. But one of the principles is that its size should be such as to make a direct participatory democracy of the population feasible. For example, with up-to-date communications technology a population of up to 100,000 (i.e., 20,000 to 30,000 families) may be viewed as reasonable, although this does not imply that the community size may increase in proportion to the technical efficiency of the computer. This is the size significantly larger than an Owenite settlement or an Israeli kibbutz, but requires no cumbersome bureaucracy or technocracy for its administration. It is neither too small to make its inhabitants parochial nor too large to dilute their sense of belonging. Each community must, in principle, be self-sufficient on an ecologically sustainable agriculture. Hence an area large and fertile enough to be able to feed the population must belong to the community. Given the present population statistics, there should be about 2,400 such communities in the United States, 1,250 in Japan, and 250 in Canada.[29] If a nation is divided up into less than 3,000 autonomous communities, it is an easy matter to coordinate their activities. Although inside the communities political decisions must be made on the basis of direct democracy, a method of representative democracy may be applied to decide on legislations pertaining to inter-communal affairs.

There are bound to be urbanized areas in each community which may be called cities or towns. But "cities" in the above *tableau* refer to metropolitan cities in which highly specialized or skilled professionals live,[30] rather than to local cities which are already integrated into the communities. They are not meant to be commercial centers but pools of human resources which both the communities and the state factories may tap. Cultural, educational, health-care, and other service facilities beyond the scope of communities will be concentrated in "cities," to the extent that such concentrations are either necessary or desirable. But the whole idea of the new economic organization is to reverse the unhealthy trend toward excessive urbanization that is present in all industrial societies. There is nothing wrong with a small number of metropolitan cities priding themselves in supplying advanced and sophisticated labor services. But most people should return to local eco-communities where agriculture, manufacture, and services should form an integrated whole. In fact, what is called labor services in the *tableau* refers to skilled and professional services, and not to simple and ordinary productive labor.

One of the purposes of socialism is to abolish simplified ordinary labor which is unfulfilling drudgery and competes poorly with machines. In the "state factories" which produce "quantitative" intermediate goods automated and robotized processes are the rule. Human intervention is needed only in the computer programming of such processes, and the managers and the programmers of the state factories will come from the cities. It must be understood very clearly, however, that the technocratic activity of the state factories should be subordinated to the creative activity of the communities, not the other way round. If one represents the state economic activity $X$ in the style of Leontief's input-output system: $X = (I - A)^{-1} Y$, where $A$ is the matrix of technological coefficients and $Y$ the vector of final demands, it must not be the central planners who determine $Y$. The vector of final demands must be found from the aggregation of annual orders for quantitative goods placed by the many free communities making up the state.[31]

The crucial institution presupposed by the present *tableau* is the ownership of all land by the communities, not by individuals nor by the state. Since the communities are the sole landlords in the system, they can control the economic activities of both the state factories and the cities in such a way as to minimize the environmental destruction. For example, landowning communities may refuse to renew the tenancy contract if the state factory continues to spew harmful chemicals from its smokestacks. They may also control the operation of the factory by being part of its board of directors.[32] In the council of the tenant city the communities most certainly retain some voting power, so that the city may have to agree to fairly stiff environmental restrictions. Once this form of land-ownership is established, it does not really matter to whom "produced" means of production (capital goods) inside the communities belong, so long as the "workers free in the double sense" are prevented from emerging *en masse*.[33] The communities should own not only the land on which they exist, but also distant and outlying lands normally leased to cities and state factories, or left in their natural state as conservation areas or sanctuaries. Several communities, not too many in number, should jointly manage each of such lands, and control how the tenants if any may use the land.

## V

The thumbnail sketch of a community-based future society such as the above tends to be rejected almost instantly by the "practically minded" believers of industrial society as another unrealistic and retrogressive utopianism of the village socialists. But what appears to be unrealistic and utopian today may suddenly become necessary and inevitable tomorrow; and what appears practical today may no longer be even practicable tomorrow. History teaches us that the crunch frequently arrives unannounced. Not that everyone is taken by surprise, but the majority chooses to be unperturbed by the danger signals and refuses to be moved by alarmist counsels. In order therefore not to panic in the hour of distress which is certain to come, it is wise to be prepared in advance.

I would like to stress that the transition from the present society to socialist society such as was outlined in the previous section can begin today. It requires no violent revolution, bloodshed, or any other form of painful social upheaval. The "communities" as described above can be introduced on a "one at a time" basis within the existing rules of the game, provided that proper laws are enacted to shelter their self-determination. Existing communities in depressed regions whose survival is increasingly in doubt are the logical candidates for reorganization. If they are to be supported by the welfare budget of the central or a regional government, they will consume millions upon millions of public money with little effect. It is much better to endow them with income properties once for all, such as real estate in large cities and/or substantial investment portfolios of securities, and *let them spend their "property incomes" only on quantitative goods from the outside*. They should in principle produce all qualitative goods locally for local consumption.[34] If there is not enough manpower let them arrange the settlement of immigrants with required skills up to their ability to locally feed the new settlers. But in return for such an agreement the sponsoring government should see to it that no supermarket chains, department stores, and other outside merchants should be permitted to overrun the communities by selling mass-produced, pseudo-qualitative goods in them.

It is not necessary to introduce hundreds of such communities at once. It is better to begin with half a dozen carefully selected experimental cases, and see what sort of problems they each will encounter in the course of their formation.[35]

Concrete examples and object lessons teach more than abstract principles. But all these communities are meant to become self-supporting in the not too distant future (say within five to ten years), after which they should cease to be a burden on the public budget. They should take care of their own employment and production problems in whatever manner they may see fit. In these communities, resident members produce as much of qualitative goods, including food, as they wish or need for their own survival and enrichment of life. All they need is (1) land productive enough to ensure the provision of food for their population, (2) skills to transform quantitative goods into qualitative goods, and (3) enough property incomes to enable them to buy quantitative goods that they need from the outside.[36] None of these communities need start in a fully finished form. Small villages may be gradually confederated into larger communities, and they may be endowed with more income properties as they expand. Since the communities are club-like and will in any case absorb a large number of present city-dwellers as new settlers, such a gradualist approach may indeed become necessary rather than merely recommended.

As some of these experimental models turn out to be successful, the government will receive applications from various existing local communities for similar reorganization. This time they should come up with a carefully worked-out plan of their own, and the part that the sponsoring government plays will be smaller. As such autonomous eco-communities multiply in number, existing corporate manufacturers will cease to produce final consumption goods gradually, and concentrate on quantitative intermediate goods. Their function will approach that of the state factories in the above *tableau*. To most existing corporate manufacturers this will be a painless transition. Only those greedy vultures who have so far specialized in consumer exploitation, whether in production or in circulation, will find their market significantly curtailed. For instance, department stores, supermarket chains, fast-food franchises, and developers will be asked to keep their hands off the emerging communities, although they may continue to serve elsewhere pending the completion of the economic organization as outlined above.[37]

The reorganization of present society in the direction of community-based socialism takes place as "technological unemployment" threatens modern industry in the wake of the micro-electronic revolution. As more and more automated and robotized processes are adopted, the corporate sector will disengage a large number of workers whom service industries in large cities cannot completely absorb. The only place they can go is the communities in which the production of qualitative goods in great variety always needs manpower, at least as much as the communities' food production capacity can support. This is the only "work-sharing" that makes sense. For no member of the community starves unless the community itself does. If the increasingly automated and labor-saving corporate sector now specializes in the production of quantitative intermediate goods, it is already close enough to be the state factories of the *tableau.* What remains is only to transfer the ownership of their shares to the communities and the state, which can be done gradually and in an orderly fashion over a certain number of years.

It is in the course of experiments over many years that an appropriate classification of use-values into qualitative and quantitative goods can be established. One cannot determine in the abstract whether a bus or a truck is a qualitative or quantitative good, or whether television sets should arrive at the community all assembled or in separate parts with a do-it-yourself assembly instruction. Air transport and public utilities are in some cases final consumption goods but may not have to be provided separately by each community. Such practical problems must, however, not obscure the theoretical distinction. The point is that as much creative human work as possible should be done in the community and as much tedious, mechanical, and boring work should be left outside it. Also such questions as what levels of professional services should belong to the cities rather than the communities cannot be determined *a priori* and once for all. The most advanced medical school or the most prestigious philharmonic orchestra of the nation will presumably be located in a metropolitan city. But there is no reason why some communities cannot vie with one another in high-level cultural and educational accomplishment. Indeed, the communities should be the source of all innovative ideas. One must not misunderstand them to be closed and isolated backwaters with little contact among themselves. On the contrary, active cultural and educational exchanges as well as trade *in qualitative goods* among them will be promoted. The production of qualitative goods is by itself an integral part of culture and must not be dealt with from the economic point of view alone, so that trade in qualitative goods which is in the nature of cultural exchanges rather than commodity exchanges will not be governed by the crass principle of comparative costs. For instance, it does make good sense to impose a restriction such as no community should be allowed to produce a qualitative good mainly or exclusively for export.[38]

I have so far dwelled on the possibility of moving peacefully and gradually toward a sustainable socialist society starting from a modern industrial state of the Western kind. But there is no reason why a communist country of the Eastern Bloc or a developing nation of the Third World cannot also try to advance in the same direction. A minimum degree of democracy is, of course, needed in any case in the sense that society's future must depend on the political will of the majority. But the problem lies more frequently in the absence of a fully articulated political vision, whether in the form of a party platform or of an individual leader's personal conviction, behind which the majority may rally. To articulate the vision of a future society it is not enough to simply denounce the existing regime. It is necessary to demonstrate the viability of its alternative. For socialists this means demonstrating the feasibility of the new economic organization in which the liberation of mankind is expected to take place. This essay is intended as a modest contribution toward that end.[39]

# Notes

1. This statement is sometimes attributed to G.D.H. Cole, although I have not been able to confirm it.

2. This idea comes originally from Kozo Uno. See his *Principles of Political Economy* (Sussex: Harvester Press, 1980), and my "An Essay on Uno's Dialectic of Capital" contained therein. See also Thomas T. Sekine, *The Dialectic of Capital*, vol. 1 (Tokyo: Toshindo Press, 1983), pp. 86–90. About Uno's writings in general see *New Palgrave*, vol. 4, under Uno, Kozo.

3. The dialectic of capital claims its objectivity for being independent of human judgment. On the "stage" of the dialectic of capital human beings do appear as capitalists, commodity-owners, workers, etc., but only as personifications of capital or as embodiments of the logic of capital, playing out as it were nothing but capital's scenario. Human beings "in flesh and blood" capable of judgments independent from capital watch as spectators what is played out on the stage, reacting to it with human emotion. This doubling of human beings into the wire-pulled puppets on the stage and the critical observers off the stage is vital to the understanding of the interpretation of Marxian economics advanced here.

4. The claim of historical materialism that capitalism is the last class-antagonistic society with which the prehistory of mankind ends smacks of Judeo-Christian theology. Such a thought cannot occur to those outside that religious tradition. A Chinese communist, for example, can adopt historical materialism in its finished form, but cannot himself invent it. Whatever may be the meaning of the religious dogma, its blind application to matters of human society is dangerous, inasmuch as it engenders the false expectation that, once set on the right track by a revolution or some such cataclysm, society automatically takes care of itself in achieving a secular paradise or a classless society known as socialism. See, below, the beginning of section IV. A sensible theory of socialism should begin with the rejection of such a questionable dogma.

5. By "the commodity-economic conception of history" Uno meant the capitalist (or liberal) outlook on history, a belief propounded by Adam Smith and shared widely by classical economists, that all (primitive) societies develop eventually into (civilized) capitalism. Marx's materialistic conception of history differs from it only in including capitalism as well in the prehistory (primitive stage) of mankind. The difference is either fundamental or trivial depending on how one interprets the history of mankind. If the most efficient use of economic resources, the unleashing of productive powers, material affluence and abundance, etc., are the goal of human society, it makes little difference whether the end product is called capitalism or socialism. The difference becomes real only when such "economistic" goals are abandoned, i.e., when such a liberal and "materialistic" outlook is overcome. What is needed is to transcend economism by coming to grips with the upside-down character (invertedness) of capitalism.

6. Capital is the god of the market. Feuerbach's theory of anthropomorphism (Ludwig Feuerbach, *Lectures on the Essence of Religion*) teaches that man creates god by extrapolating his essence and making it infinite. But once god is created, what comes from him, the lord, is surely different from what comes from man, his servant. Capital is also originally man's creation. That calculating, rational, and greedy part of man is made transcendental and infinite and called capital. Once it becomes an independent being, however, capital far exceeds man's finiteness. It has become the god of ultimate rationality who presides over the market. Studying economics is essentially experiencing how capital develops out of man. This explains why most economists acquire in the course of their training the unshakable faith in the rationality and beneficence of the market and can never again recover from their deep self-hypnotism. If the market "fails," they do not

regard it as due to any failure of its principle but to the lack of competition, free enough trade, private initiative, etc. What is to be blamed is not the god of the market but our humanly errors which may have caused monopoly, externality, decreasing cost, complementarily, etc. What makes Marx's dialectic of capital stand out amongst the body of economic theory is its awareness and critique of this subservience of man to capital as the "upside-down" character of economics.

7. Yoshiro Tamanoi, "Liberating Oneself from the Market Mentality," *York Studies in Political Economy*, 2 (1983), pp. 109–33.

8. Neoclassical economics has consistently described production as a strictly technical process of transformation of inputs into outputs with the concept of "production function." In Marxian theory production (the transformation of part of nature into use-values) is viewed as dual, consisting of both the production process and the labor process. The production process is the technical aspect of production whereas the labor process sees it as man's interface with nature. The Marxian concept is, therefore, richer than the neoclassical one, but there is a considerable measure of anthropocentrism even in the concept of the labor process, since it is specifically understood as man's purposive action on nature, i.e., as part of man's conquest of nature. The idea of "industrial" production is not only mechanical and physicalistic but also anthropocentric.

9. Nicholas Georgescu-Roegen, *The Entropy Law and the Economic Process* (Cambridge, Mass.: Harvard University Press, 1971); *Entropy and the Economic Process. A Seminar* (Science Council of Canada, 1980); Yoshiro Tamanoi, Atsushi Tsuchida, and Takeshi Murota, "Towards an Entropic Theory of Economy and Ecology," *Economie appliquée*, 37, 2 (1984), pp. 279–94. The following passage comes from the introductory section of the last item. "Going back to its original definition by Rudolf Clausius, we find the entropy as a quantitative measure of the dissipation of heat, or of matter. More intuitively speaking, it can be interpreted as a degree of dirtiness of heat or of matter. In our daily lives, we observe high entropy heat as waste heat and high entropy matter as waste materials. . . . Entropy is a fundamental attribute of heat and of matter, and it is a physical quantity having the dimension of calory/absolute temperature" (pp. 279–80).

10. Karl Polanyi, *The Great Transformation, the Political and Economic Origins of Our Time* (Boston: Beacon Press, 1971).

11. A close parallel between the positions of agriculture and women under capitalism may be pointed out here. Feminists are not always aware that the repression of women in a bourgeois society differs from that in premodern society, and attribute both to trans-historical male chauvinism. A feudal-military society expects men to command and women to obey because of its "naturalistic" conception of society. Whether this role-assignment is fair or foul, the ideology views both nature and society as hierarchical and it enjoins us against defying the "order of things." The discrimination therefore comes from the recognition of the difference of the sexes. In contrast a bourgeois society views men and women not only as equal but essentially the same (unisex). It does not recognize the difference of the sexes. When this principle is applied to the marketplace, women inevitably fall behind because they are not as "disembeddable" as men. Just as agriculture is told in vain to be like industry women too are told to be like men in order to be more successful, which advice works only in the public sphere. The liberation of women based on the bourgeois principle of unisex-ism is doomed to fail because, when it succeeds one-hundred percent, the private sphere, the source of life, has been eliminated. What is needed clearly is to liberate women in the private sphere of life rather than forcing them out of it into the public sphere. But we can see that capitalism is unlikely to accomplish this in view of its poor track record with regard to agriculture.

12. Polanyi, *Great Transformation*. Polanyi's contrast of the 1920s and the 1930s is

especially revealing. Uno also held that World War I was the last "imperialist" war, the outbreak of which foretold the end of capitalism. See Sekine, *Dialectic of Capital*, vol. 1, pp. 90ff.

13. I owe the idea of this diagram to Dr. Kazuki Kumamoto. Actually I have fashioned this one by bringing together several of his diagrams which he used to explain much the same factual development in greater detail in an unpublished monograph.

14. There is no shortage of perception and imagination as such, as the following interesting books attest: Rudolf Bahro, *From Red to Green* (London and New York: Verso, 1984); André Gorz, *Farewell to the Working Class* (London: Pluto Press, 1982); idem, *Paths to Paradise* (London, 1983).

15. Tamanoi's extensive writings in Japanese on the economy of the living system have not yet been translated into English. However, apart from the item quoted in note 7, a short article entitled "Economy of the Living System" is being translated by Tamanoi's student, Mr. Makoto Maruyama, and will be made available shortly.

16. This is not a place to expand on the concept of value. But according to the teaching of the Uno School a commodity relation first arises between two more or less self-sufficient communities and then, once it becomes regular, makes inroads into them. If in those communities labor power too is transformed into a commodity, the communities become saturated with commodity relations and become capitalist societies. Their substantive economic life is "subsumed" by the mercantile principles which come from the outside. This process of subsumption is the process of value prevailing over use-values, i.e., the process in which the merchant's indifference to use-values subordinates the consumer's concern over use-values. In capitalism commodities are not produced as use-values but simply as value. Value in this sense is the basic principle that governs capitalist society.

17. Polanyi, *Great Transformation*.

18. Sekine, *Dialectic of Capital*, vol. 2, pp. 376–87.

19. "A tenant of a holding shall have full right to practise any system of cropping of the arable land on the holding and to dispose of the produce of the holding without incurring any penalty, forfeiture, or liability, provided that he shall have previously made suitable and adequate provision to protect the holding from injury or deterioration, which provision shall in the case of disposal of the produce of the holding consist in the return to the holding of the full equivalent manurial value to the holding of all crops sold off or removed from the holding in contravention of the custom, contract, or agreement." T.C. Jackson, *The Agricultural Holdings Acts, 1908–1914* (London: Sweet and Maxwell, 1917), p. 113.

20. Indeed, contrary to what economic theory presupposes, there was no easy intersectoral flow of human resources between agriculture and industry. The work ethos of the agriculturalist and the industrialist being different, the mobility of people between the country and the cities always involved painful sociological experience.

21. Garrett Hardin, "The Tragedy of the Commons," *Science*, 162 (1968), pp. 1243–48, reprinted in Herman E. Daly (ed.), *Economics, Ecology, Ethics* (San Francisco: W.H. Freeman, 1973), pp. 100–14. It must be remarked, however, that the "tragedy" does not occur on a commons, unless "as a rational being, each herdsman seeks to maximize his gain" (p. 104). It was not simply because "the numbers of both man and beast [were kept] well below the carrying capacity of the land" that overgrazing could be averted in premodern societies. It was also because the herdsman was not yet corrupt by the "worship of filthy lucre."

22. This expression comes from Wendell Berry, *The Gift of Good Land* (San Francisco: North Point Press, 1981). The author emphasizes the difference in the philosophies of agriculture and of mining.

23. James Burnham, *The Managerial Revolution, What is Happening in the World?* (New York: John Day, 1941); John K. Galbraith, *The New Industrial State* (New York, 1967). Burnham's book published on the eve of America's entry into World War II contains brilliant analyses which are still very apropos, even though its failure to predict the overwhelming influence of Keynes renders it somewhat obsolete. Galbraith recapitulates many of Burnham's ideas in a more urbane and academic fashion, but perhaps with less penetration and incisiveness.

24. It is well to recall that Uno stated in an article published in 1950 (Kozo Uno, "Sekaikeizai-Ron no Hoho to Mokuhyo," which may be translated into "The Methodology and the Objective of the Theory of the World Economy") that socialism in order to be viable must solve not only the internal contradiction of capitalism, i.e., class conflict, but also its external contradiction, i.e., agricultural problems.

25. See note 4 above. Burnham, *Managerial Revolution*, quite rightly objects to the Marxist's "assumption" that "socialism is the only alternative to capitalism" a great number of times. The abolition of capitalism does not guarantee automatically the coming of socialism.

26. N. Berdyaev, *The Destiny of Man* (London: G. Bles, The Centenery Press, 1937), p. 106.

27. That is to say, the context in which Mayo's "spontaneous cooperation" can be obtained and maintained must become the basis of socialism. Elton Mayo, *The Social Problems of an Industrial Civilization* (Boston: Division of Research, Graduate School of Business Administration, Harvard University, 1945).

28. The fundamental distinction between "qualitative" and "quantitative" goods has not been sufficiently emphasized. In an industrial society the general tendency is to mass-produce even final consumption goods as if they were quantitative intermediate goods. But this means that the whole society is taken hostage by the production managers and designers. In the case of sophisticated consumer durables whose operation needs to be learned through reading a thick user's manual, this may be to some extent unavoidable. In such a case, the consumer needs to decide only whether he wants the thing or not, and how much he is prepared to spend. For the rest his choice is academic. If this trend is universalized, eventually the consumer needs to declare only "I want to live and this is my income." An expert can decide for him how he should live, making the best of his money's worth. Not much room will be left for the philosophy of "free to choose."

29. These estimates are at the outside, since the "cities" should also absorb a considerable portion of the population, say, between one-quarter to one-fifth. It is outside the scope of this paper to speculate what sort of population policy the communities and the cities may sensibly adopt in the future society. I only assume that the nation is self-sufficient in food.

30. The civil servants of the state including the operators of the state factories are to reside in metropolitan cities.

31. This is another way to safeguard against the domination of the consumer by the producer. See note 28 above.

32. The shares of the state factories may in part be owned by the state, and in part by communities. In fact, it is important that the communities whose environment is directly affected by the activity of the state factory should own its shares in addition to being its landlord. Then the communities have enough stake in the operation of the state factory to adequately control its choice of techniques. It is true that the control of the planet-threatening pollution requires not only national but international legislation. But the source of pollution is always local. If there is no local incentive to control pollution at the source, a piece of legislation would remain a dead letter and the cost of policing would be prohibitive.

33. Even if all the capital goods in the community are owned privately and all the products are sold in a free market inside the community, that does not make the community a small capitalist nation. The community can produce only qualitative goods, mainly for internal consumption. In order to accumulate, more quantitative goods must be purchased. But since they are purchased in the first instance by the community with its property income, they are not immediately at the disposal of the private entrepreneurs. The community is a club-like organization which determines the allocation of its resources through the mechanism of direct democracy.

34. I mean "mainly for local consumption" since eventually the communities must produce qualitative goods for "cities" as well. Many Canadians react to this idea by asserting that Florida oranges and California grapefruits are indispensable items of their consumption. If so the community may democratically elect to spend some of its property income on American citrus fruit instead of quantitative goods. If the "trade-off" is reasonable the members of the community may perpetuate their relatively recent addiction.

35. In order to make the first several experiments successful a board of highly educated individuals and other wise people should be established in each case not only to oversee and monitor the coming into being of the community, but also to be ready on hand to assist it in every possible way if and when any difficulty arises in the course of its development.

36. As far as possible an equal distribution of property incomes among the communities must be ensured so that no community should be either too rich or too poor per capita of its population relative to the average. But since the use of property incomes is limited in principle to the purchase of quantitative goods from the outside, what remains as savings may be taxed heavily by the state for transfer to other communities with negative savings. Concrete strategies are to be worked out in light of actual experience.

37. As already stated large corporations should not be in the sphere of direct consumer services (whether in the production of final consumption goods or in the provision of services) anyway. Hence the faster they withdraw from this sphere the better. See note 28 above.

38. This provision is to ensure that the scope of the market in qualitative goods is properly circumscribed. Notice that in the picture of the future society all of what Polanyi called the methods of economic integration: reciprocity, redistribution, and exchange are at work, but none overwhelming the others. These may be alternatively called the principles of cooperation, planning, and the market. The socialists have tirelessly talked about planning versus the market as if they were the only two principles of economic organization. I have instead emphasized the third principle of cooperation or mutual aid. This is what the anarchists have always demanded, especially Kropotkin and his followers. Originally, socialism and anarchism were closely related. They should again be reunited. For by separating from each other they have both become ineffective as a plausible alternative to the existing society.

39. Due to the limitation of space certain concrete problems of vital importance such as defense, international trade, administration of justice, human rights, provisions in case of a natural calamity, etc., could not be discussed in this paper. But I see no reason why they cannot be satisfactorily worked out, once the viability of the state is in principle ensured.